# Essentials of Processes, Systems, and Information

**with SAP Tutorials**

**Earl McKinney Jr.**
Bowling Green State University

**David M. Kroenke**

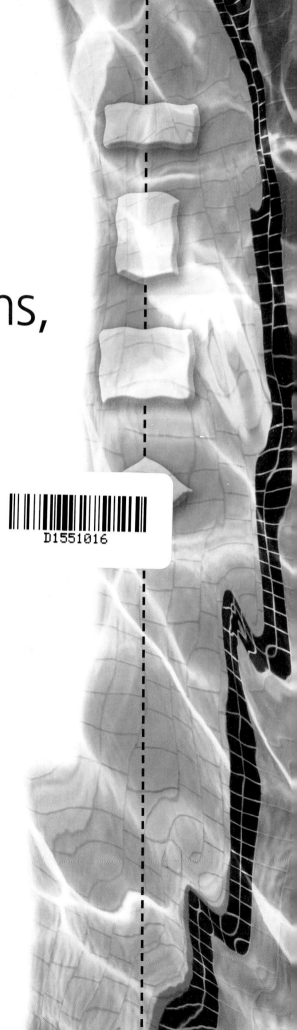

**PEARSON**

Boston   Columbus   Indianapolis   New York   San Francisco
Upper Saddle River   Amsterdam   Cape Town   Dubai   London
Madrid   Milan   Munich   Paris   Montreal   Toronto   Delhi
Mexico City   Sao Paulo   Sydney   Hong Kong   Seoul   Singapore
Taipei   Tokyo

**Editor in Chief:** Stephanie Wall
**Executive Editor:** Bob Horan
**Editorial Project Manager:** Kelly Loftus
**Editorial Assistant:** Ashlee Bradbury
**Director of Marketing:** Maggie Moylan
**Senior Marketing Manager:** Anne Fahlgren
**Senior Managing Editor:** Judy Leale
**Production Project Manager:** Ann Pulido
**Operations Specialist:** Maura Zaldivar
**Art Director:** Jayne Conte

**Cover Designer:** Bruce Kenselaar
**Interior Designer:** Karen Quigley
**Editorial Media Project Manager:** Alana Coles
**Production Media Project**
  **Manager:** Lisa Rinaldi
**Full-Service Project Management**
  **and Composition:** Integra
**Printer/Binder:** Courier/Kendallville
**Cover Printer:** Courier Kendallville
**Text Font:** 10/12 Times LT Std

Credits and acknowledgements borrowed from other sources and reproduced, with permission, in this textbook appear on the appropriate page within text.

Microsoft and/or its respective suppliers make no representations about the suitability of the information contained in the documents and related graphics published as part of the services for any purpose. All such documents and related graphics are provided "as is" without warranty of any kind. Microsoft and/or its respective suppliers hereby disclaim all warranties and conditions with regard to this information, including all warranties and conditions of merchantability, whether express, implied or statutory, fitness for a particular purpose, title and non-infringement. In no event shall Microsoft and/or its respective suppliers be liable for any special, indirect or consequential damages or any damages whatsoever resulting from loss of use, data or profits, whether in an action of contract, negligence or other tortious action, arising out of or in connection with the use or performance of information available from the services.

The documents and related graphics contained herein could include technical inaccuracies or typographical errors. Changes are periodically added to the information herein. Microsoft and/or its respective suppliers may make improvements and/or changes in the product(s) and/or the program(s) described herein at any time. Partial screen shots may be viewed in full within the software version specified.

Microsoft® and Windows® are registered trademarks of the Microsoft Corporation in the U.S.A. and other countries. This book is not sponsored or endorsed by or affiliated with the Microsoft Corporation.

This publication contains references to the products of SAP AG. SAP, R/3, SAP NetWeaver, Duet, PartnerEdge, ByDesign, SAP BusinessObjects Explorer, StreamWork, and other SAP products and services mentioned herein as well as their respective logos are trademarks or registered trademarks of SAP AG in Germany and other countries. Business Objects and the Business Objects logo, BusinessObjects, Crystal Reports, Crystal Decisions, Web Intelligence, Xcelsius, and other Business Objects products and services mentioned herein as well as their respective logos are trademarks or registered trademarks of Business Objects Software Ltd. Business Objects is an SAP company. Sybase and Adaptive Server, iAnywhere, Sybase 365, SQL Anywhere, and other Sybase products and services mentioned herein as well as their respective logos are trademarks or registered trademarks of Sybase, Inc. Sybase is an SAP company.

SAP AG is neither the author nor the publisher of this publication and is not responsible for its content. SAP Group shall not be liable for errors or omissions with respect to the materials. The only warranties for SAP Group products and services are those that are set forth in the express warranty statements accompanying such products and services, if any. Nothing herein should be construed as constituting an additional warranty.

Many of the designations by manufacturers and sellers to distinguish their products are claimed as trademarks. Where those designations appear in this book, and the publisher was aware of a trademark claim, the designations have been printed in initial caps or all caps.

**Library of Congress Cataloging-in-Publication Data is on file at the Library of Congress**

10 9 8 7 6 5 4 3 2 1

ISBN 10:    0-13-340675-X
ISBN 13: 978-0-13-340675-7

# Brief Contents

# Contents

# Preface

ERP skills are essential for business school graduates. Studies consistently show that, for all business disciplines, students with ERP training earn more than students without such training. This textbook provides students with no background in the subject an opportunity to learn and apply the basics of ERP systems. No prerequisite knowledge of ERP or even of business processes is assumed.

We believe the best way to teach students to learn to use ERP systems is to provide a context—the essential concepts and principles explained within a business story—and a set of tutorials to see those concepts in action. Therefore, we introduce ERP fundamentals and then allow students to apply their knowledge through hands-on tutorials. Most introductory ERP books shy away from using ERP tutorials, seeing them as too complex for students.

Earl, the author of the tutorial exercises, has been teaching SAP for six years at Bowling Green State University. During that time, these exercises were extensively tested in a lab setting. In addition, Earl has written a detailed teaching guide that includes his tips for using the exercises most effectively and his experience about where students are most likely to struggle.

Over these years, Earl learned that it is far too easy for the students to slip into "monkey-see, monkey-do" mode when completing SAP exercises, without any clear understanding of what they are doing or why. Students who memorize simulation steps without reflecting on what the ERP system is doing are particularly prone to this behavior. Based on this classroom experience, we believe that the setup to procurement and sales in Chapters 4 and 5, together with the exercises themselves, help the student move beyond simple copy mode and learn the nature of process-oriented software and its role in organizations in addition to SAP keystrokes. These chapters and tutorials have recently been adopted by a wide variety of colleges and universities as part of another text, *Processes, Systems, and Information, An Introduction to MIS*.

For students to understand ERP systems, one of the essential concepts is the business process—how it works toward objectives, how it is supported by IS, and how it can be improved. This book starts with processes, then introduces information systems and how they relate to processes, and finally applies these concepts to ERP systems.

We believe this book works well in an Introduction to MIS course. It is also intended for use outside MIS, wherever processes or ERP systems are taught. The chapters and tutorials on the procurement and sales processes make this book a good fit for introductory supply chain courses and marketing classes that seek to explain processes and ERP systems. Other potential adopters of this textbook are departments that make business processes a key component or thread through their curricula. This market includes all universities that are part of the SAP University Alliance or the Microsoft Dynamics Academic Alliance as well as other institutions emphasizing a business process orientation. Chapters 4 and 5 provide specific examples of the use of SAP, and the Active Cases that conclude each of those chapters provide tutorial exercises that use the SAP University Alliance Global Bikes Inc. (GBI) simulation.

## Text Features

A challenge of teaching from a process orientation is that few students have significant business or process experience; they have been lifeguards or baristas. When we attempt to talk about, say, the impact of process change on departmental power, that discussion goes over the heads of most students. The students may memorize the terms, but they often lose the essence of the discussion. The features of this text are designed, in part, to address this problem.

### Opening Vignettes

Each chapter opens with a short vignette about one of two different organizational settings: Chuck's Bikes, a bicycle manufacturer that competes with Global Bikes, or Central Colorado State, a fictitious university. Each vignette illustrates the use of the chapter's contents in an applied setting. Most contain a problem that requires knowledge of the chapter to understand and solve.

## In-Class Exercises

Every chapter includes a group exercise for use in the classroom that will engage students with the chapter's knowledge. These exercises are part lab and part case in nature. In our experience, many of them lead to spirited discussions that could run for two or three class periods if time permits! The instructor's guide provides teaching and coaching suggestions that will show how the exercise can make the chapter's content more vivid.

## SAP Tutorial Exercises

The appendices to Chapters 4 and 5 contain process exercises that involve the SAP Alliance's GBI simulation. These are valuable components for professors whose institutions are members of the alliance. However, because not every department using this book is a member of that alliance, we have made these exercises optional appendices; instructors can omit the exercises without any loss of continuity.

The exercises are, we hope, purposeful yet simple to do. Teaching assistants and faculty members who have not been able to attend the SAP university training can still conduct the exercises by utilizing the extensive instructor support materials we provide.

By the way, Chapters 4 and 5 use the example of Chuck's Bikes, in the main text, rather than GBI. We made this change at the request of the SAP Alliance, which prefers that authors not add new material to GBI, change any characters, make videos, and so forth. We created CB so as to comply with that request while still providing more detailed business scenarios that are compatible with the GBI client.

## Question-Based Pedagogy

Research by Marilla Svinicki at the University of Texas Psychology Department indicates that today's students need help managing their time. She asserts that we should never give homework assignments to read a prescribed amount of text, such as pages 75–95. The problem, she says, is that students will fiddle with those pages for 30 minutes but will not know when they're done accomplishing the objectives of the assignment. Instead, she recommends that we give a list of questions; when the student can successfully answer all the questions, the assignment is complete, and the student is done studying. We have used this approach in our classrooms, and we believe that it is most effective. Students like it as well. Hence, we have organized each chapter as a list of questions.

## Ethics Guides

We believe that business ethics is a critically important component of the introduction to MIS course and that the best way to teach ethics is in the context of case-like situations. We also believe that ethics ought not to be relegated to a single chapter or section, as this could lead to the inoculation theory of education: "We don't need to discuss ethics; we've already done that." Accordingly, each chapter contains a two-page spread called an Ethics Guide. These guides are shown in the table of contents; to sample just one of them, turn to page 20.

## Collaboration Exercises

Collaboration is a key skill for today's business professionals, so we believe that teaching collaboration, collaboration processes, and collaboration information systems is critical. To that end, each chapter includes a collaboration exercise to be accomplished by a student team. We recommend that students use modern collaboration tools for the majority of their collaboration exercises rather than meeting face-to-face. We prefer requiring the students to use Office 365 and SharePoint. Using Google Drive and related tools is another possibility.

## End-of-Chapter Cases

The chapter-opening scenarios are based on real-life experience, but the organizations they describe are fictitious. We want the students to be able to learn from organizational mistakes and, at times, even organizational foolishness. However, we have not found many real companies that will allow us to "air their laundry" in this way. In any case, we feel it is unfair to ask for an organization's cooperation and then turn around and publish its problems.

However, we do believe students need to see examples of the role of MIS in actual organizations to help them bridge the chapter content to the real world. Hence, each chapter concludes with a case that illustrates some aspect of the chapter's contents in a real world company. Unlike the introductory vignettes, these cases all have happy endings.

### Active Reviews

The concluding material at the end of each chapter includes an Active Review. These reviews help students ensure they have learned the most essential material. They also serve as lists of potential test questions, thus helping students to prepare for exams.

## Chapter Outline

Chapter 1 defines and illustrates processes, information systems, and information. It uses the university intramural league to illustrate the relationship of processes and information systems. It utilizes the Gregory Bateson definition of information as any difference that makes a difference.

Chapter 2 provides an overview of departmental and cross-departmental processes. It discusses process adaptation and improvement as well as the use of process objectives and measures in making process changes. Chapter 3 is a survey of EAI and ERP information systems, their benefits, and their challenges.

Chapters 4 and 5 are "applied" chapters. They show how SAP is used in two representative processes—procurement and sales. Two processes were chosen so that students could begin to see what is common to all processes and what might differ between processes. We specifically selected these two processes, buying and selling, because they are fundamental to business and widely used. Each chapter also includes a student lab exercise appendix that uses the SAP alliance's GBI simulation.

## Supplements

The following supplements are available at the Online Instructor Resource Center, accessible through *www.pearsonhighered.com/mckinney*.

### Instructor's Manual

The instructor's manual, prepared by Timothy O'Keefe of the University of North Dakota, includes a chapter outline, list of key terms, suggested answers to the MIS InClass questions, and answers to all end-of-chapter questions.

### Test Item File

This Test Item File, prepared by ANSR Source, Inc., contains over 500 questions, including multiple-choice, true/false, and essay questions. Each question is followed by the correct answer, learning objective it ties to, page reference, AACSB category, and difficulty rating.

### PowerPoint Presentations

The PowerPoints, prepared by Robert Szymanski of Georgia Southern University, highlight text learning objectives and key topics and serve as an excellent aid for classroom presentations and lectures.

### Image Library

This collection of the figures and tables from the text offers another aid for classroom presentations and PowerPoint slides.

### TestGen

Pearson Education's test-generating software is available from *www.pearsonhighered.com/irc*. The software is PC/MAC compatible and preloaded with all of the Test Item File questions. You can manually or randomly view test questions and drag and drop to create a test. You can add or modify test bank questions as needed. Our TestGens are converted for use in several course management systems, including Blackboard and WebCT. These conversions can be found on the Instructor's Resource Center.

## CourseSmart

CourseSmart eTextbooks were developed for students looking to save on required or recommended textbooks. Students simply select their eText by title or author and purchase immediate access to the content for the duration of the course using any major credit card. With a CourseSmart eText, students can search for specific keywords or page numbers, take notes online, print out reading assignments that incorporate lecture notes, and bookmark important passages for later review. For more information or to purchase a CourseSmart eTextbook, visit *www.coursesmart.com.*

## Acknowledgements

First, we thank the numerous reviewers of a previous version of this text. In particular, we thank the following people:

Yvonne Antonucci, *Widener University*

Cynthia Barnes, *Lamar University*

John Baxter, *SAP*

William Cantor, *Pennsylvania State University–York Campus*

Gail Corbitt, *SAP*

Darice Corey, *Albertus Magnus College*

Mike Curry, *Oregon State University*

Heather Czech, *SAP*

Janelle Daugherty, *Microsoft Dynamics*

Peter DeVries, *University of Houston, Downtown*

Lauren Eder, *Rider University*

Kevin Elder, *Georgia Southern University*

John Erickson, *University of Nebraska at Omaha*

Donna Everett, *Morehead State University*

David Firth, *The University of Montana*

Jerry Flatto, *University of Indianapolis*

Kent Foster, *Microsoft*

Biswadip Ghosh, *Metropolitan State College of Denver*

Bin Gu, *University of Texas at Austin*

William Haseman, *University of Wisconsin–Milwaukee*

Jun He, *University of Michigan–Dearborn*

Mark Hwang, *Central Michigan University*

Gerald Isaacs, *Carroll University*

Stephen Klein, *Ramapo University*

Ben Martz, *University of Northern Kentucky*

William McMillan, *Madonna University*

Natalie Nazarenko, *SUNY College at Fredonia*

Timothy O'Keefe, *University of North Dakota*

Tony Pittarese, *East Tennessee State University*

Martin Ruddy, *Bowling Green State University*

James Sager, *California State University–Chico*

Narcissus Shambare, *College of Saint Mary*

Robert Szymanski, *Georgia Southern University*

Lou Thompson, *University of Texas, Dallas*

Ming Wang, *California State University*

We wish to thank the incredible production team that helped us to bring this book into existence. First and foremost, we thank Bob Horan, our editor, for his long-standing encouragement for a process-oriented text and for his untiring support throughout the process. We especially thank Kelly Loftus for returning to the fold to help us marshal this text and all its supplements through the Pearson production process and Angel Chavez for her management of the project as well. We also thank Janet Slowik, art director, and her team for designing this book.

We thank our friend and colleague Chuck Yoos of Fort Lewis College for his groundbreaking work on the meaning of information and the role of information in organizations today. Chuck is responsible for the helpful distinction between *perceiving data* and *conceiving information* and many other insights that have shaped this text's material. Chuck's Bikes is named in his honor.

Finally, we are most grateful to our wives and families who have lovingly supported us through these processes.

Earl McKinney
*Bowling Green, Ohio*

David Kroenke
*Seattle, Washington*

# About the Authors

**Earl McKinney Jr.** Teaching the Introduction to MIS course has been Earl McKinney's passion for 20 years. He first caught the bug at his alma mater, the U.S. Air Force Academy, and has continued his addiction during his tenure at Bowling Green State University. While teaching that class and other undergraduate and graduate classes, Earl has also introduced a half-dozen new courses on BI, security, social media, ERP, and information. He has been awarded a number of department and college teaching awards by students and fellow faculty. His interest in the broader context of the business curriculum is reflected in several of his publications and by the Decision Science Institute's National Instructional Innovation Award.

Earl's research in e-commerce and small team communication during a crisis as well as theoretical work on the notion of information has been published in *Behaviour and Information Technology, Human Factors, Information and Management,* and *MIS Quarterly.* Along with James Hall, the former head of the NTSB, he consults for British Petroleum, the U.S. Forest Service, and several Air Force agencies on human factors and aviation communication issues.

Earl holds an undergraduate economics degree from the Air Force Academy, a Master's of Engineering from Cornell University, and a PhD in MIS from the University of Texas. A former Air Force fighter pilot, Earl lives in Bowling Green with his wife and has two grown sons.

**David Kroenke** David Kroenke has many years of teaching experience at Colorado State University, Seattle University, and the University of Washington. He has led dozens of seminars for college professors on the teaching of information systems and technology; in 1991 the International Association of Information Systems named him Computer Educator of the Year. In 2009, David was named Educator of the Year by the Association of Information Technology Professionals-Education Special Interest Group (AITP-EDSIG).

David worked for the U.S. Air Force and Boeing Computer Services. He was a principal in the start-up of three companies. He was also vice president of product marketing and development for the Microrim Corporation and was chief of technologies for the database division of Wall Data, Inc. He is the father of the semantic object data model. David's consulting clients have included IBM, Microsoft, and Computer Sciences Corporations, as well as numerous smaller companies. Recently, he has focused on the use of information systems for collaboration in education and industry.

David's text *Database Processing* was first published in 1977 and is now in its 12th edition. He has also published many other textbooks, including *Database Concepts,* 6th ed. (2013), *Using MIS,* 6th ed. (2014), *Experiencing MIS,* 4th ed. (2014), *MIS Essentials,* 3rd ed. (2014), *SharePoint for Students* (2012), and *Office 365 in Business* (2012). David lives in Seattle. He is married and has two children and three grandchildren.

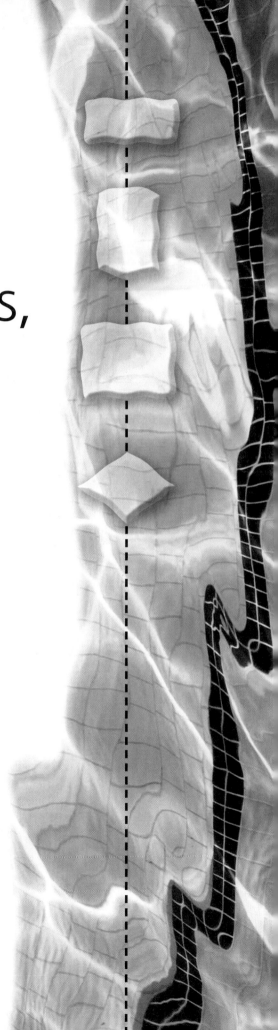

# Essentials of
# Processes, Systems,
# and Information

## with SAP Tutorials

"What do you mean I'm not a valid student?" Carter Jackson, a student at Central Colorado State, is trying to check out soccer equipment from the university intramural center and is talking with Dirk Johansen, one of the center's part-time employees.

"Valid? Yeah, I did say that. Sorry. Look, you might be a fine student for all I know, but this computer is telling me you haven't paid your bill." Dirk looks at the long line forming behind Carter.

"What bill?"

"I don't know. It doesn't tell me."

"Look," Carter is trying to be patient, "I'm the coach of the Helicopters, the best soccer team in the league. The team will be here in 30 minutes. We need to practice. I need the soccer gear, the shirts, the cones, all the stuff to get started."

"Yeah, I've heard of the Helicopters. Good team...at least last year."

"So, gimme the gear and I'll get out of here," Carter sees a ray of hope.

"Can't do it. I can't check out any gear to anyone who's not in good standing with university accounting...or whoever is on the other end of this computer." Dirk is adamant.

"Look, accounting is closed. I can't fix this problem now."

"Right. You should have paid your bill earlier."

"I did pay my bill. I don't know what this is about. Just *loan* me the gear."

"I can't." Dirk looks at the even longer line of people behind Carter.

"OK. I see one of our players coming in from the lot. Let me call her over here and you can check it out to her."

"Is her name Carter Jackson?"

"No, you idiot. *My* name is Carter Jackson. I already told you that." Carter is angry now.

"Hey, don't get snippy. I'll call security."

"OK, sorry. My name is Carter Jackson. Her name is Heather Nealey."

"I'm sure she's a nice person, but she's not getting any soccer gear. The only person on the Helicopters who can check out equipment is the team captain, someone named Carter Jackson." Dirk sounds like he's talking to a 2-year-old.

"That's me!"

"Right. And you haven't paid your bill, so, no equipment until you do."

"I'm sure I've paid all my bills. I don't know what's going on, but I'll fix it tomorrow. How about if I give you a credit card?" Carter's getting desperate.

"We don't take credit cards here. Just university IDs."

"I already gave you my ID."

"Right. The bogus one."

"IT ISN'T BOGUS, YOU NITWIT!"

"Carter, Heather, whatever your name is, get out of here. There's 10 people in line behind you. Move on and let me get these people their equipment."

"Yeah, buddy, stop yelling and let us get our stuff," says someone waiting in line.

"Oh, he's the Helicopters' coach. Probably complaining that he didn't get new balls. Thinks he can get away with anything," says another person in line.

The next day at the accounting office...

"Hi, my name's Carter Jackson. I'm here to take care of whatever problem there is on my account."

"OK. Give me your student card." June Marble has been working in the accounting office for 30 years.

"Sure."

June scans the card and looks at her computer. "What problem are you here about?" June asks.

"I'm not sure. I was trying to check out equipment for the Helicopters last night..."

"Helicopters? You in the right place?" June can't resist teasing him.

"It's an intramural soccer team. OK? Anyway, I was trying to check out equipment and this nitwit told me that I have a past due bill."

"Hmmm. I don't see any problem with your account. You've got a few charges this month, but we haven't sent out this month's bills. Don't worry about it." June starts to turn away from the counter.

"But he thinks my account is bad or something."

"Tell him to call me."

"He doesn't come in till 6:30 tonight."

"Oh, I leave at 5:00." June looks back at her computer screen. "Hey, wait. There's another Carter Jackson who left...oh, I can't tell you the story, but I suspect they confused your accounts somehow."

**Q1.** What is a business process?

**Q2.** What is an information system?

**Q3.** How do business processes and information systems relate?

**Q4.** What is information?

**Q5.** What factors drive information quality?

**Q6.** How do structured and dynamic processes vary?

## Chapter Preview

MIS is the management and use of business processes, information systems, and information to help organizations achieve their strategies. This chapter describes that definition's three fundamental terms: business process, information system, and information. We begin with business processes, describing their components, and then introduce you to BPMN, the standard way of documenting business processes. Next we will define information systems and describe their components. Then we will explain how business processes and information systems relate. Following that, we will present several different definitions of information and ask where and how information is created. Finally, we will discuss factors that influence information quality and then return to the question of how organizations use information systems. We will wrap up by explaining how these concepts will be treated in the rest of this text.

## Q1. What Is a Business Process?

A **business process** is a sequence of activities for accomplishing a function. For example, your university has business processes to:

- Add a class to the business curriculum
- Add a new section to a class schedule
- Assign a class section to a classroom
- Drop a class section
- Record final grades

An **activity** is a task within a business process. Examples of activities that are part of the record final grades process are:

- Compute final grades
- Fill out grade reporting form
- Submit the grade recording form to the departmental administrator

Business processes also involve resources, such as people, computers, data and document collections, and so forth. To understand those, consider the business process for checking out equipment that opened this chapter.

### An Example Business Process

Dirk, the student who was issuing sports equipment at the start of this chapter, was following a business process. As yet, we don't know exactly what the process was, but clearly it involved checking out equipment only to team captains and ensuring that those captains were in good standing with the university's accounting office.

DOCUMENTING BUSINESS PROCESSES  To talk meaningfully about business processes, we need some way of documenting them. We need to create an *abstraction* of business processes. The computer industry has created dozens of techniques for documenting business processes over the years, and this text will use one of them known as the **Business Process Management Notation (BPMN) standard.** We use this technique both because it is a global standard and also because it is widely used in industry. Microsoft Visio Premium,[1] for example, includes templates for creating process drawings using BPMN symbols.

---

[1] Visio is a diagram-drawing product licensed by Microsoft. If your university belongs to the Microsoft Academic Alliance (which is likely), you can obtain a copy of Visio for free. If you want to draw diagrams that use BPMN symbols, be certain that you obtain the Premium version of this product, which is available from the Academic Alliance.

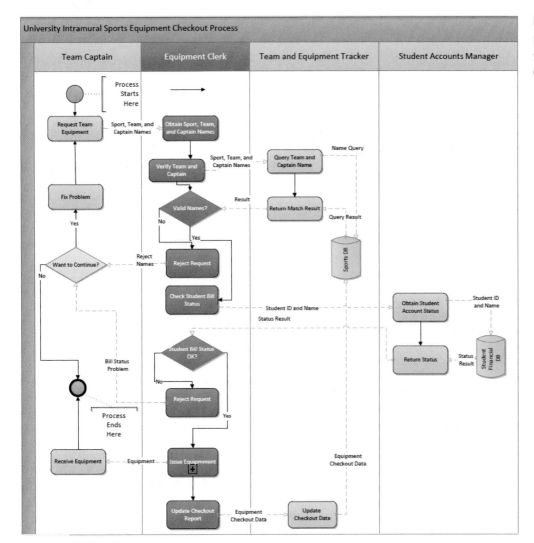

**FIGURE 1-1**

**University Intramural Sports Equipment Checkout Process**

Figure 1-1 is a BPMN model, or abstraction, of the business process used by the intramural sports league. Each of the long columns is headed by a name such as *Team Captain* and *Equipment Clerk*. That name identifies a **role,** which is a subset of the activities in a business process that is performed by a particular actor. **Actors** can be people; in the opening vignette, Dirk was fulfilling the role of Equipment Clerk. As you will learn, actors can also be computers, but that's getting ahead of the story.

The long columns in Figure 1-1 are called **swimlanes**; each such lane contains all the activities for a particular role. Swimlanes make it easy to determine which roles do what. According to the BPMN standard, the process starts at a circle with a narrow border and ends at a circle with a heavy border. Thus, in Figure 1-1, the business process starts at the top of the *Team Captain* swimlane and ends at the heavy-bordered circle near the end of that swimlane. The BPMN standard defines dozens of symbols; the symbols we will use in this text are summarized in Figure 1-2.

Activities are shown in rectangles with rounded corners, and decisions are shown by diamonds. A solid arrow shows the flow of action; the solid arrow between the Obtain Sport, Team, and Captain Names and Verify Team and Captain activities means that once the Equipment Clerk has obtained the names, the next task in the process is to verify them.

Dotted arrows show the flow of the data that is named on the arrow. Thus, the dotted arrow between the Request Team Equipment activity and the Obtain Sport, Team, and Captain Names activity means that the data items named on that arrow are sent from one activity to another.

**FIGURE 1-2**

**Summary of BPMN Symbols**

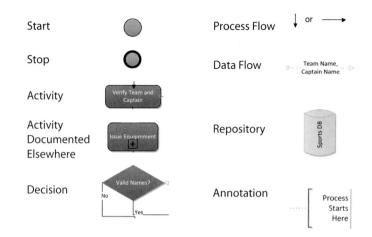

In this case, the Request Team Equipment activity is sending Team Name and Captain Name to the Obtain Sport, Team, and Captain Names activity.

A **repository** is a collection of something, usually the collection of records of some type. In Figure 1-1, the symbol that looks like a small tin can represents a repository. Here, we have one repository named *Sports DB* and a second named *Student Financial DB*. As hinted in those names, a repository is often a database (DB), but it need not be. It might be a cardboard box full of records. And some repositories, like inventories, are collections of things other than data.

**HOW MUCH DETAIL IS ENOUGH?**  As an abstraction, a business process diagram shows some details and omits others. It has to, otherwise it would be hundreds of pages long and needlessly so because many details are obvious. We don't need to show that the equipment clerk should open the checkout window before talking to customers or that he or she must turn on a computer before using it. However, we need to show sufficient detail so as to avoid ambiguity. The process with one big activity named Check Out Equipment leaves out too much detail. Such a diagram would not show, for example, that only authorized team captains can check out equipment.

To simplify process diagrams, the details of some activities are documented separately. In Figure 1-1 examine the activity Issue Equipment (near the bottom of the Equipment Clerk swimlane). The activity is shown with a plus sign enclosed in a small box. That notation signifies that the details of the Issue Equipment activity are documented elsewhere. As stated, such external documentation is used to simplify a diagram; it is also used when the details of the subprocess are unimportant to the process under study or when those details are unknown. For example, the details of an activity that is performed by an external agency like a credit bureau would be unknown.

### Why Do Organizations Standardize Business Processes?

Other than very small businesses, most businesses choose to standardize business processes. For one, standard processes enable the business to enforce policies. The intramural sports league has decided that equipment is to be checked out only to authorized and identified team captains and that those captains must have a problem-free account with the university's accounting's office. If every equipment clerk had a different process, there would be no way to enforce those policies.

Second, standardized business processes produce consistent results. When every employee follows the same process steps, the results will be the same, regardless of who is staffing the window. Third, standardized processes are scalable. If the intramural sports league decides to open a third or fourth center at a remote campus, it can do so more easily if its business processes are standardized.

Finally, standardized business processes reduce risk. When every employee follows the same process, the opportunities for error and serious mistakes are greatly reduced.

You might be wondering that if such standardized processes are so great, why didn't Carter get his team's equipment? To answer that question, you need to understand information systems and their relationship to business processes, so we will consider them next. Be patient, you will see what happened to Carter very soon.

## Q2. What Is an Information System?

A **system** is a group of components that interact to achieve some purpose. As you might guess, an **information system (IS)** is a group of components that interact to produce information. That sentence, although true, raises another question: What are these components that interact to produce information?

Figure 1-3 shows the **five-component framework**—a model of the components of an information system: **computer hardware, software, data, procedures,** and **people.** These five components are present in every information system, from the simplest to the most complex. For example, when you use a computer to write a class report, you are using hardware (the computer, storage disk, keyboard, and monitor), software (Word, WordPerfect, or some other word-processing program), data (the words, sentences, and paragraphs in your report), procedures (the methods you use to start the program, enter your report, print it, and save and back up your file), and people (you).

Consider a more complex example, say an airline reservation system. It, too, consists of these five components, even though each one is far more complicated. The hardware consists of dozens or more computers linked together by telecommunications hardware. Furthermore, hundreds of different programs coordinate communications among the computers, and still other programs perform the reservations and related services. Additionally, the system must store millions upon millions of characters of data about flights, customers, reservations, and other facts. Hundreds of different procedures are followed by airline personnel, travel agents, and customers. Finally, the information system includes people, not only the users of the system, but also those who operate and service the computers, those who maintain the data, and those who support the networks of computers.

Notice the symmetry in these five components. Hardware and people are actors; they do things. Programs and procedures are instructions. Programs tell the hardware what to do, and procedures tell the humans what to do. Data is the bridge between the machine side (hardware and software) and the human side (procedures and people).

The important point here is that the five components in Figure 1-3 are common to all information systems, from the smallest to the largest. As you think about any information system, learn to look for these five components. Realize, too, that an information system is not just a computer and a program, but rather an assembly of computers, software, data, procedures, and people.

Also, problems develop if any one of these five components is overlooked. A common mistake is to assume that hardware and software are the only costs of a new system. In fact, the costs of designing and documenting procedures and the labor costs of training employees to use those procedures can far exceed the hardware and software costs for a new system.

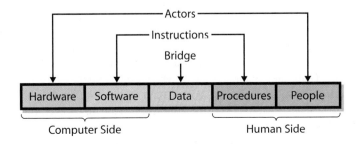

**FIGURE 1-3**

**Five Components of an Information System**

# MIS InClass 1

## Recognizing Processes Close to Home

The management and use of business processes is crucial to your success as a business professional. Although you may not realize it, business processes are all around us. To help you understand this fact, work with a group of students to complete the following tasks:

1. Identify three important business processes used at your university. Choose one process that involves finances, one process that involves operations, and one process that involves marketing.
2. Complete the following for each process:
   a. Name the process.
   b. Identify and briefly describe three to five key activities for the process.
   c. Describe performance measures that management can use to assess the process.
   d. If the process is assisted with information systems, describe how. If you don't know if the process is assisted by information systems, describe how you think information systems could be used.
3. Present the results of your group's work to the rest of the class.

Source: © Jinlide/Dreamstime.com.

These five components also mean that many different skills are required besides those of hardware technicians or computer programmers when building or using an information system. People are needed who can design the databases that hold the data and who can develop procedures for people to follow. Managers are needed to train and staff the personnel for using and operating the system. We will return to this five-component framework later in this chapter, as well as many other times throughout this book.

Before we move forward, note that we have defined an information system to include a computer. Some people would say that such a system is a **computer-based information system.** They would note that there are information systems that do not include computers, such as a calendar hanging on the wall outside of a conference room that is used to schedule the room's use. Such systems have been used by businesses for centuries. Although this point is true, in this book we focus on computer-based information systems. To simplify and shorten the book, we will use the term *information system* as a synonym for *computer-based information system.*

## Q3. How Do Business Processes and Information Systems Relate?

To understand this crucial question, look again at Figure 1-1. Who are the actors playing the roles in that diagram? The team captain role is a human who is recognized by the league as a captain of a sports team in the league. What about equipment clerk? From the opening vignette, and from the discussion in this chapter, the equipment clerk role is played by one or more part-time employees. But, does this role have to be performed by a human? Could it be performed by some computer-based system? Yes, it could. It could all be done in a browser. The only activity that is likely to require a human is Issue Equipment, and that is a subactivity that could be placed into a role of its own. The rest could be done by a computer-based system.

What about the Team and Equipment Tracker and the Student Accounts Manager roles? Could they be performed by humans? Of course, and in the 1950s and earlier all such roles were performed by humans accessing data in filing cabinets. Thus, the entire business process in Figure 1-1 could be done by humans. However, because of the very low cost of computers and the nearly zero cost of data storage and data communications, in 2013 and beyond most such roles are performed by computers, following instructions in software. Grocery stores have a similar example. It used to be that a human was required for checkout. Now, at many stores, you can scan your groceries yourself; the role of checker has been taken over by scanners and computers.

## Information Systems in the Context of Business Processes

Let's assume that the Team and Equipment Tracker and the Student Accounts Manager roles are performed by computers. To understand them, consider Figure 1-4, which extracts those two roles along with the activities that access them from Figure 1-1. Consider the activity Check Student Bill Status in the Equipment Clerk role. It generates and sends Student ID and Name to the Obtain Student Account Status activity.

Check Student Bill Status uses a computer-based system, and procedures need to be written to instruct the clerk how to invoke that system and transmit the data. Let's assume those procedures tell the clerk how to access and fill out the data entry form in Figure 1-5. The Obtain Student Bill Status activity is performed by a computer, which means that the activity is encoded in a computer program. That program accesses the Student Financial DB to obtain the student's account status.

Notice how the five components are integrated into the business process. Computers and humans are actors who play roles in the business process. The particular techniques for using the computer system to perform an activity are encoded in procedures for human actors, and they are encoded in programs for computer actors. Data is bridging the two types of actors.

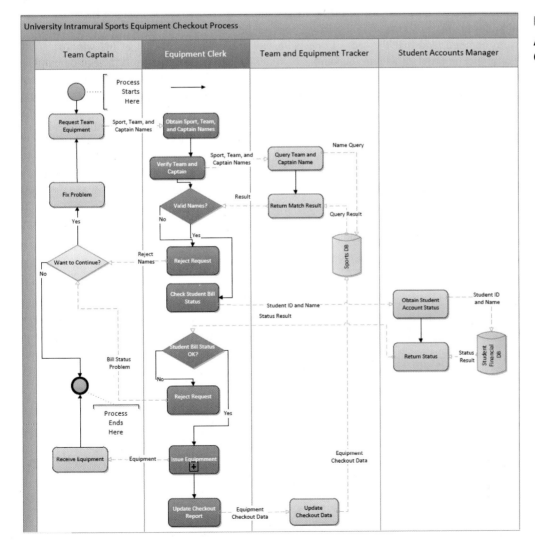

**FIGURE 1-4**

**Activities That Involve Computer Actors**

**FIGURE 1-5**

**Account Status Request Data Input Form**

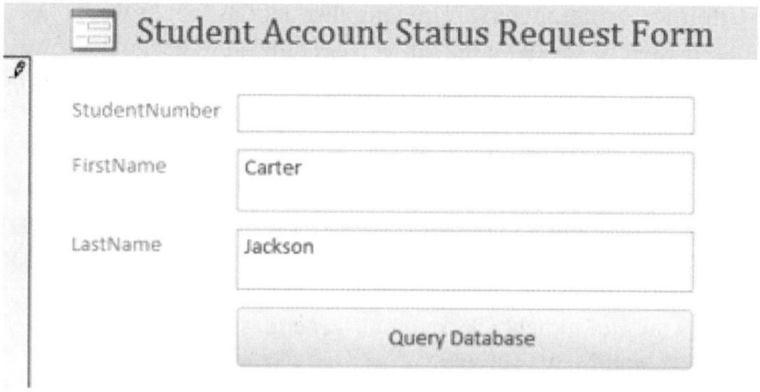

All of this brings us to why the Helicopters' equipment request was denied. The procedures for using the information system to check student account status include two modes of access. If the form shown in Figure 1-5 includes a value for *StudentNumber* (what *Student ID* is called within the information system), then the Obtain Student Bill Status program returns one account (or none if there is no match). However, if the form in Figure 1-5 does not include a *StudentNumber*, then that program returns all accounts that match values for first and last name.

Figure 1-6 shows the data that were returned from the program executing the Return Status activity. As you can see, the bottom of the form indicates that two records were returned. According to the procedures of the system, if the input does not include a value for *StudentNumber*, then the user of the system is supposed to verify the student's ID with the returned value of *StudentNumber*. Had Dirk done so, he would have seen that two student records were returned, and that the second one belonged to the Carter in front of his window. That Carter had no problem with his account and would have been able to receive the equipment that he was authorized to receive.

What caused this problem? One could say that Dirk was improperly trained, or that he didn't know procedures for doing his job. Or, maybe, given the long line in front of his window, he was hasty and made a mistake. Or, one could say the system that performs this role is improperly designed; it ought not to have two modes of access. Or possibly the form in Figure 1-6 is poorly designed. Something other than a tiny little number at the bottom of the form should be used to indicate that more than one account was returned. For our purposes here, it doesn't matter, except that, as a future manager, you should understand the importance of training employees to use information systems according to their designed procedures.

Figure 1-7 brings activities of the business process and the five-component model together. You can see how each of the components of the information system relates to elements of the business process.

**FIGURE 1-6**

**Student Account Status Return Form**

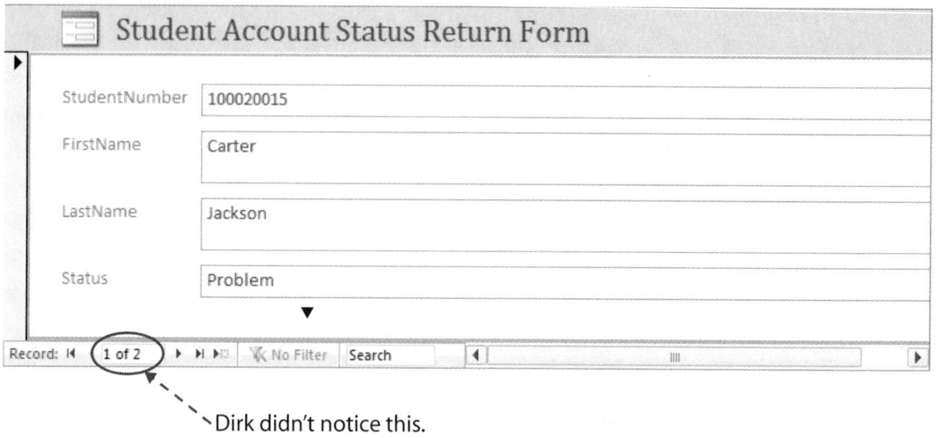

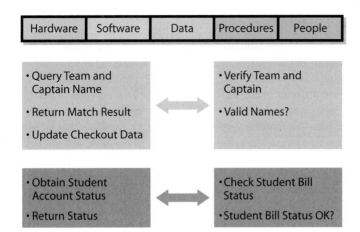

**FIGURE 1-7**

**Five Components and Activities**

This example also shows an aggravating reality. The intramural sports league refers to student identifiers as *Student ID*s. The university's student accounting system refers to student identifiers as *StudentNumbers*. These entities have two names for the same thing. Why? There could be many different reasons. Perhaps they were developed by different teams of people at different times, or StudentNumber was thought to be less confusing than StudentID. Whatever the reason, such synonyms are common when using different information systems. You and the people you manage may find such multiplicity of names frustrating and confusing, but rest assured that you will find them.

## Business Processes and Information Systems Have Different Scope

Before we move on, notice something that is very confusing to many students and that, in fact, is misunderstood by many business professionals. The scope of business processes and the scope of information systems are different. The business process in Figure 1-1 uses two different information systems: a local one and a university-wide one. In general, a business process may use zero, one, or many different information systems.

Similarly, although not shown, each of the two information systems in Figure 1-1 is used by many other business processes. The system that plays the Team and Equipment Tracker role also plays a role in other business processes, such as the Check In Equipment process and the Schedule Teams process. The system that plays the Students Account Manager role also plays a role in processes such as the Buy Athletic Tickets process and the Pay Dorm Bill process, and so forth. In general, an information system plays a role in from one to many business processes.

Thus, the scope of business processes and information systems that support them overlap, but they are different, as shown in Figure 1-8.

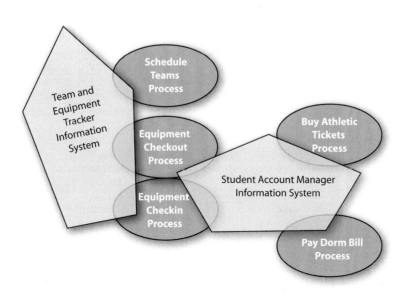

**FIGURE 1-8**

**Overlap of Process and IS Scope**

## Q4. What Is Information?

*Information* is one of those fundamental terms that we use every day but that turns out to be surprisingly difficult to define. Defining information is like defining words such as *alive* and *truth*. We know what those words mean, or at least we pretend we do in normal conversation. Nonetheless, they are difficult to define.

Probably the most common definition is that **information** is knowledge derived from data, whereas *data* is defined as recorded facts or figures. Thus, the facts that employee James Smith earns $17.50 per hour and that Mary Jones earns $25.00 per hour are *data*. The statement that the average hourly wage of all the equipment clerks is $22.37 per hour is *information*. Average wage is knowledge that is derived from the data of individual wages.

Another common definition is that *information is data presented in a meaningful context.* The fact that Jeff Parks earns $10.00 per hour is data.[2] The statement that Jeff Parks earns less than half the average hourly wage of the equipment clerks, however, is information. It is data presented in a meaningful context.

Another definition is that *information is processed data,* or sometimes, *information is data processed by sorting, filtering, grouping, comparing, summing, averaging, and other similar operations.* The fundamental idea of this definition is that we do something to data to produce information. The list of orders in Figure 1-9(a) is data; that data has been sorted,

**FIGURE 1-9**

**Information Produced by Processing**

| Adams, James | JA3@somewhere.com | 1/15/2012 | $145.00 |
|---|---|---|---|
| Angel, Kathy | KA@righthere.com | 9/15/2012 | $195.00 |
| Ashley, Jane | JA@somewhere.com | 5/5/2012 | $110.00 |
| Austin, James | JA7@somewhere.com | 1/15/2011 | $55.00 |
| Bernard, Steven | SB@ourcompany.com | 9/17/2012 | $78.00 |
| Casimiro, Amanda | AC@somewhere.com | 12/7/2011 | $52.00 |
| Ching, Kam Hoong | KHC@somewhere.com | 5/17/2012 | $55.00 |
| Corning,Sandra | KD@somewhereelse.com | 7/7/2012 | $375.00 |
| Corning,Sandra | SC@somewhereelse.com | 2/4/2011 | $195.00 |
| Corovic,Jose | JC@somewhere.com | 11/12/2012 | $55.00 |
| Daniel, James | JD@somewhere.com | 1/18/2012 | $52.00 |
| Dixon, James T | JTD@somewhere.com | 4/3/2011 | $285.00 |
| Dixon,Eleonor | ED@somewhere.com | 5/17/2012 | $108.00 |
| Drew, Richard | RD@righthere.com | 10/3/2011 | $42.00 |
| Duong,Linda | LD@righthere.com | 5/17/2011 | $485.00 |
| Garrett, James | JG@ourcompany.com | 3/14/2012 | $38.00 |
| Jordan, Matthew | MJ@righthere.com | 3/14/2011 | $645.00 |
| La Pierre,Anna | DJ@righthere.com | 12/7/2011 | $175.00 |
| La Pierre,Anna | SG@righthere.com | 9/22/2012 | $120.00 |
| La Pierre,Anna | TR@righthere.com | 9/22/2011 | $580.00 |
| La Pierre,Anna | ALP@somewhereelse.com | 3/15/2011 | $52.00 |
| La Pierre,Anna | JQ@somewhere.com | 4/12/2012 | $44.00 |
| La Pierre,Anna | WS@somewhere.com | 3/14/2011 | $47.50 |
| Lee,Brandon | BL@somewhereelse.com | 5/5/2010 | $74.00 |
| Lunden,Haley | HL@somewhere.com | 11/17/2009 | $52.00 |
| McGovern, Adrian | BL@righthere.com | 11/12/2010 | $47.00 |
| McGovern, Adrian | AM@ourcompany.com | 3/17/2011 | $52.00 |
| Menstell,Lori Lee | LLM@ourcompany.com | 10/18/2012 | $72.00 |
| Menstell,Lori Lee | VB@ourcompany.com | 9/24/2012 | $120.00 |

**(a)** Data

| CustomerName | Number of Orders | TotalPurchases |
|---|---|---|
| La Pierre,Anna | 6 | $1,018.50 |
| Rikki, Nicole | 2 | $330.00 |
| Menstell,Lori Lee | 2 | $192.00 |
| McGovern, Adrian | 2 | $99.00 |
| Corning,Sandra | 2 | $570.00 |

**(b)** Information

[2] Actually the word *data* is plural; to be correct we should use the singular form *datum* and say "The fact that Jeff Parks earns $10 per hour is a datum." The word *datum* however, sounds pedantic and fussy, and we will avoid it in this text.

filtered, grouped, and computations have been made upon it to create the information in Figure 1-9(b).

A fourth definition, created by the psychologist George Bateson, is that information is *a difference that makes a difference.* At the start of this chapter, Dirk perceived that Carter's account was in arrears or had some other problem. That perception was a difference. Now, because of the intramural sport's league's policy, encoded in its business process, that difference made a difference.

None of these definitions is perfect; each can be useful in certain circumstances, and they all have problems. For now, consider the four of them as four sides of a boundary of what the term *information* means.

However, one characteristic of information may surprise you. Understanding this characteristic will make you a far better consumer of MIS. We begin by asking the question "Where is information?"

## Where Is Information?

Examine the data in Figure 1-10. Put that data in front of your family dog. Does this information mean anything to your dog? No. They mean nothing to Fido. Fido may perceive information, but it will have to do with scents on the book, as in "someone had tacos for lunch."

Now, put that same data in front of someone who leads a weekly Weight Watcher's group. Ask that person to interpret the data. He will most likely say that the first column contains the name of a person, the second the person's current weight, and the third the number of pounds lost. If that person looks closely, he may also find information: People who weigh the most tend to lose the most. (In this data, for the most part, the bigger the value in the second column, the bigger the value in the third.)

Now, put that same data in front of someone who manages an IQ testing center for adults. Ask that person to interpret the data. She will most likely say the first column contains the name of a person, the second the person's IQ test score, and the third the person's age. Furthermore, she may also find the information that, according to this data, IQ increases with age.

We can continue this thought experiment to the manager of a bowling league, but you get the point: At least in these cases, the information resides in the head of the person who perceives the data. Does this occur here only because the data are not labeled? Had we put labels on the

| Christianson | 140 | 42 |
|---|---|---|
| Abernathy | 107 | 25 |
| Green | 98 | 21 |
| Moss | 137 | 38 |
| Baker | 118 | 32 |
| Jackson | 127 | 38 |
| Lloyd | 119 | 29 |
| Dudley | 111 | 22 |
| McPherson | 128 | 33 |
| Jefferson | 107 | 24 |
| Nielsen | 112 | 33 |
| Thomas | 118 | 29 |

**FIGURE 1-10**
**Sample Data**

**FIGURE 1-11**

**Data Processing and Information**

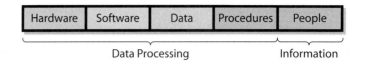

| Hardware | Software | Data | Procedures | People |
|----------|----------|------|------------|--------|

Data Processing      Information

columns of data in Figure 1-10 would the information have been on the piece of paper? No. Labeled columns of data are still just marks on a paper. All the interpretation, and any information constructed, will occur in the mind of the person confronted with the data. In this text, we will say humans *perceive* data but *conceive* information.

Look at Figure 1-11, which again shows the five components of an information system. According to this figure, hardware runs software that processes data to produce a data display. That display is then perceived by a human and is conceived into information by the thinking process of that human. That conceiving process is guided by procedures, but involves critical-thinking skills that go beyond basic procedures.

Thus, for our purposes, it is only the human component of an information system that produces and understands information. Perhaps within the next 30 years the field of artificial intelligence will create machines that emulate humans' ability to conceive information. However, even if such systems exist today, they are rare and we can safely ignore them in mainstream commerce.

## Q5. What Factors Drive Information Quality?

Figure 1-12 summarizes the factors that influence information quality. Some of the factors concern the data that is used to conceive the information, and some concern the abilities and characteristics of the human creating the information.

### Data Factors

First, data must be accurate. It must be a correct and complete measure of whatever it is supposed to measure. If the data has been processed, it must have been processed correctly, in accordance with expectations and standards.

Second, data must be timely. A monthly report that arrives 6 weeks late is most likely useless. The data arrives long after the decisions have been made that needed related information. An information system that tells you about poor credit of a customer to which you have already shipped goods is unhelpful and frustrating. Notice that timeliness can be measured against a calendar (6 weeks late) or against events (before we ship).

When you participate in the development of an information system, timeliness will be part of the requirements that you specify. You need to give appropriate and realistic timeliness needs. In some cases, developing systems that provide data in near real time is much more difficult and expensive than producing data a few hours later. If you can get by with data that is a few hours old, say so during the requirements specification phase.

Consider an example. Suppose you work in marketing and you need to be able to assess the effectiveness of new online ad programs. You want an information system that not only will deliver ads over the Web, but that also will enable you to determine how frequently customers click on those ads. Determining click ratios in near real time will be very expensive;

**FIGURE 1-12**

**Factors That Affect Information Quality**

| Data | Human |
|------|-------|
| • Accurate | • Knowledge |
| • Timely | • Criteria |
| • Correct granularity | |
| • Easy to use | |

saving the data in a batch and processing it some hours later will be much easier and cheaper. If you can live with data that is a day or two old, the system will be easier and cheaper to implement.

Third, data must be of the appropriate granularity. Data that is too fine-grained has too many details; data that is too coarse is too highly summarized. A file that contains records of millions of clicks on a Web page is too fine-grained for an analysis of revenue generated by different page designs. A file of national sales data is too coarse-grained for an analysis of the relative performance of city sales regions. Ideally, data is detailed enough to serve the purpose at hand, but just barely so.

It is possible to group data that is too fine into appropriate granularity; however, data that is too coarse cannot be subdivided into its constituents. Hence, when specifying requirements, if you are going to err, err on the side of being too fine-grained.

Finally, data needs to be easy to use. The data in Figure 1-6 is correct, timely, and at the right level of granularity, but it is not easy to use. The 2 is presented subtly and is difficult to find. An easier-to-use presentation would show, for example, a picture of the two students named Carter Jackson so that it would be obvious that two different student records have been returned.

## Human Factors

Again, in this text we will say that humans perceive data and conceive information. Thus, the quality of the information produced is at least as much determined by characteristics of the human involved than it is by the data utilized.

The first factor of importance when conceiving information is knowledge. Decades of psychological research indicate that what humans know greatly influences what they perceive. So, the data that you pay attention to is determined, in part, by your knowledge. Additionally, once you have perceived a difference, your knowledge will help you determine which differences make a difference to the problem at hand. So, what you know about a domain will determine the quality of the information you conceive.

A second human factor that affects information quality is the **criteria** used to interpret the data. To understand this, consider a marketing analyst who wants to conceive information from the sales data in Figure 1-9(a). Figure 1-13 shows data that has been filtered, grouped, and summed from that raw data.

The analyst has used several criteria to construct the report. First, customers with only one purchase have been filtered out of this report, so one criterion is "Consider only repeat customers."

**FIGURE 1-13**

**Applying Criteria to Data**

| Customer Name | Number of Orders | Total Purchases |
|---|---|---|
| La Pierre, Anna | 6 | $1,018.50 |
| Corning, Sandra | 2 | $570.00 |
| Rikki, Nicole | 2 | $330.00 |
| Menstell,Lori Lee | 2 | $192.00 |
| McGovern, Adrian | 2 | $99.00 |

**(a)** Data Sorted by Total Purchase Amount

| Customer Name | Number of Orders | Total Purchases | Average Order Total |
|---|---|---|---|
| La Pierre, Anna | 6 | $1,018.50 | $169.75 |
| Corning, Sandra | 2 | $570.00 | $285.00 |
| Rikki, Nicole | 2 | $330.00 | $165.00 |
| Menstell,Lori Lee | 2 | $192.00 | $96.00 |
| McGovern, Adrian | 2 | $99.00 | $49.50 |

**(b)** Data with Average Order Total

Given that the report is shown in descending order of total purchases, it would appear that another criterion in use is "Consider customers with the largest order total first." Now suppose that the marketing analyst notices there seems to be only one male name in this list. That suggests another criterion: "Consider sales grouped by sex of customer."

Figure 1-13(b) shows this same data, but includes the computation of the average order total. Notice that the order of customers has changed. Considering average order total, Sandra Corning is the top customer; considering only total purchases, Anna La Pierre is the top customer. So, average order seems to make a difference in the relative merit of customers. If the analyst is concerned with increasing the total number of orders, then he or she might use the criteria "average." At this point, we have four criteria for determining which differences make a difference:

- Include only repeat customers
- Consider order of total or average purchases
- Group customers by sex
- Use average order total

Is this a good set of criteria? It is if it helps the business professional to be more successful. It will be if it helps her to make better decisions, to deal more effectively with employees and customers, or to construct better strategies and tactics.

This subject is both rich and deep, and there is a good deal more to explore.[3] Alas, we need to move on. For now, the most important point for you to remember is that data is external, objective, and similar for all. Information is internal, depends on the person, and can be different for all. Thus, two people can perceive the same data, but conceive different information from that data.

### How Do Groups Conceive Information?

"Wait a minute," you may be saying. "Hold on. If every human conceives his or her own version of information from a personal perspective, how do we ever get anything done? Why aren't groups constantly disagreeing about everything? How could I ever manage a group like that?"

Because information is conceived personally, it might be that everyone always disagrees about everything. It is, however, unlikely. Why? Because we all share the same mental apparatus. In fact, the biologist Humberto Maturana claims that cognition and communication evolved only to allow us to organize our collective behavior.[4] He believes that because we have the same hardware, we will conceive information the same way, and thus be able to organize ourselves into groups that have a selective advantage over other groups.

So, given that we share the same mental apparatus, perceive the same data, and use the same criteria, we will tend to conceive information in the same way. Often, however, the more interesting case occurs when we do not conceive information in the same way. If everyone is engaged in the process and communicating honestly, then that can only occur when people perceive the data differently (someone notices something that others have not) or when people are using different criteria. The latter case may occur because they have found a criterion that others have not found or that they stress on one criterion more than others do.

See the Ethics Guide on pages 20–21 to learn one technique that business professionals use to obtain a common definition of a problem.

You can apply this insight the next time you are in a group that is having a discussion that is going round and round and getting nowhere. Ask the group members what data they perceive. Ask them what criteria they are using to make their statements. If you can start a discussion

---

[3] See, for example, Earl McKinney and Chuck Yoos, "Information About Information, a Taxonomy of Views," *MIS Quarterly,* 2010, Volume 24, pp. 329–344.

[4] Humberto R. Maturana, *The Tree of Knowledge* (Boston: Shambhala Publications, 1992).

about criteria, it will often lead to a discussion of why you are using those criteria. This technique is a useful and valuable way of getting a group unstuck. Try it.

## Q6. How Do Structured and Dynamic Processes Vary?

Businesses have dozens, hundreds, even thousands of different processes. Some processes are stable, almost fixed, in the flow among their activities. For example, the process of a sales clerk accepting a return at Nordstrom, or other quality retail store, is fixed. If the customer has a receipt, take these steps.…If the customer has no receipt, take these other steps.…The process needs to be standardized so that customers are treated correctly, so that returned goods are accounted for appropriately, and so that sales commissions are reduced in a way that is fair to the sales staff.

Other processes are less structured, less rigid, and sometimes creative. For example, how does Nordstrom's management decide what women's clothes to carry next spring? They can look at past sales, consider current economic conditions, and make assessments about women's acceptance of new styles at recent fashion shows, but the process for combining all those factors into orders of specific garments in specific quantities and colors is not nearly as structured as that for accepting the return of goods.

There are two broad categories of processes. **Structured processes** are formally defined, standardized processes. Most structured processes support day-to-day operations: accepting a return, placing an order, computing a sales commission, and so forth. **Dynamic processes** are less specific, more adaptive, and even intuitive. Using Twitter to generate buzz about next season's product line is an example of a dynamic process. Deciding whether to open a new store location or how best to solve a problem of excessive returns are other examples of dynamic processes.

### Characteristics of Structured Processes

Figure 1-14 summarizes the major differences between structured and dynamic processes. Structured processes are formally defined with specific detailed activities arranged into fixed, predefined sequences, like that shown in the BPMN diagram in Figure 1-4. Changes to structured processes are slow, made with deliberation, and are difficult to implement. Control is critical in structured processes. For example, at Nordstrom's item returns must be done in a consistent, controlled fashion so that, among other reasons, sales commissions are reduced appropriately. Innovation of structured processes is not expected, nor is it generally appreciated or rewarded. "Wow, I've got four different ways of returning items" is not a positive accomplishment in retail sales.

For structured processes, both efficiency and effectiveness are important, and we will define them in Chapter 3. For now, assume that *efficiency* means accomplishing the process with minimum resources, and *effectiveness* means that the process contributes directly to the organization's strategy. Reducing time required to sell an item at a grocery store by 1 second would be a huge efficiency gain. If, at Nordstrom's, the competitive strategy is to treat customers as royalty, then a return process that humiliates customers is ineffective.

Finally, information systems for structured processes are prescriptive. They clearly delimit what the users of the system can do and under what conditions they can do it. In Chapters 4 and 5, you will see how information systems based on SAP, an enterprise-wide IS, constrain human activity to specific tasks at specific points in procurement, sales, or other processes. Variations on those tasks will not be tolerated, as you will learn.

### Characteristics of Dynamic Processes

The second column of the table in Figure 1-14 summarizes characteristics of dynamic processes. First, such processes tend to be informal. This does not mean that they are unstructured; rather it means that the process cannot be reduced to fixed steps taken in a specific control flow every time. BPMN diagrams of dynamic processes are always highly generic. They have activities with generalized names like "gather data," "analyze past sales," and "assess fashion shows." Human intuition plays a big role in a dynamic process.

**FIGURE 1-14**

**Differences Between Structured and Dynamic Processes**

| Structured Processes | Dynamic Processes |
|---|---|
| Formally defined process | Informal process |
| Process change slow and difficult | Process change rapid and expected |
| Control is critical | Adaptation is critical |
| Innovation not expected | Innovation required |
| Efficiency and effectiveness are important | Effectiveness is important |
| IS are prescriptive | IS are supportive |

Dynamic processes, as their name implies, change rapidly. If structured processes are cast in stone, dynamic processes are written in sand on a windy beach. "We'll try it this way. If it works, great, if not, we'll do something else." A good example is the process for using Twitter to generate buzz for the spring fashions. Which employees tweet? And how? And what? And how frequently? The team will measure results and change their process as needed. Such rapid change is expected.

Rather than controlled, dynamic processes are adaptive; they must be so to evolve with experience. Dynamic process actors collaborate; they give feedback to each other, and over time the process evolves into one that no single person might have envisioned, and one that works better than anyone could have created on their own ahead of time.

Adaptation requires innovation. Whereas innovation on a structured process like computing commissions is likely to get you fired, innovating with Twitter to forecast sales will be highly rewarded.

For the most part, dynamic processes are evaluated on effectiveness more than efficiency. Did the process help us accomplish our strategy? This is not to say that efficient use of resources does not matter; rather, dynamic processes change so fast that it is not possible to measure efficiency over time. Typically, costs are controlled by budget: "Get the best result you can with these resources."

Finally, information systems for dynamic processes are supportive rather than prescriptive. Information systems provide a platform, an infrastructure, to facilitate dynamic processes. Microsoft's Office 365, for example, includes a videoconferencing product named Lync and a resource-sharing product called SharePoint. IS that use those products provide a forum for group work. They enable team members to easily communicate and share documents, files, wikis, and so on, and thus support whatever process the team is engaged upon. Business intelligence systems enable teams to gather intelligence needed to support decisions within a dynamic process.

This structured–dynamic distinction is important. For one, the behavior you choose as a business professional depends on the type of process in which you are involved. Innovation will be expected in dynamic processes, but discouraged in structured processes. Rigid structure will be appreciated in critical manufacturing processes, but disdained in collaboration.

For information systems, this distinction is important in the nature and character of the system. As stated, when SAP is used to support structured processes it will restrict your behavior and readily (and successfully) frustrate any attempts at innovation. In contrast, SharePoint is an open book. Put anything in it you want; control that content in whatever way you think is appropriate.

# Ethics Guide

## Egocentric Versus Empathetic Thinking

As stated earlier, a problem is a perceived difference between what is and what ought to be. When developing information systems, it is critical for the development team to have a common definition and understanding of the problem. This common understanding can be difficult to achieve, however.

Cognitive scientists distinguish between egocentric and empathetic thinking. Egocentric thinking centers on the self; someone who engages in egocentric thinking considers his or her view as "the real view" or "what really is." In contrast, those who engage in empathetic thinking consider their view as one possible interpretation of the situation and actively work to learn what other people are thinking.

Different experts recommend empathetic thinking for different reasons. Religious leaders say that such thinking is morally superior; psychologists say that empathetic thinking leads to richer, more fulfilling relationships. In business, empathetic thinking is recommended because it is smart. Business is a social endeavor, and those who can understand others' points of view are always more effective. Even if you do not agree with others' perspectives, you will be much better able to work with them if you understand their views.

Consider an example. Suppose you say to your MIS professor, "Professor Jones, I couldn't come to class last Monday. Did we do anything important?" Such a statement is a prime example of egocentric thinking. It takes no account of your professor's point of view and implies that your professor talked about nothing important. As a professor, it is tempting to say, "No, when I noticed you weren't there, I took out all the important material."

To engage in empathetic thinking, consider this situation from the professor's point of view. Students who do not come to class cause extra work for their professors. It does not matter how valid your reason for not attending class; you may actually have been contagious with a fever of 102. But, no matter what, your not coming to class is more work for your professor. He or she must do something extra to help you recover from the lost class time.

Using empathetic thinking, you would do all you can to minimize the impact of your absence on your professor. For example, you could say, "I couldn't come to class, but I got the class notes from Mary. I read through them, and I have a question about establishing alliances as competitive advantage....Oh, by the way, I'm sorry to trouble you with my problem."

Before we go on, let's consider a corollary to this scenario: Never, ever, send an e-mail to your boss that says, "I couldn't come to the staff meeting on Wednesday. Did we do anything important?" Avoid this for the same reasons as those for missing class. Instead, find a way to minimize the impact of your absence on your boss.

Empathetic thinking is an important skill in all business activities. Skilled negotiators always know what the other side wants; effective salespeople understand their customers'

needs. Buyers who understand the problems of their vendors get better service. And students who understand the perspective of their professors get better....

## DISCUSSION QUESTIONS

1. In your own words, explain how egocentric and empathetic thinking differ.
2. Suppose you miss a staff meeting. Using empathetic thinking, explain how you can get needed information about what took place in the meeting.
3. How does empathetic thinking relate to problem definition?
4. Suppose you and another person differ substantially on a problem definition. Suppose she says to you, "No, the real problem is that..." followed by her definition of the problem. How do you respond?
5. Again, suppose you and another person differ substantially on a problem definition. Assume you understand his definition. How can you make that fact clear?
6. Explain the following statement: "In business, empathetic thinking is smart." Do you agree?

Source: Artur Bogacki/Shutterstock.

# Active Review

Use this Active Review to verify that you understand the material in the chapter. You can read the entire chapter and then perform the tasks in this review, or you can read the text material for just one question and perform the tasks in this review for that question before moving on to the next one.

## Q1. What is a business process?

Define *business process* and give an example of two business processes not in this text. Define *activity* and give examples of five activities. Explain the need for an abstraction of a business process and describe the purpose of the BPMN notation. Define *role* and *actor* and explain their relationship. Identify four swimlanes in Figure 1-1 and explain their utility. Explain the meaning of each of the symbols in Figure 1-2. Give an example of two repositories. Describe criteria for deciding how much detail is enough in a process diagram. Describe four reasons that organizations standardize business processes.

## Q2. What is an information system?

Define *system* and *information system*. Name and describe the five components of an information system. Describe, as best you know at this time, the five components of an information system required to buy a product online. Explain why a variety of skills are required to develop an information system.

## Q3. How do business processes and information systems relate?

Using Figure 1-1 as an example, explain how all of the roles in that process could be played by human actors. Explain which of the roles could be played by computer actors. Explain where procedures appear in a business process diagram. In general, how many information systems can a business process use? In general, in how many business processes does a particular IS appear? Explain Figure 1-8.

## Q4. What is information?

Give four different definitions for *information* and explain the problem of each. According to this text, explain where information resides. Do you agree? Why or why not? Which definition of information will be used in this text, and why? Summarize the data factors that drive information quality.

## Q5. What factors drive information quality?

Summarize the human factors that drive information quality. Define *criteria* and explain how they pertain to information. Explain why this definition of information does not necessarily lead different people to different information. Describe a practical application of criteria for group discussions that are stuck in a discussion rut.

## Q6. How do structured and dynamic processes vary?

In your own words, describe and characterize structured processes. Describe and characterize dynamic processes. Describe the differences in expected employee behavior for each type of process. Summarize differences in the character of IS that support each category of process.

# Key Terms and Concepts

Activity   *4*
Actor   *5*
Business process   *4*
Business Process Management
  Notation (BPMN) standard   *4*
Computer-based information system   *8*
Computer hardware   *7*

Criteria   *15*
Data   *7*
Dynamic processes   *17*
Five-component framework   *7*
Information   *12*
Information system (IS)   *7*
People   *7*

Procedures   *7*
Repository   *6*
Role   *5*
Software   *7*
Structured processes   *17*
Swimlane   *5*
System   *7*

# Using Your Knowledge

1. Consider Dirk's error in the opening vignette of this chapter.
   a. List four possible solutions to this problem.
   b. Of your four solutions, which is the most effective? Why?
   c. Of your four solutions, which is the cheapest? Which is the easiest to implement? Explain.
   d. Describe the cost of Dirk's error to the intramural league and to each of the actors in the story.

2. Explain, in your own words, the relationship between business processes and information systems. Assume you are going to give your explanation to a business professional who knows little about information systems.

3. In Figure 1-8, the team and equipment tracker information system is used exclusively by processes within the intramural sports organization. The student account manager information system is used university-wide. Given these two different scopes:
   a. Which will be the easier system to change? Why?
   b. If problems occur with either of these systems, which system is more likely to provide a rapid fix?
   c. If the intramural sports league wants a change to the form in Figure 1-6, how do you think they should proceed?
   d. If the university IS department decides to change the student account manager information system, how might that change affect the business process in Figure 1-1? Is it likely that the intramural sports organization can stop any change that will adversely impact its processes? Why or why not?

4. Consider some of the ramifications of the way in which information is defined in this chapter.

   a. Why, according to this chapter, is it incorrect to say, "Consider the information in Figure 1-10?" Where is the information?
   b. When you read a news article on the Web, where is the news? When you and a friend read the same news, is it the same news? What is going on here?
   c. Suppose you are having a glass of orange juice for breakfast. As you look at the juice, where is it? Is the thing that you know as orange juice on the table, or is it in your mind? After you drink the orange juice, where is it?
   d. Suppose I say that a glass of orange juice is a collection of molecules arranged into structures. When pressed, suppose I say a molecule is a collection of atoms, arranged according to certain principles. When further pressed, suppose I say that atoms are collections of electrons and neutrons, and, when pressed even more, I say, well, electrons are assemblies of quarks and leptons, and so on, and that they, in turn, are collections of differential equations. In saying all this, have I said anything about the orange juice? Or, have I just made statements about constructs in my mind? What do you think?
   e. Consider the statement, "Words are just tokens that we exchange to organize our behavior; we don't know anything, really, about what it is they refer to, but they help us organize our social behavior. Reality is a mutual hallucination. It only looks the way it does because all of us have the same, more or less, mental apparatus, and we act as if it's there." Do you agree with this statement? Why or why not?
   f. Describe how you might use insights from this sequence of questions to become a better business professional.

**5.** Using Figure 1-14 as a guide, identify two structured processes and two dynamic processes at your university. Explain how the degree of structure varies in these processes. How do you think change to these processes is managed? Describe how the nature of the work performed in these processes varies. Explain how information systems are used to facilitate these processes. How do you think the character of the information systems supporting these processes varies?

# Collaboration Exercise 1

Collaborate with a group of fellow students to answer the following questions. For this exercise do not meet face to face. Your task will be easier if you coordinate your work with SharePoint, Office 365, Google Docs with Google+ or equivalent collaboration tools. Your answers should reflect the thinking of the entire group, and not just that of one or two individuals.

The purpose of this exercise is to compute the cost of class registration. To do so, we will consider both class registration processes as well as information systems that support them.

1. Class registration processes:
    a. List as many processes involved in class registration as you can. Consider class registration from the standpoint of students, faculty, departments, and the university. Consider resources such as classrooms, classroom sizes, and requirements for special facilities, such as audiovisual equipment, labs, and similar needs. Also consider the need for departments to ensure that classes are offered in such a manner that students can complete a major within a 4- or 5-year time period. For this exercise, ignore graduate schools.
    b. For each process, identify human actors. Estimate the number of hours each actor spends in the roles that he or she plays per enrollment period. Interview, if possible, two or three actors in each role to determine the time they spend in that role, per term.
    c. Estimate the labor cost of the processes involved in class registration. Assume the fully burdened (wages plus benefits plus applicable taxes) hourly rate of clerical staff is $50 per hour, that of professorial staff is $80. Determine the number of departments involved in registration, and estimate the number of clerical and professional actors involved in each. Use averages, but realize that some departments are much larger than others.
2. Information systems:
    a. For each process identified in question 1, list supporting information systems. Consider information systems that are used university-wide, those used by departments, and those used by individuals.
    b. For each information system identified in part a, above, describe the five components of that information system.
    c. List sources of cost for each of the five components identified in your answer to part a. Consider both development and operational costs. Explain how some of the personnel costs in your answer here may overlap with the costs of actors in processes. Why will only some of those costs overlap? Do all of the costs of class registration information systems apply to the cost of class registration business processes? Why or why not?
    d. As a student, you have no reasonable way to estimate particular information systems costs in your answer to part c, above. However, using your best judgment, estimate the range of total costs. Would it be closer to $10,000? $100,000? $1,000,000? More? Justify your answer.
3. Effectiveness and efficiency:
    a. What does the term *effectiveness* mean when applied to business processes? List as many pertinent effectiveness objectives for class registration as possible. List possible measures for each objective.
    b. What does the term *efficiency* mean when applied to business processes? List as many pertinent efficiency objectives for class registration as possible. List possible measures for each objective.
4. The quarter system. Many universities operate on a four-term quarter system that requires class registration four times per year as opposed to semester systems that require class registration just three times per year. As of 2011, the state of Washington has experienced large tax revenue reductions and has severely cut the budget of state universities, resulting in substantial increases in student tuition and fees, yet the University of Washington continues to operate on a quarter system.
    a. Assume that you work for a university using a quarter system. Justify that system. Can your argument be based upon registration process efficiency? Why or why not? Can it be based on registration process effectiveness? Why or why not?
    b. Assume you attend a university on a quarter system. Using your answers to questions 1 and 2, write a two-page memo explaining the advantages of converting to a semester system.
    c. Considering your answers to questions 1 and 2, do you think it would be wise for universities to convert to semester systems? Why or why not? Would you recommend a national policy for universities to use the semester system?
    d. If converting from a quarter system to a semester system is advantageous, why not convert to a

one-term system? What would be the advantages and disadvantages of such a system? Would you recommend one if it reduced your tuition by 25 percent? 50 percent? 75 percent?

e. At present, there has been no public outcry to convert the University of Washington to a semester system. There has been, however, considerable public anguish about the increasing costs of tuition. Why do you suppose this situation exists?

f. Given all of your answers to these questions, which type of term system (e.g., quarter, semester, year) does your team believe is best? Justify your answer.

## CASE STUDY 1

## An Amazon of Innovation

On November 29, 2010, Amazon.com customers ordered 13.7 million items worldwide, an average of 158 items per second. On its peak order fulfillment day, Amazon.com shipped more than 9 million units, and over the entire 2010 holiday season it shipped to 178 countries.[5] Such performance is only possible because of Amazon.com's innovative use of information systems. Some of Amazon.com's major innovations are listed in Figure 1-15.

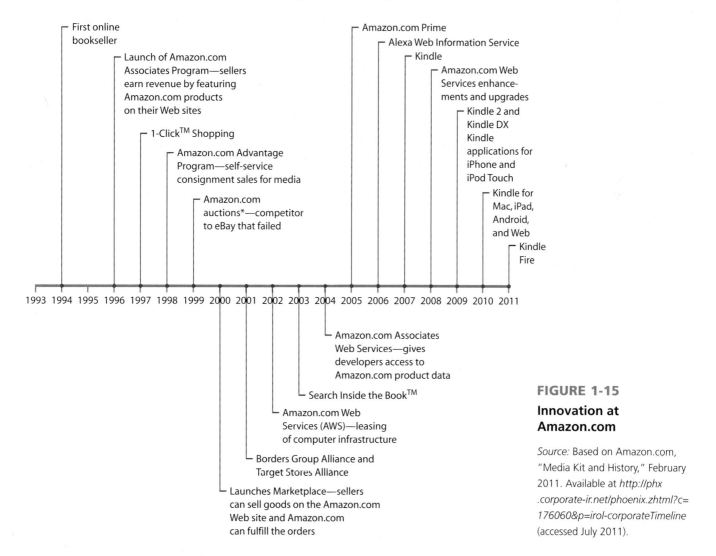

**FIGURE 1-15**

**Innovation at Amazon.com**

*Source:* Based on Amazon.com, "Media Kit and History," February 2011. Available at *http://phx .corporate-ir.net/phoenix.zhtml?c= 176060&p=irol-corporateTimeline* (accessed July 2011).

---

[5] Amazon.com, "Third-Generation Kindle Now the Bestselling Product of All Time on Amazon Worldwide," News release, December 27, 2010. Available at *http://phx.corporate-ir.net/phoenix.zhtml?c=176060&p=irol-newsArticle&ID=1510745&highlight=* (accessed June 2011).

You may think of Amazon.com as simply an online retailer, and that is indeed where the company has achieved most of its success. To achieve that success, Amazon.com had to build enormous supporting infrastructure—just imagine the information systems, processes, and infrastructure needed to ship 9 million items on a single day. That infrastructure, however, is only needed during the busy holiday season. Most of the year, Amazon.com is left with excess infrastructure capacity. Starting in 2000, Amazon.com began to lease some of that capacity to other companies. In the process, it played a key role in the creation of what is termed *the cloud* and *cloud services*. For now, just think of cloud services as Internet-based computer resources that are leased on flexible terms. Today, Amazon.com's business can be grouped into three major categories:

- Online retailing
- Order fulfillment services
- Cloud services

Consider each.

Amazon.com created the business model for online retailing. It began as an online bookstore, but every year since 1998 it has added new product categories. In 2011, the company sold goods in 29 product categories. Undoubtedly, there will be more by the time you read this.

Amazon.com is involved in all aspects of online retailing. It sells its own inventory. It incentivizes you, via its Associates program, to sell its inventory as well. Or, it will help you sell your own inventory within its product pages or through one of its consignment venues. Online auctions are the only major aspect of online sales in which Amazon.com does not participate. It tried auctions in 1999, but it could never make inroads against eBay.[6]

Today, it's hard to remember how much of what we take for granted was pioneered by Amazon.com. "Customers who bought this, also bought"; online customer reviews; customer ranking of customer reviews; book lists; Look Inside the Book; automatic free shipping for certain orders or frequent customers; and Kindle books and devices were all novel concepts when Amazon.com introduced them.

Amazon.com's retailing business operates on very thin margins. Products are usually sold at discounts from the stated retail price, and 2-day shipping is free for Amazon Prime members (frequent buyers). How does Amazon.com do it? For one, Amazon.com drives its employees incredibly hard. Former employees complain of long hours, severe pressure, and a heavy workload. But a company can only drive its employees so hard.

What else explains those thin margins? Another major factor is efficient business processes. When you are shipping 13 million items a day, saving a tenth of a cent in operations expense on each item saves $130,000 a day! Amazon.com also has been able to find ways to use the benefits of Moore's Law and the innovative use of nearly free data processing, storage, and communication to improve its business processes.

The second major category of Amazon.com products is order fulfillment services. You can ship your inventory to an Amazon.com warehouse and have Amazon.com manage it and ship to your customers. Amazon.com also can handle your customers' returns. All for a small processing fee. Your information systems can access Amazon.com's information systems just as if they were your own. Using a technology known as Web services, your order processing information systems can directly integrate, over the Web, with Amazon.com's inventory, fulfillment, and shipping applications. Your customers need not know that Amazon.com played any role at all.

Why is Amazon.com able to do all this for a small fee? Because it uses the same, highly tuned and efficient business processes for fulfilling your orders as it does its own. Amazon.com is, in essence, leasing its process expertise to you.

The third product category is Amazon Web Services (AWS). With AWS, organizations can lease time on Amazon.com's computer equipment in very flexible ways. Amazon.com's Elastic Cloud 2 enables organizations to expand and contract the computer resources they need within minutes. Amazon.com has a variety of payment plans, and it is possible to buy computer time for less than a penny an hour. This dynamic, elastic leasing is only possible because the leasing organization's computer programs interface directly with Amazon.com's computer programs to programmatically scale up and scale down the resources leased. For example, if a news site publishes a story that causes a sudden surge of traffic, that news site can, programmatically, request, configure, and use more computing resources for an hour, a day, a month, whatever. Amazon.com also uses its cloud to support Silk, the innovative browser on the Kindle Fire.

## Questions

1. In what ways does Amazon.com, as a company, evidence the willingness and ability to collaborate?
2. In what ways does Amazon.com, as a company, evidence the willingness and ability to experiment?
3. In what ways do you think the employees at Amazon.com must be able to perform systems and abstract thinking?

---

[6] For a fascinating glimpse of this story from someone inside the company, see "Early Amazon: Auctions" at *http://glinden.blogspot.com/2006/04/early-Amazon.com-auctions.html* (accessed June 2011).

4. Describe, at a high level, the principal roles played by each of the five components of an information system that supports Amazon.com's order fulfillment information systems.

5. Summarize the importance of business processes to Amazon.com's success.

6. Choose any five of the innovations in Figure 1-15 and explain how you think Moore's Law facilitated that innovation.

7. Suppose you work for Amazon.com or a company that takes innovation as seriously as Amazon does. What do you suppose is the likely reaction to an employee who says to his or her boss, "But, I don't know how to do that!"?

8. Using your own words and based on your own experience, what skills and abilities do you think you need to have to thrive at an organization like Amazon.com?

Sarah sits in the student union at Central Colorado State drinking coffee and eating her morning bagel when the question suddenly occurs to her, "How did this stuff get here? The milk? The coffee? The bagel? How did it get here?"

Somewhere there must be a cow that produced the milk that's in her coffee. Where is that cow? Who owns that cow? Who milked that cow? Who decided to ship that particular milk to the union that morning? Who delivered the milk? On what truck? How was the truck routed to customers? Who trained the truck driver?

For that matter, how did the coffee get there? It was grown in Kenya, shipped to the United States, roasted in New Jersey, packaged by a vendor, and delivered to the union. How did all of that happen?

What about the bagel? Who baked it? When? How many bagels did they bake? How did they make that decision?

What about the chair she is sitting on? The wood was grown in Brazil and shipped to China, where the chair was manufactured, and then it was delivered to an import/export business in San Francisco. How did it get here? Who bought it? For whom did they work? Who paid them? How?

The more Sarah thinks about it, the more she realizes that a near miracle occurred just to bring her to this experience. Hundreds, if not thousands, of different processes had successfully interacted just to bring her a simple bagel and coffee.

It's truly amazing. And those processes had to do more than just work. They had to work in such a way that all of the economic entities involved obtained a payment to cover their costs and make a profit. How did that occur? Who set the prices? Who computed the quantity of non-fat milk to be shipped in the night before? How does all of this come about?

In truth, all of this activity comes about through the interaction of business processes. The union has a process for ordering, receiving, storing, and paying for ingredients like milk and coffee. The coffee roaster has a process for assembling demand, ordering its raw materials, and making deliveries. All of the other businesses have processes for conducting their affairs as well.

**Q1.** What are the fundamental types of processes in organizations?

**Q2.** What are examples of common business processes?

**Q3.** How can organizations improve processes?

**Q4.** How can organizations use IS to improve processes?

**Q5.** How can an IS hinder a process?

**Q6.** How can SOA improve processes?

## Chapter Preview

Although processes help explain Sarah's miracle, they go largely unnoticed. Processes are not exciting—no one makes a movie, creates a Facebook page, writes a bestseller, or says to a friend, "Hey, check out that process." Many IS professionals once took them for granted, too. After all, computers were going to change everything—the new tricks, rapidly improving performance, and mind-numbing speeds made them the star, not the processes they supported. Those days are over.

Processes are now the most common way to think of business. Further, processes, along with IS and information, are now the foundation of MIS. Because processes are so central to business and MIS, we devote this chapter to processes and how they can be improved. We strongly believe that it is vital for you to be able to see business operations as processes and learn how IS can make these processes better.

To grasp why processes have become so important, let's look at another example. Sarah has a part-time job at a pizza place that is part of a larger pizza chain. Each month, employees are asked to submit suggestions for process improvement. Such improvements are important. If that national pizza chain sells a million pizzas a month, and if Sarah finds a way to improve that process a single penny each time, the company would save $10,000 a month, every month, on that improvement alone.

## Q1. What Are the Fundamental Types of Processes in Organizations?

Let's review what we already know about processes. In Chapter 1, we defined a **business process** as a sequence of activities for accomplishing a function. We also defined an **activity** as a task within a business process and **resources** as the items, such as people, computers, data, and document collections, necessary to accomplish an activity. **Actors** are resources who are either humans or computers. Finally, a **role** is a subset of the activities in a business process that is performed by a particular actor.

### Examples of Processes

At Sarah's pizza restaurant, five processes are needed to fulfill a pizza order. These five, shown in Figure 2-1, are Order, Assemble, Bake, Package, and Deliver.[1] For each of the five processes, activities, roles, resources, and actors can be specified. The five processes are accomplished by the Cashier, Chef, and Driver roles, as shown. Further, each process can be deconstructed into activities. For example, the Assemble process has three main activities—Prepare Dough, Add Sauces, and Add Toppings. Within the Prepare Dough activity, Sarah, an actor, plays the role of Chef and uses resources such as a Recipe and Utensils. Processes and their activities are both depicted by rectangles, because in practice the terms are sometimes used interchangeably. For example, Add Sauces could be considered a process with activities Add Tomato Sauce and Sprinkle on Spices.

A student's life is full of processes. Some of these processes, similar to making a pizza, occur in the same sequence. For example, making it to class might include the processes of getting to the bus stop, taking the bus, getting off the bus, and walking to class. Other processes, such as planning parties, paying bills, doing laundry, or reading MIS textbooks, are not as sequential.

IS can be used to improve processes. For example, students use IS to improve both sequential processes and independent processes. In the past, you used to call people to invite them to

---

[1] From Larry Pervin, "Manufacturing and Work Processes," University of Illinois at Urbana-Champaign, September 2009. Available at *http://www.ler.illinois.edu/sociotech/*.

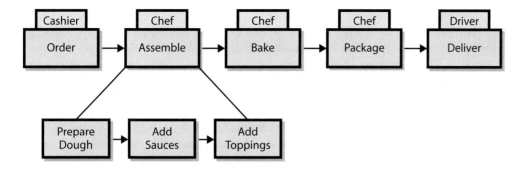

| Assemble Process Activities | Resources | Role |
|---|---|---|
| Prepare Dough | People, Recipe, Utensils, etc. | Chef |
| Add Sauces | People, Measuring Cup, Scales, etc. | Chef |
| Add Toppings | People, Quantity of Toppings, Sequence List, etc. | Chef |

**FIGURE 2-1**

**Five Sequential Processes, Resources, Actors, and Roles at the Pizza Shop**

an event, now Facebook makes that easier; you used to do your taxes by hand, now TurboTax makes that more accurate; and you used to buy greeting cards at a store and mail them at the post office, now e-cards make that process faster.

Although you manage a few important processes in your life, the manager of the pizza shop may have a dozen key processes to oversee, such as hiring employees, closing the store at night, depositing receipts at the bank, taking deliveries, and running promotions. Next door, Walmart managers operate many of the same processes and thousands of others. In both companies, business professionals constantly look for ways to improve or correct process deficiencies. As you will see in this and the next three chapters, IS can help improve business processes much as they have helped you improve your personal processes.

## Scope of Processes

Before we can discuss how IS can improve processes, let's organize the landscape of business processes. That way, we can better understand the wide variety of processes in common use in organizations today. We organize processes in Figure 2-2 into the three categories first introduced in Chapter 1: strategic, managerial, and operational.

**FIGURE 2-2**

**Scope and Characteristics of Processes**

| Scope | Characteristics | Mix of Actors | Frequency | Examples | IS Supporting This Type of Process |
|---|---|---|---|---|---|
| Strategic | Broad-scope, organizational issues | More people than other processes | Low | Decide on new restaurant location, corporate budgeting | Executive support system (ESS) |
| Managerial | Allocation and use of resources | Mix | Medium | Assess seasonal promotions, plan and schedule cashiers | Management information system (MIS) |
| Operational | Common, routine, day-to-day | More computers than other processes | High | Order supplies, pay bills, check out customers | Transaction processing system (TPS) |

**Operational processes** are commonplace, routine, everyday business processes. At the pizza shop these include ordering supplies, paying bills, and ringing up customers. These processes may be executed hundreds or thousands of times a day across all the restaurants in the local franchise. The procedures, or instructions, for these processes are changed very infrequently. Typically, operational processes rely more on computerized actors than do other types of processes. Finally, because many actors contribute to this process, changing them is more difficult than changing other types of processes. Information systems that facilitate operational processes are sometimes called **transaction processing systems (TPS)**.

**Managerial processes** concern resource use. These processes include planning, assessing, and analyzing the resources used by the company in pursuit of its objectives. Managerial processes occur much less frequently and with many fewer computerized actors than operational processes have. At the pizza franchise, these processes include assessing seasonal promotions, planning and scheduling cashiers, and determining which personnel to promote. Information systems that facilitate managerial processes are sometimes called **management information systems (MIS)**, which, by the way, is a second meaning for the term *MIS*.

**Strategic processes** seek to resolve issues that have long-range impact on the organization. These processes have broad scope and impact most of the firm. Because judgment and a tolerance for ambiguity are important, strategic processes typically have more human actors than do operational or managerial processes. Examples of strategic processes include determining where to locate a new restaurant, setting a business's budget, and introducing a new product. Information systems that support strategic processes are sometimes called **executive support systems (ESS)**.

### Objectives of Processes

The operational–managerial–strategic distinction is an important way to classify a process. A second valuable way to understand how processes differ is to consider their objectives, as shown in Figure 2-3. An **objective** is a desired goal an organization has decided to pursue. These objectives can be classified as effective or efficient.

An **effective** objective helps achieve organizational strategy. Sarah's pizza shop depends heavily on pizza sales to college students. As a result, one objective of the Sales process is to sell to freshmen.

A second type of objective is efficiency. An **efficient** objective seeks more output with the same inputs or the same output with fewer inputs. The pizza shop might try to improve the efficiency of the Deliver process. To do so, the shop may specify an objective of reducing unnecessary delays.

To summarize effective objectives help achieve company strategy and efficient objectives seek to conserve limited resources. In other words, efficiency is doing things right, whereas effectiveness is doing the right things.

These two categories of process objectives—efficiency and effectiveness—can occur at any of the three levels of processes—operational, managerial, or strategic. That said, the most common combinations are operational processes with efficiency objectives and strategic processes with effectiveness objectives.

**FIGURE 2-3**

**Process Objectives and Measures**

| Objective Category | Definition | Example Process and Objective at Pizza Shop |
|---|---|---|
| Effectiveness | Achieve organizational strategy | Sales process: Sell to freshmen |
| Efficiency | Create more output with same input or same output with fewer inputs | Deliver process: Reduce unnecessary delays |

| Primary Activity | Description | Support Activity | | |
|---|---|---|---|---|
| Inbound Logistics | Receiving, storing, and disseminating inputs to products | Human Resources | Technology | Infrastructure |
| Operations | Transforming inputs into final products | | | |
| Outbound logistics | Collecting, storing, and physically distributing products to buyers | | | |
| Sales and marketing | Inducing buyers to purchase products and providing a means for them to do so | | | |
| Customer service | Assisting customer's use of products and thus maintaining and enhancing the products' value | | | |

**FIGURE 2-4**

**The Value Chain**

## Q2. What Are Examples of Common Business Processes?

So far, we have classified processes by their scope—strategic, managerial, and operational, and by their objectives—effectiveness and efficiency. A third characteristic of processes is their place within the value chain. A value chain is a series of value-adding activities.[2] As shown in Figure 2-4, a value chain is composed of five primary activities and several support activities. The primary activities are inbound logistics, operations, outbound logistics, sales and marketing, and service. The support activites include human resources, technology, and infrastructure (which includes legal, finance, general management, and other functions). The supporting activites support each of the primary activities.

Figure 2-5 highlights a variety of processes in each of the primary activities and two of the support activities. This overview of business processes will help you see the variety of processes at a typical firm within the context of the value chain—a framework that is common in business. You will learn more about these business processes and value chains in other business school courses.

### Inbound Logistics Processes

Inbound logistics receives, stores, and disseminates product input.[3] Processes in inbound logistics listed in Figure 2-5 include Procurement, Manage Inventory, and Evaluate Potential Suppliers. **Procurement** is an operational process that acquires goods and services. Procurement activities at the pizza shop include ordering ingredients and boxes, as well as receiving and paying for those items. This Procurement process is the subject of Chapter 4. Inventory management processes use past data to compute stocking levels, reorder levels, and reorder quantities in accordance with inventory policy. An example of a strategic inbound logistics process is the evaluation of potential suppliers. When the pizza shop orders ingredients, it only uses suppliers who were previously approved by the strategic process called Supplier Selection.

### Operations Processes

Operations transform inputs into outputs. Operations processes schedule the equipment, people, and facilities necessary to build or assemble a product or provide a service. Assembling and baking pizzas are two operational operations processes. An example of a management operations process is scheduling maintenance on the ovens. Strategic processes evaluate if the pizza company should open another restaurant or change its menu.

---

[2] Warning: Porter uses the term *activities* to describe these categories. We use the term *activity* in our definition of a process as a series of activities.

[3] Definitions of value chain activities are from Michael Porter's *Competitive Advantage* (New York: Simon and Schuster, 1998).

**FIGURE 2-5**

**Value Chain Activities
and Process Examples**

| Value Chain Activity | Operational Process | Managerial Process | Strategic Processes |
|---|---|---|---|
| **Primary Activities** | | | |
| Inbound logistics | Procurement (*Chapter 4*) | Manage inventory | Evaluate potential suppliers |
| Operations | Assemble product | Schedule maintenance | Open new restaurant |
| Outbound logistics | Sales (*Chapter 5*) | Award refund | Determine payment policy |
| Sales & marketing | Mail promotion | Evaluate promotional discounts | Launch new product |
| Service | Track orders | Evaluate complaint patterns | Evaluate outsourcing options |
| **Support Activities** | | | |
| Human resources | Recruit employees | Plan future needs | Determine pay scales |
| Technology development | Test software | Estimate milestones | Evaluate acquisition options |

### Outbound Logistics Processes

**Outbound logistics processes** collect, store, and distribute products to buyers. Outbound logistics processes concern the management of finished-goods inventory and the movement of goods from that inventory to the customer. Outbound logistics processes are especially prominent for nonmanufacturers, such as distributors, wholesalers, and retailers.

An operational outbound process is the **Sales process** that records the sales order, ships the product, and bills the customer. Other operational outbound logistics processes at the pizza shop include the Order, Package, and Deliver processes. A managerial outbound logistics process is Award a Refund. A strategic outbound logistics process is Determine Payment Policy, such as deciding if the shop will accept personal checks.

### Sales and Marketing Processes

Sales and marketing provide the means and incentives for customers to purchase a product or service. The primary objective of sales and marketing processes is to find prospects and transform them into customers by selling them something. The end of the sales and marketing process is the beginning of the Sales process mentioned earlier. When the pizza chain mails promotions to prospects it is executing its operational Promotion process. Evaluate Promotional Discounts is a managerial marketing process. Examples of strategic marketing processes are Launch New Product or Open New Restaurant.

### Service Processes

Providing after-sales support to enhance or maintain the value of a product is called *service*. Operational customer service processes include Track Orders, Customer Support, and Customer Support Training. Customers call customer service to ask questions about their order status, to query and report problems with their accounts, and to receive assistance with product use. When a customer calls the pizza shop about a late delivery, the store manager initiates a service process. This process records some of the key circumstances for later analysis and awards the customer a discount on a future purchase or the immediate delivery of another pizza. A management service process evaluates customer complaints to determine if there are patterns to the complaints, such as day of the week or a particular delivery person. Evaluating outsourcing service options is a strategic service process.

### Human Resources Processes

**Human resources processes** assess the motivations and skills of employees; create job positions; investigate employee complaints; and staff, train, and evaluate personnel. Operational human resources processes recruit, compensate, and assess employee performance for the organization. In a small company such as the pizza shop, posting a job may be a simple process requiring one or two approvals. In a larger, more formal organization, posting a new job may involve multiple levels of approval requiring use of a tightly controlled and standardized process. Management processes address the development and training of the organization's workforce and planning for future needs. Strategic processes in human resources determine pay scales, authorize types of incentives, and decide organizational structure.

### Technology Development Processes

**Technology development processes** include designing, testing, and developing technology in support of the primary activities. An operational technology development process tests whether newly developed software can handle tens of thousands of possible keystroke entries. A managerial technology development process is a milestone development process that estimates time required for each step in a software development process. A strategic technology development process decides if a particular technology will be purchased or developed by the company.

## Q3. How Can Organizations Improve Processes?

You can fill a library with books on the topic of improving processes. Here we simplify some of these suggestions into general categories. Then, in Q4, we add to this list several ways that IS can help improve a process. Figure 2-6 shows three fundamental steps in a process for improving processes. We call this process the **OMIS model**, for **O**bjectives, **M**easures, and **I**nformation **S**ystems.

### Process Objectives

Each process has one or more objectives. The first step in the OMIS model, as shown in Figure 2-7, is to specify and, if possible, improve the objectives for the process.

As mentioned earlier, process objectives can be classified as either efficient or effective. For example, the Sales process at the pizza shop has two objectives. One is an efficiency objective—reduce the time needed to place an order by phone—and the other is an effectiveness objective—sell to freshman.

Often a process will have unstated objectives. The OMIS model requires that each process have explicitly stated objectives. At other times, businesspeople may disagree about the objectives, and this step will force them to resolve these differences. Finally, processes may have stated objectives that are vague or inappropriate. For example, a vague objective would be to have a great sales process. Inappropriate objectives are objectives not matched to strategy. If the strategic plan of the pizza shop is to target freshman, but the only two promotional process objectives are to promote multitopping pizzas and salad orders, the promotional process objectives are inappropriate for the stated strategy.

In today's Information Age, process improvement can cross over a line into evading someone's personal privacy. Read the Ethics Guide on pages 46–47 to consider this dilemma.

| To improve a process: |
|---|
| • **O**bjectives: Specify and improve |
| • **M**easures: Specify and improve |
| • **IS**: Implement IS improvements |

**FIGURE 2-6**

**Steps in the OMIS Model**

**FIGURE 2-7**

**Options for Improving
the Objectives of a
Process**

**FIGURE 2-7**

**Options for Improving
the Objectives of a
Process**

**To improve a process:**

• **O**bjectives: Specify and improve
   Classify objectives as effectiveness or efficiency
   Make objectives explicit
   Obtain agreement about objectives
   Ensure that objectives are not vague or inappropriate

• **M**easures: Specify and improve

• **IS**: Implement IS improvements

### Process Measures

The second step in the OMIS model, as shown in Figure 2-8, is to specify and, if possible, improve how each objective is measured. **Measures**, also called **metrics**, are quantities assigned to attributes. For example, a measure of the deliver process is the elapsed time from leaving the store until arrival at the customer's location. This attribute is measured using the quantity of minutes and seconds.

Some measures are common, others can be unique. Some processes have commonly accepted ways to measure them, like delivery time for a pizza. Other processes have measures that are created by managers for that particular process. In either case, the second step of the OMIS model requires that the measures be clearly identified and improved, if possible.

Selecting and creating measures can be difficult. Many of the objectives of a process are difficult to quantify. For example, the pizza shop wants to sell to freshmen so that these students become frequent customers over their time at the university. However, it is hard to know which customers are freshmen. As a result, the pizza shop decides to measure the number of deliveries to the dorms as an approximation. Freshmen are not the only dorm residents, but this is the only measure that is available to the pizza shop.

Although measuring dorm sales is clearly not a perfect measure of freshmen sales, the pizza shop owner realizes that all measures are imperfect to some degree. Einstein once said, "Not everything that can be counted counts, and not everything that counts can be counted." When considering measures, recognize they all have limitations and that the key business challenge is to select the best ones available and to know their limits.

The best measures are reasonable, accurate, and consistent. A reasonable measure is a measure that is valid and compelling. It is reasonable to approximate freshmen pizza orders with dorm orders. Accurate measures are exact and precise. An accurate measure is 26 pizzas, a less accurate one is "more than last week." To accurately assess an objective, it may be appropriate to have multiple measures. For example, to assess selling to freshmen the pizza shop might also record the number of pizzas delivered to campus during the freshmen orientation weekend. A final characteristic of a good measurement is consistency. A business should develop measures of processes that are reliable; that is, the measure returns the same value if the same situation reoccurs.

Having specified and improved the stated objectives and measures, we can now consider how to improve a process with IS. The results of the improvement will be apparent in the specified measures.

**FIGURE 2-8**

**Options for Improving
the Measures of a
Process**

**To improve a process:**

• **O**bjectives: Specify and improve

• **M**easures: Specify and improve
   Ensure that measures are:
      –Reasonable
      –Accurate
      –Consistent

• **IS**: Implement IS improvements

# Q4. How Can Organizations Use IS to Improve Processes?

Today, information systems are playing an increasingly important role in business processes. Think about Sarah in the student union, virtually all the organizational processes she is considering depend heavily on IS. Look around you. Did any man-made item in your sight get there without an IS helping that process along? Probably not.

An IS can support a process in a number of ways. Here we consider three ways, as shown in Figure 2-9.

## Three Ways IS Improve Processes

One way to improve a process with IS is to improve the efficiency or effectiveness of the activities. Earlier in this chapter we suggested that Facebook, TurboTax, and e-cards are examples of improving an activity with an IS. Similarly, the pizza shop can equip each delivery vehicle with a GPS with traffic updates. This would help to reduce unnecessary delays in this activity in the Deliver process. As a result, the measure of this objective—delivery time—is improved.

At Central Colorado State one strategic objective is to expand the use of education technology. In one process, the Teaching process, the classroom teaching activity is improved with a new IS in the classroom that can display online material, DVD resources, and other content. One measure of the Teaching process is frequency of use of educational technology.

Information systems can also improve a process by improving the links among activities either in the same process or among activities in different processes. The impact of one activity on another activity is called a **linkage**. For example, consider the new IS the pizza shop installed to record pizza orders as they are phoned in. This IS improved an activity in the Order process, and it improved the link between Order activities and Deliver activities. The system displays new orders in real time on all the drivers' GPS displays. Using this data, drivers can make better plans about when to stop for gas or when to wait for one more pizza to finish cooking before heading out on deliveries. As a result, delivery time is again improved with this IS.

At Sarah's university, Moodle, a learning management IS, was implemented to improve the linkage among a variety of educational processes. For example, students can collaborate on the system using the discussion board and submit the results of their collaboration for evaluation without leaving Moodle. The processes of Collaboration and Evaluation are jointly improved—the objective of increasing collaboration and reducing time spent submitting evaluation material are both improved.

A third way that IS can improve a process is to improve control of the process. In general, **control** limits behavior. A process is like a river; controls are like dams and sidewalls that limit and direct the flow of the river. Like a dam that maintains a steady flow for the river, controls

**To improve a process:**

• **O**bjectives: Specify and improve

• **M**easures: Specify and improve

• **IS**: Implement IS improvements.
      Improvements can enhance:
         –An activity
            Pizza shop: GPS improves offsite Deliver process

         –Linkages among activities
            Pizza shop: Order display improves offsite Deliver process

         –Control of an activity
            Pizza shop: Order input control improves in restaurant Deliver process

**FIGURE 2-9**

**Options for Improving the Use of IS in a Process**

help reduce wide variations in a process so that it runs consistently and smoothly. In other words, the process provides consistent results. One common control used in organizations is standardization, another is IS.

Control is vital to business processes. Controls at the pizza shop help make every pizza the same size, keep the oven at a consistent temperature, and allow only the manager to void sales on the cash register. An example of an IS control is the computer added recently to the in-restaurant Order process. Waiters and waitresses now input orders on the computer rather than on handwritten slips. One control on this process is that incomplete orders are not sent to the kitchen. For example, if a waiter fails to enter three pizza toppings for a three-topping pizza or a dressing is not specified for a salad, the system alerts the waiter to enter the missing data. The kitchen is not given the order until it is corrected by the waiter. This control helps reduce delivery time, in this case, for in-restaurant orders.

At Central Colorado State an example of using an IS to improve control is the recent procedural change to the Login process. The old procedure required users to login with both a username and password; now the procedure takes the user's e-mail as the username. With fewer inputs, there are fewer errors. Fewer errors are a sign of improved control. The objectives of the Login process—accurate authentication and reducing time—are both improved.

These examples show some of the possibilities for improving processes with information systems. IS support of processes will continue to grow as the price–performance ratio of computers continues to plummet, new technologies and ideas continue to enter the business world, and young professionals join the workforce who are more comfortable with technology than any previous generation. The most significant technology for improving business processes has emerged over the past decade. These are multimillion-dollar ERP systems that are designed to support and coordinate a wide range of company processes.

For you to be able to contribute in such an environment, hone your ability to visualize and assess business processes. That is, once you isolate a particular process, determine its objectives, assess the quality of its measures, and determine if IS can support that process. To this end, the OMIS model is designed to equip you with a series of questions you can ask to better understand a current process and to make suggestions for improvement.

### Non-IS Process Improvements

We would be remiss if we did not include a discussion of how processes can be improved by non-IS means. In Figure 2-10, we present the two general categories: add more resources and change the structure of the process.

A business can improve a process by adding resources to a given process without changing its structure. One way to reduce delays in the Delivery process is to simply add more drivers. Similarly, some processes can be improved by reducing resources. If the pizza shop has drivers sitting around talking, their productivity may increase by reducing the driving staff.

A second way of altering a business process is to change its structure. Process designers can change the arrangement of the activities of a process without changing resource allocations. An example of changing a structure can be seen in the Assemble process. Currently, each chef rolls dough, adds toppings, then loads his or her own pizza into the oven and takes it out when it is finished. On busy nights, a better structure to the process would be to specialize the jobs. That

**FIGURE 2-10**

**Non-IS Process Improvements**

| Improvement Category | Process | Examples in Pizza Shop | Objective | Measure |
|---|---|---|---|---|
| Add more resources | Delivery | Hire more drivers | Reduce unnecessary delays | Average time in minutes |
| Change the structure | Make | Specialize cooks | Reduce unnecessary delays | Average time in minutes |

is, one chef rolls dough for all the pizzas, another adds ingredients, and a third moves pizzas in and out. This helps reduce delays, an objective of the Assemble process.

Although it is convenient to describe process improvement as IS and non IS, in practice the two frequently overlap. Often a process structure is redesigned to take advantage of new IS. For example, the process of sharing academic content with students has changed structure with on-line content. Once the process was for students to buy a textbook at the college bookstore; now the process includes that activity but also includes online supplements.

Keep in mind that there are always ways to improve processes. The issue is whether it is worth the cost and if the improvements help the process better achieve the firm's strategy. For example, the pizza shop can always add more drivers or use Twitter to take orders, but managers must decide if these improvements are better than other choices that might be less expensive or time consuming and achieve the strategy better.

Although our OMIS model is a good way to begin your process education, the most common approach to process improvement, particularly in the manufacturing industry, is called Six Sigma. **Six Sigma** seeks to improve process outputs by removing causes of defects and minimizing variability in the process. Each Six Sigma project follows a very structured sequence of steps with quantified financial measures. Six Sigma gets its name from its goal that 99.99966 percent of process outputs will be free from defects. Without such high quality processes, Six Sigma proponents argue that we would be without electricity 10 minutes each week, 810 commercial airliners would crash every month, and 50 newborn babies would be dropped at birth by a doctor every day.[4]

## Participants and Diagrams in Process Improvement

Whether achieved through Six Sigma, the OMIS model, or other approaches, process improvement at medium-to-large organizations always involves a team. Typically, the process includes the users who are the actors in the process, managers, and business analysts. Managers help by coordinating the changes, acquiring the necessary resources, and motivating participants. Business analysts contribute by understanding the fundamentals of process change and by creating diagrams of processes.

Unless the process is very simple, like assembling or baking a pizza, diagramming a process is typically necessary in order for team members to understand the process and to identify activities that must be changed. It is necessary for the redesign team to understand how the current process works and what the intended process should look like. Diagrams of the current process are typically called **as-is diagrams** and diagrams of suggested improvements **ought-to-be diagrams**. Diagrams can take many forms, but as mentioned in Chapter 1, we will use the current gold standard, BPMN.

To better understand BPMN diagramming, consider the Select New Supplier process for Sarah's pizza shop. This is the process used by the pizza franchise company that owns and operates Sarah's pizza shop and a dozen other outlets in the same region. The company must find and select suppliers for fresh pizza items, cleaning supplies, uniform cleaning, office supplies, and waste removal. The objectives of this managerial process are to find low-cost but good-quality suppliers. The measures for these objectives are shown in Figure 2-11.

| Objectives | Measures |
|---|---|
| **Good Quality**<br>Effectiveness | Difference in scheduled and actual delivery time<br>Number of returned purchases |
| **Low Cost**<br>Efficiency | Supplier price at or below industry average |

**FIGURE 2-11**

**Objectives and Measures of the New Supplier Process**

---

[4] J. Harrington and K. Lomax, *Performance Improvement Methods: Fighting the War on Waste* (New York: McGraw-Hill), p. 57.

The Select New Supplier process is shown in Figure 2-12. It begins when the franchise communicates a request for proposal (RFP) to potential suppliers (the Request Proposal from Supplier activity). This activity, completed by the warehouse manager, finds potential suppliers, performs a cursory investigation of their products, and contacts the potential supplier's sales office. If the supplier responds positively, the next step is the Receive Proposal from Supplier activity. In this activity, a supplier provides address and contract data and a list of products the supplier expects to sell to the franchise if the supplier is approved. This application data and product data are inserted as new supplier data in a resource labeled Warehouse DB. Once this activity is complete, the warehouse manager evaluates the potential supplier's product list to determine items that may be appropriate. While this activity is happening, an accountant is also evaluating the supplier's credit policies in the Evaluate Supplier Credit Policies activity. The data generated about the supplier's credit policies is stored in the Accounting DB. This data will be used later by the accounting department in payment processes. Accounting also collects other data on the supplier in order to reach an approve/disapprove supplier decision. This activity is called Evaluate Supplier Financial Strength. If the accountants approve the potential supplier, a Complete the Application activity is initiated that specifies the potential products to be ordered. Finally, after the first month, the final activity, Evaluate Supplier Performance, is accomplished. The franchise strives to determine quickly whether a supplier is working out.

**FIGURE 2-12**

**BPMN Diagram of the New Supplier Process**

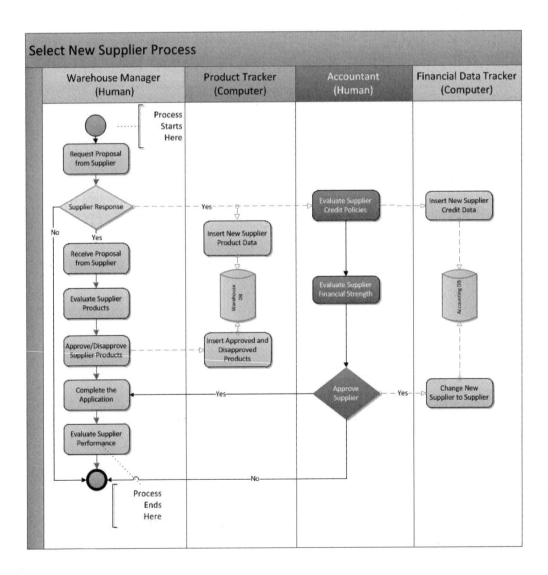

# Q5. How Can an IS Hinder a Process?

As we have seen, an IS can be used to improve a process. However, an IS can also reduce process efficiency and effectiveness and limit its improvement. Notice that the objectives of the Select New Supplier process are to select suppliers that are low cost and good quality. The final activity in the Select New Supplier process is Evaluate New Supplier Performance. To evaluate the new supplier, an analyst must obtain data on the new supplier's deliveries to the pizza shops. One measure of good quality is the timeliness of delivery—the difference in time between scheduled delivery and actual delivery. Unfortunately, the scheduled delivery times are stored in the franchise database system, but actual delivery times are stored in spreadsheets at the different shops. Storing data in multiple places can hinder a process and make it difficult to improve. The data could be stored in multiple places for a number of reasons, and we will consider these shortly.

## Information Silos

Sharing data is essential to improving a process. The key disadvantage of maintaining data in multiple places is that the data are difficult to share. This situation is called **information silos**, a condition that exists when data are isolated in separated information systems or when data are duplicated in various files and databases. When duplicated, the data can become inconsistent if changes are made to just one copy. Stated from a process point of view, the data needed by one process are stored in an information system designed and used in another process. (Isolated systems are referred to as *silos* because when drawn in diagrams they appear as long vertical columns—like silos.) Because they operate in isolation from one another, they create islands of automation or information silos that can diminish the efficiency and effectiveness of a process and limit the opportunities to improve it.

Information silos can make processes inefficient. For example, the Evaluate New Supplier activity is very inefficient. An analyst must first find the actual delivery times and then enter these times into the same database that tracks scheduled delivery times in order to calculate the timeliness of delivery. The same situation occurs when the franchise runs the Evaluate Promotional Campaign process. Redeemed promotional coupons are collected at each store. However, the number of pizzas sold during the campaign is kept in the franchise sales database.

Information silos can also make processes ineffective. Anytime data is transcribed from one place to another or entered in two places errors can occur. With errors, the measures calculated for some new suppliers and promotions will be incorrect, making these processes less effective than if the data were in one place.

The most obvious fix to eliminate information silos is to store a single copy of data in a shared database and revising business processes to use that database. A single-copy database solution is a feature of the ERP systems that we will discuss in the next three chapters.

## Why Information Silos Exist

Information silos at the pizza franchise are caused, in part, by the physical separation of the stores from the franchise headquarters. However, this information silo problem occurs even when all the data is under the same roof. For example, at the franchise office, one database stores data on restaurant sales while another database keeps track of the inventory and deliveries. In each database, the data are compiled at the end of the day and shared with the other database. This delay normally does not impact the franchise; however, several times a year sales are quite unusual, and this delay leads to running out of items at the restaurants or unneeded deliveries. If the data were all in one system, these problems would be less likely to occur.

If the problems of information silos are so evident and the ERP solution so clear, why does this issue ever arise? Organizations store data in separate databases for several reasons.

First, organizational departments prefer to control the systems they use. Departmental personnel like to control how databases are set up, what the data will look like, and how the database will be updated. Also, one department may have very different objectives than other departments in the firm. These objectives might be to minimize inventory or serve customers. Therefore, a department system that helps accomplish this one objective might be deemed better by the department than an enterprise system that does not support that objective as well.

Another reason departments set up their own databases is that they analyze the costs and benefits of the system using their own, fairly narrow measures. Using their own narrow department measures, the advantages of an enterprise system may not be evident. Only when many processes in many departments all rely on the same IS do the savings really accumulate.

There are also more legitimate reasons for a department to use its own database. Some processes use sensitive data not needed in other processes, such as tax data for accounting processes and health care claims data for the HR department. Also, a department system can be purchased and implemented more quickly than most enterprise solutions. Finally, departmental IS are much more affordable; enterprise systems can cost as much as 10 to 50 times as much as a single-department application.

In the past, the choice was frequently to use a department IS to support a department process, because cross-department IS were rare. Today, the expectation is to share data among departments as organizations seek to improve their processes, not just in one pizza franchise, but across a global enterprise.

## Q6. How Can SOA Improve Processes?

Data trapped in silos limit process improvements. Although enterprise systems can address this problem, another approach is SOA, or *services-oriented architecture*. SOA is a new IS approach designed to make it easier to share data among process activities.

Earlier we stated that an IS can improve process activities, linkages, and control. SOA, like an IS, improves a process by facilitating data sharing and by improving control by enforcing standards. We close the chapter with this topic because it is a valuable approach to combat information silos and an interesting current example of how IS can improve processes.

SOA was originally used to design interacting, widely distributed, Internet-based computer programs. SOA enables the development of *middleware*, software that sits between two computer programs and facilitates interprogram communication and data sharing. More recently, systems designers have applied SOA principles to business process activities, whether those activities are manual, partly automated, or fully automated. SOA offers great flexibility, ease of use, and adaptability, and we can expect that it will see even greater use as organizations continue the trend toward integrating processes.

To begin, SOA is not a piece of software or hardware. It is a design philosophy. Two previous design philosophies were standalone computers and client-server architecture. **Service-oriented architecture (SOA)** is a design in which every activity is modeled as an encapsulated service and exchanges among those services are governed by standards. This definition has three key terms: *service, encapsulation,* and *standards*. Consider each.

### Service

First, a **service** is a repeatable task that a business needs to perform. A service is similar to an activity in a process, a very common activity that may be used by many processes. A service needs access to data to be efficient. At a bookstore, the following are examples of services:

- Calculate a tax amount.
- Pay another business.
- Check inventory of a book.

Each of these services is performed frequently at the bookstore, and each requires data. Further, each of these services is an activity in several processes. Prior to SOA, checking inventory might be hardwired into each process in a slightly different fashion, making the code and activity difficult to use in different processes. If the process designers treat these services as standalone, independent activities, these activities can be plugged into various processes without rewriting code.

# MIS InClass 2

## Improving the Process of Making Paper Airplanes[5]

The purpose of this exercise is to demonstrate process concepts. In this exercise, students will form assembly lines to create paper airplanes. Each assembly line will have the same four activities, each called a Work Center (WC), as shown in Figure 2-13. Raw material is a stack of plain paper, finished goods are the folded airplanes, and WIP is "Work in Progress," which is the output of the WC prior to the next WC.

One student is assigned to each of the four WCs in the assembly line. Student 1 (in WC 1) creates the first fold, as shown at the top of Figure 2-14. Student 2, at WC 2, folds the corners, also shown in Figure 2-14. The location and assembly instructions for Students 3 and 4 are also shown in Figure 2-14. In addition to the four students who fold the planes, seven other students observe, time, and record each assembly line, as listed below, using the three forms in Figure 2-15:

*Source: Benis Arapovic/Shutterstock.*

**Observer 1:** Use Form 1, record WC 1 task times.

**Observer 2:** Use Form 1, record WC 2 task times.

**Observer 3:** Use Form 1, record WC 3 task times.

**Observer 4:** Use Form 1, record WC 4 task times.

**Observer 5:** Use Form 2, record cycle time at the end of the line.

**Observer 6:** Use Form 3, record colored sheet throughput time.

**Observer 7:** Count WIP at the end of each run.

Each assembly line is run to construct 20 airplanes. Prior to beginning the process, each line will run a practice session of four or five planes. Then, clear the line, start the clock, and make the 20 airplanes. Each WC continues to work until the 20th plane is finished, which means that more than 20 will be started because there will be WIP when the 20th is finished. About halfway through the run, the instructor will insert a colored piece of paper as raw material. Each student assembler works at his or her own pace. As workers build planes, they should work at a comfortable pace and not speed. This is not a contest for maximum output, but for quality.

After the first run is completed, make a second run of 20 planes with all the same roles. However, each student can work only when there is an airplane in their inbox (WIP) and no airplane in their outbox (WIP). Again, midway through the run the instructor will insert a colored sheet of paper.

After the runs:

1. In teams, diagram the process using BPMN symbols such as roles, swimlanes, activities, and decisions. Name resources assigned to roles.
2. Apply the OMIS model to improve this process. Discuss the objectives of the assembly line. If you were in charge of the assembly line like this one, do you think your objectives would be efficiency or effectiveness? Specify the measures used to monitor progress toward your objective(s).
3. Assume that the WC folding is done by four machines. In that scenario, the second run uses different software than the first run. Does this new IS improve an activity, linkage, or control?
4. Are any data in an information silo on the first or second runs?
5. Which measure changed most significantly from the first to the second run? Did you anticipate this? Are other processes with other measures just as subject to change with a similar minor change in information?
6. Were there any controls on the assembly process? Could an IS improve the process by improving control? On which measure(s) will this improvement appear?

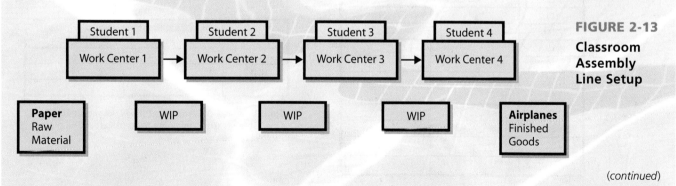

**FIGURE 2-13**

**Classroom Assembly Line Setup**

*(continued)*

---

[5] Based on "A Classroom Exercise to Illustrate Lean Manufacturing Pull Concepts," by Peter J. Billington, in *Decision Sciences Journal of Innovative Education*, 2(1), 2004, pp. 71–77.

**FIGURE 2-14**

**Assembly (Folding) Instructions**

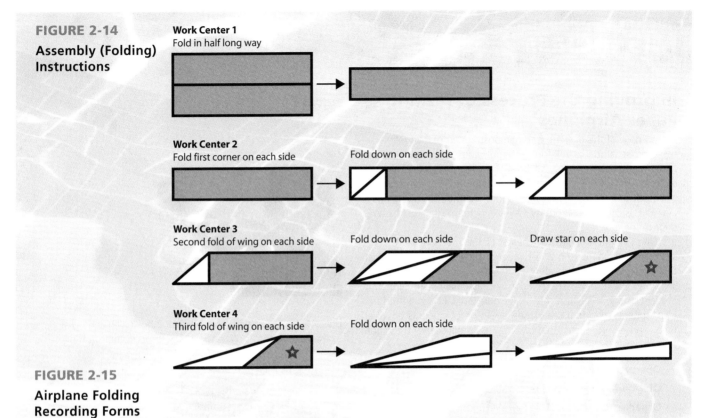

**Work Center 1**
Fold in half long way

**Work Center 2**
Fold first corner on each side        Fold down on each side

**Work Center 3**
Second fold of wing on each side        Fold down on each side        Draw star on each side

**Work Center 4**
Third fold of wing on each side        Fold down on each side

**FIGURE 2-15**

**Airplane Folding Recording Forms**

## Work Center _____ (1, 2, 3, or 4)

| Unit | Run 1 (seconds) | Run 2 (seconds) |
|------|-----------------|-----------------|
| 1 | | |
| 2 | | |
| 3 | | |
| 4 | | |
| 5 | | |
| 6 | | |
| 7 | | |
| 8 | | |
| 9 | | |
| 10 | | |
| 11 | | |
| 12 | | |
| 13 | | |
| 14 | | |
| 15 | | |
| 16 | | |
| 17 | | |
| 18 | | |
| 19 | | |
| 20 | | |
| Sum | | |
| Average | | |

**Form 1:** Airplane manufacturing task time. Observers 1, 2, 3, and 4 use this form to record assembly times for each Work Center.

| System | Throughput Time for 20 Sheets Run 1 | Throughput Time for 20 Sheets Run 2 |
|--------|-------------------------------------|-------------------------------------|
| Run 1 | | |
| Run 2 | | |
| | | |

**Form 2:** Airplane manufacturing cycle time for 20 airplanes. Observer 5 uses this form to record start and finish time for entire run of 20 planes.

| System | Throughput Time for Colored Sheets Run 1 | Throughput Time for Colored Sheets Run 2 |
|--------|------------------------------------------|------------------------------------------|
| Run 1 | | |
| Run 2 | | |
| | | |

**Form 3:** Paper airplane manufacturing color sheet throughput time. Observer 6 uses this form to record start and finish time for colored sheet.

## Encapsulation

Now consider *encapsulation,* the second key term in the SOA definition. **Encapsulation** hides details inside a container. In networks, encapsulation is used to allow devices to communicate containers (packets) of data without being concerned about the data inside. SOA uses encapsulation in much the same way, hiding data within containers so that services can communicate. Figure 2-16 shows the interactions of two services at Hard Books, Inc., a book supplier for the bookstore. The Process Credit Order service is part of a business Order process. Authorize Credit is a second service that is part of a different business process called Credit Authorization. Using SOA principles, each service will be designed to be independent; neither will be aware of how the other does its work and neither will need to know. Instead, these services need only agree on how they will exchange data and what that exchange means.

The Process Credit Order service sends customer credit data to the Authorize Credit service. It receives back a credit authorization that contains an approval or rejection and other data. The Credit Authorization process could involve flipping a coin, throwing darts, or performing some sophisticated data mining analysis on the customer's data. Process Credit Order does not know, nor does it need to know, how that authorization is made.

When the logic for some service is isolated in this way, the logic is said to be encapsulated in the service. Encapsulation places the logic in one place, which is exceedingly desirable. For one, all other services know to go to that one place for that service. Even more important, if the managers of the credit department decide to change how they make credit authorizations, Process Credit Order is not affected. As long as the structure and meaning of customer credit data and credit authorization data do not change, Process Credit Order is completely isolated from changes in Authorize Credit or any other service in the Credit Authorization process.

Because of encapsulation, service implementations can be readily adapted to new requirements, technologies, and methodologies. In fact, it does not matter who performs the services or where they are performed. Credit authorization could be done by a single company department on a single computer. Later, it could be changed to be performed by a different company, on different computers, in another part of the world. As long as the interface between Process Credit Order and Authorize Credit does not change, Authorize Credit is free to change its implementation.

## Standards

The third key term in the SOA definition is *standards.* Data, and more generically, messages, are exchanged among services using standardized formats and techniques, which are referred to as **SOA standards**. In the past, the programmers of the Process Credit Order program would meet with the programmers of the Authorize Credit program and design a unique, proprietary means for exchanging data via this interface. Such a design is expensive and time consuming. Consequently, the computer industry developed standard ways for formatting messages and describing services and standard protocols for managing the exchanges among services. Those standards eliminated the need for proprietary designs and expanded the scope and importance of SOA.

SOA can improve the efficiency and effectiveness of a process in the same ways an IS improves processes. SOA makes activities easier and hence less costly to access. Further, SOA improves control because it limits the messages exchanged by using standards. Standards help control the exchange of messages.

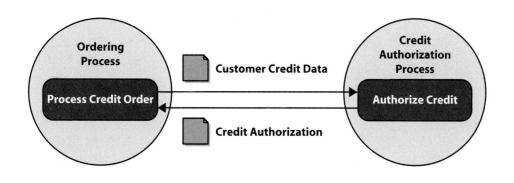

**FIGURE 2-16**

**Example of Two Independent Encapsulated Services**

# Ethics Guide

## Process Improvement or Privacy Problem?

A new type of IS, a vehicle tracking system is improving many company processes, and at the same time, raising privacy issues. These vehicle tracking systems are typically used by companies on their fleet of vehicles. They are becoming increasingly common in food delivery and car rental companies.

These companies use the systems to better track their fleet of vehicles, improve routing and dispatch, prevent theft, and improve vehicle retrieval. Some hotel companies are using the systems to ensure that special guests are appropriately welcomed upon arrival at the hotel.

These systems typically include the wireless device attached to the vehicle and some type of GPS tracking server that receives data from the device, stores it and creates reports for analysis. Two types of systems are in use. Active systems collect data and transmit the data to the server in real time via cellular networks. Passive systems store the data on board for later download to the server.

Automobile insurance companies are beginning to offer discounts to drivers willing to install a wireless computer device on their cars. This device can measure distance traveled, acceleration, speed, turning forces, and braking. If these measures indicate a cautious driver, some insurance companies give 20 to 30 percent discounts. Many cautious drivers hail this improvement as a just reward for their good driving. They also might like to see this device on all vehicles in order to increase public safety on the roads. Others, particularly privacy advocates, see it as yet another example of an invasion of privacy.

### DISCUSSION QUESTIONS

1. Would you install such a device to get a discount? What if the discount was 50 percent? 70 percent?
2. Is it appropriate for parents not to tell their 16-year-old driver that they installed this device on their cars in order to secretly learn from the insurance company how cautiously the teen drives?
3. Is it ethical for a company to sell this data to a car manufacturer? The insurance company never specifically asked its customers if it could share this data, and the car company does not want any customer-identifying data, just the driver's age and the measures for each driver.
4. Should the legal system be able to subpoena this data from the insurance company as evidence in a court case? Would your answer change if you were being falsely accused of a hit-and-run accident?

5. Car rental and food delivery companies are required to tell their drivers when these systems are in place. In what ways can these systems lead to abuse and how could the systems be designed to limit these abuses?

6. Should Sarah's pizza franchise require this device for all vehicles used by its drivers? It would not be used for insurance purposes, but to determine better delivery routes and to encourage delivery drivers to be more cautious.

7. For the pizza franchise, this device is an IS that improves a process. The business process is Delivery. What are the objectives of the Delivery process? What measures would the IS improvement make available?

8. Is this IS improvement an improvement in activity, linkage, or control?

9. In this scenario, improving a process with IS reduces privacy. Do all IS improvements involving processes with employees or customers reduce privacy? Can you think of processes with sensitive employee or customer data in health care, finance, or social media where improving the process with IS does not threaten privacy?

# Active Review

Use this Active Review to verify that you understand the material in the chapter. You can read the entire chapter and then perform the tasks in this review, or you can read the text material for just one question and perform the tasks in this review for that question before moving on to the next one.

## Q1. What are the fundamental types of processes in organizations?

Define *business process* and the key terms that describe business processes: *activity, resource, role,* and *actor*. Name the term that can be fulfilled by either a human or computer. Explain what business professionals constantly seek to do with their processes. List the three main categories of process scope, and explain how each one is different from the others. Give examples of processes in each of the categories. Define *efficiency* and *effectiveness*. What things are efficient and effective?

## Q2. What are examples of common business processes?

Explain a process in each of the primary activities of the value chain. Explain a support activity process in HR and accounting. Specify if that process is operational, managerial, or strategic and explain why you classified it that way. Describe a procurement process and a sales and marketing process.

## Q3. How can organizations improve processes?

Explain the OMIS model. Explain vague and inappropriate objectives. Explain measures and discuss why they are difficult to develop. Give examples of reasonable, accurate, and consistent process measures.

## Q4. How can organizations use IS to improve processes?

Explain the three ways IS can be used to improve a particular process. Specify a process and explain how an IS can improve that process. Specify measures and objectives for the process. Give an example of a process where an activity can be improved using an IS. Define *linkage* and explain how IS can improve linkage in a process. Explain why control is important for a business process. Describe an example of how IS can improve control in a process. Explain the two categories of non-IS process improvement and give an example of each. Describe why, in practice, IS and non-IS improvements frequently overlap. State the goal of Six Sigma. Identify common participants in a process improvement team. Describe the two types of BPMN diagrams.

## Q5. How can an IS hinder a process?

Describe how IS configuration in a company can hamper a process and limit its improvement. Describe an information silo. Explain the impact of silos on process objectives. Explain the most common fix to the silo problem. Describe why departments like to control the systems they use. Explain why a department may legitimately seek to keep its data in multiple databases.

## Q6. How can SOA improve processes?

Describe, in general, the two ways that SOA can improve a process (e.g., improve an activity, supply a linkage, or implement a control). Explain the term *service*. Give examples of services in an example process. Describe encapsulation. Give an example of two encapsulated services in a process. Explain how the independence of each encapsulated service makes process improvement possible. Describe how messages used to be exchanged between services and the role standards play in making this exchange better. Give an example of an SOA standard.

# Key Terms and Concepts

# Using Your Knowledge

1. Use OMIS to improve the following processes. That is, specify objectives and measures and an IS that will improve the process.
   a. Selecting a job after college
   b. Planning and executing a wedding or a funeral
   c. Taking photos at college, uploading the photos to Facebook, then showing the photos to relatives on their TV using a Wii or Xbox for Internet access.
   d. The process the pizza shop uses to buy supplies

2. For the processes presented in question 1, suggest how each could be improved by non-IS means; that is, by adding resources or changing the process structure.

3. For the processes presented in question 1, classify each IS improvement as improving an activity, improving the linkages among activities, or improving control.

4. When you go to a restaurant, that restaurant must execute several operational processes. Apply the OMIS model to several of these processes. These processes might include seating, ordering, cooking, delivering, and paying. For each process specify objectives and measures and an IS that will improve the process.

5. How can your college use IS to make its processes better? Can you think of ways to use new IS tools, such as smartphones and social media, to make college processes better? Specify the objectives and measures that these IS help improve. Does your college have information silos? Which departments keep data needed by processes outside the department?

6. When you order a meal at McDonald's that data is stored in an enterprise IS to be used by various processes. Make a list of the McDonald's processes your Happy Meal purchase will appear in. You may want to review the value chain processes discussed in Q2.

7. Make a Facebook cause (*www.facebook.com/causes*). Invite several friends to join. Using paper and pencil or diagramming software, make a BPMN diagram of the three or four key activities in this promotional process. Specify objectives and measures for this process and explain how Facebook (IS) improves the promotional process.

8. Create a BPMN diagram of the five to seven key activities in the process of getting your suitcase to its destination. Specify objectives and measures for this process.

# Collaboration Exercise 2

Collaborate with a group of fellow students to answer the following questions. For this exercise do not meet face to face. Your task will be easier if you coordinate your work with SharePoint, Office 365, Google Docs with Google+ or equivalent collaboration tools. Your answers should reflect the thinking of the entire group, and not just that of one or two individuals.

The county planning office issues building permits, septic system permits, and county road access permits for all building projects in an eastern state. The planning office issues permits to homeowners and builders for the construction of new homes and buildings and for any remodeling projects that involve electrical, gas, plumbing, and other utilities, as well as the conversion of unoccupied spaces such as garages into living or working space. The office also issues permits for new or upgraded septic systems and permits to provide driveway entrances to county roads.

Figure 2-17 shows the permit process that the county used for many years. Contractors and homeowners found this process to be slow and very frustrating. For one, they

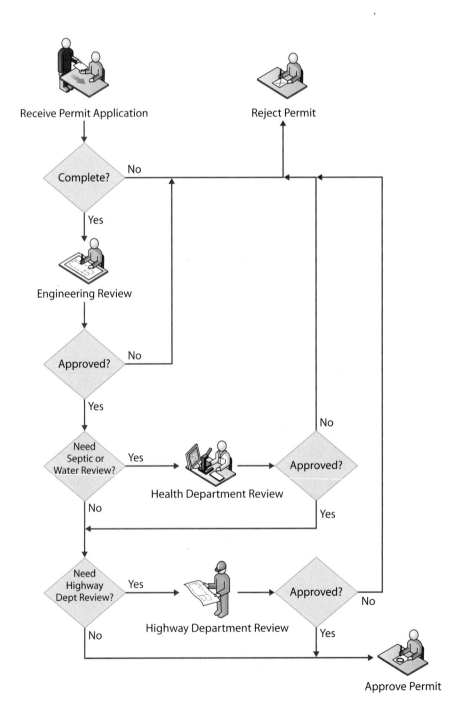

**FIGURE 2-17**

**Sequential Permit Review Process**

did not like its sequential nature. Only after a permit had been approved or rejected by the engineering review process would they find out that a health or highway review was also needed. Because each of these reviews could take 3 or 4 weeks, applicants requesting permits wanted the review processes to be concurrent rather than serial. Also, both the permit applicants and county personnel were frustrated because they never knew where a particular application was in the permit process. A contractor would call to ask how much longer, and it might take an hour or more just to find which desk the permits were on.

Accordingly, the county changed the permit process to that shown in Figure 2-18. In this second process, the permit office made three copies of the permit and distributed one to each department. The departments reviewed the permits in parallel; a clerk would analyze the results and, if there were no rejections, approve the permit.

Unfortunately, this process had a number of problems, too. For one, some of the permit applications were lengthy; some included as many as 40 to 50 pages of large architectural drawings. The labor and copy expense to the county was considerable.

Second, in some cases departments reviewed documents unnecessarily. If, for example, the highway department rejected an application, then neither the engineering nor health departments needed to continue their reviews. At first, the county responded to this problem by having the clerk who analyzed results cancel the reviews of other departments when he or she received a rejection. However, that policy was exceedingly unpopular with the permit applicants, because once an application was rejected and the problem corrected, the permit had to go back through the other departments. The permit would go to the end of the line and work its way back into the departments from which it had been pulled. Sometimes this resulted in a delay of 5 or 6 weeks.

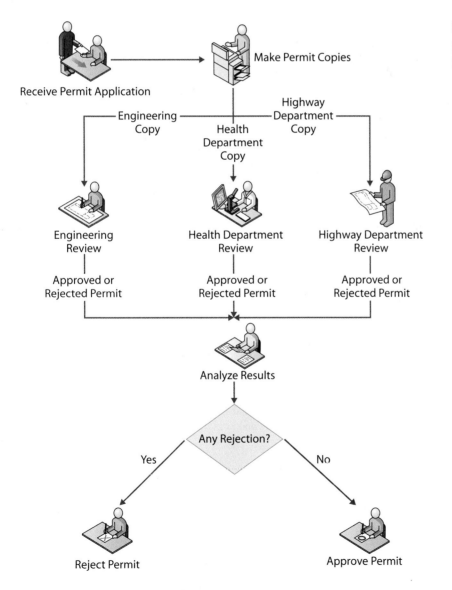

**FIGURE 2-18**

**Parallel Permit Review Process**

Canceling reviews was unpopular with the departments as well, because permit-review work had to be repeated. An application might have been nearly completed when it was cancelled due to a rejection in another department. When the application came through again, the partial work results from the earlier review were lost.

1. Is this process an operational, managerial, or strategic process?

2. Apply the OMIS model to the parallel permit process. Identify at least one flaw in each measure.

3. For your proposed IS improvements, specify if they are activity, linkage, or control improvements.

4. Where are the information silos? Why did these silos develop over the years? Are there good reasons to convert to an enterprise system?

5. Draw the new process using BPMN.

## CASE STUDY 2

# Process Cast in Stone

Bill Gates and Microsoft were exceedingly generous in the allocation of stock options to Microsoft employees, especially during Microsoft's first 20 years. Because of that generosity, Microsoft created 4 billionaires and an estimated 12,000 millionaires as Microsoft succeeded and the value of employee stock options soared. Not all of those millionaires stayed in the Seattle/ Redmond/Bellevue, Washington, area, but thousands did. These thousands of millionaires were joined by a lesser number who made their millions at Amazon.com and, to a lesser extent, at RealNetworks, Visio (acquired by Microsoft), and Aldus (acquired by Adobe). Today, some Google employees who work at Google's Seattle office are joining these ranks.

The influx of this wealth had a strong impact on Seattle and the surrounding communities. One result has been the creation of a thriving industry in high-end, very expensive homes. These Microsoft and other millionaires are college educated; many were exposed to fine arts at the university. They created homes that are not just large and situated on exceedingly valuable property, but that also are appointed with the highest-quality components.

Today, if you drive through a small area just south of central Seattle, you will find a half dozen vendors of premium granite, marble, limestone, soapstone, quartzite, and other types of stone slabs within a few blocks of each other. These materials cover counters, bathrooms, and other surfaces in the new and remodeled homes of this millionaire class. The stone is quarried in Brazil, India, Italy, Turkey, and other countries and either cut at its origin or sent to Italy for cutting. Huge cut slabs, 6 feet by 10 feet, arrive at the stone vendors in south Seattle, who stock them in their warehouses. The stone slabs vary not only in material, but also in color, veining pattern, and overall beauty. Choosing these slabs is like selecting fine art. (Visit *www.pentalonline.com* or *www .metamarble.com* to understand the premium quality of these vendors and products.)

Typically, the client (homeowner) hires an architect who either draws plans for the kitchen, bath, or other stone area as part of the overall house design or who hires a specialized kitchen architect who draws those plans. Most of these clients also hire interior decorators who help them select colors, fabrics, furniture, art, and other home furnishings. Because selecting a stone slab is like selecting art, clients usually visit the stone vendors' warehouses personally. They walk through the warehouses, often accompanied by their interior designer, and maybe also their kitchen architect, carrying little boxes into which stone vendor employees place chips of slabs in which the client expresses interest.

Usually, the team selects several stone slabs for consideration, and those are set aside for that client. The name of the client or the decorator is written in indelible ink on the side of the stone to reserve it. When the client or design team makes a final selection, the name is crossed out on the stone slabs they do not purchase. The purchased slabs are set aside for shipping.

During the construction process, the contractor will have selected a stone fabricator, who will cut the stone slab to fit the client's counters. The fabricator will also treat the stone's edges, possibly repolish the stone, and cut holes for sinks and faucets. Fabricators move the slabs from the stone vendor to their workshops, prepare the slab, and eventually install it in the client's home.

**Questions**

1. Identify the key actors in this scenario. Name their employer (if appropriate) and describe the role that they play. Include as a key player the operations personnel who move stones in the warehouse as well as those who load stones on the fabricators' trucks.

2. Apply the OMIS model to the stone fabricator's process. Identify at least one flaw in each measure.

3. For your proposed IS improvements, specify if they are activity, linkage, or control improvements.

4. Where are the information silos? Why did these silos develop over the years? Are there good reasons to convert to an enterprise system?

5. Draw the new process using BPMN.

"Are they out of their minds?" asks Pat Smith, the athletics director at Central Colorado State.

"I'm not sure Pat, but I will tell you the university is serious about this," replies Jenna Thurman, Pat's assistant.

"University Central Administration wants us to go through them for every purchase?"

"Well not all the purchases, but the ones above $500, yes. But they say that this new ERP software will save the university over a half million dollars in the first year."

"Did they say how?"

"Apparently, other places on campus did dumb things. You read about the fraud at the bookstore and the cost overruns with the new computers in the union. The university also mentioned our little adventure with that T-shirt maker. They say we should have known that company used child labor. Oh, and they claim we paid 50 percent more per jersey than the intramural department."

Visibly angry, Pat nearly screams, "And so the great solution is to go through purchasing for everything. Every order will take a month!"

"Well, they claim this new ERP system will shorten the time. They approve a list of all the suppliers for everyone on campus and they negotiate the prices for each item, and we're free to order through the system as we see fit."

"Wait, did I hear you say 'each item'? We order thousands of different things!!"

"They did admit this will take a while."

"Did they really say we paid more for our jerseys than intramurals?!! Do they have any idea how impossible it would be to recruit Division I players and say, 'and you'll look great in this 8-dollar jersey.'"

"But, boss, on the positive side they said that when other universities went to this system the suppliers worked harder to stay on everyone's good side because they had more to lose.

They did sort of point out that our soccer team jersey problem probably wouldn't have happened if that supplier had other contracts with the school they wanted to protect."

"So now what do we have to do?"

"They said start making lists of items you expect to buy this year. I'm invited to configuration meetings every Monday for the rest of my life. And starting in the fall we all have training sessions on the new software to look forward to."

"Thanks Jenna. And I thought keeping the boosters' club happy after last year was going to be my biggest headache."

As Jenna leaves, Pat admits to himself that the prospect of saving hundreds of thousands of dollars was too good for the administration to pass up in this time of rising tuition. The school had to save where it could. He is suspicious though; this new buying process might limit his flexibility to award contracts to suppliers who were consistent givers to the sports program or keep him from buying decent jerseys. Pat thinks the idea of a single way to buy everything on campus wouldn't be a good thing for the athletics department. He knows that no one at the university understands how different an athletics department is from other departments.

Q1. What problem does an ERP system solve?

Q2. What are the elements of an ERP system?

Q3. What are the benefits of an ERP system?

Q4. What are the challenges of implementing an ERP system?

Q5. What types of organizations use ERP?

Q6. Who are the major ERP vendors?

Q7. What makes SAP different from other ERP products?

**Chapter Preview**

The athletics director was right. The university has to try to save money, and using an ERP system might help achieve that objective. Clearly, ERP systems can reduce costs, but successfully installing an ERP system is exceptionally challenging. It can take years to implement and can cost hundreds of millions of dollars. These systems also require an organization to make difficult changes in the way it does things. It is a long road the university is heading down.

In the previous chapter, we looked at business from a process perspective and used the OMIS model to better understand how to make processes more efficient and effective. Here we discuss the same issue of IS and business process improvement, but from the IS point of view. More specifically, we investigate how large-scale ERP systems like the one implemented at the university can improve processes across an entire organization. To do so, we will examine the benefits and challenges of implementing an ERP system, but first we revisit the information silo problem from Chapter 2.

## Q1. What Problem Does an ERP System Solve?

To appreciate the popularity of ERP systems today, consider how businesses operated before they were introduced. Businesses were much like Central Colorado State—their departments ran their own processes using their own information systems and databases. Furthermore, many of these department processes were not well designed; they were relatively ineffective and inefficient, and, to make matters worse, they were hard to integrate with processes in other departments.

Then the Web flattened the world with fiber optic cable that carried data at speeds unimaginable just years before. Reality caught up with imagination when software engineers at SAP realized that this new network and advances in database storage allowed them to create large, centralized, well-connected databases that spanned entire companies. To use this new information system, businesses would also have to adopt processes designed by SAP. These processes were based on best industry-practices and designed from the start to be easily integrated with each other. Large firms saw an opportunity to implement one IS that would help improve and integrate their many processes.

The key to ERP systems is that data are consolidated in one central database. Recall from Chapter 2 that an information silo occurs when data are isolated and replicated in separated information systems. With information silos, the data needed by one process are stored in an information system designed and used in another process. Because information silos exist in isolation from one another, they create islands of automation that can diminish the efficiency and effectiveness of processes and make process integration difficult.

The silo problem is solved by ERP systems. We explain this approach in the rest of the chapter. However, before we get there, we briefly consider another approach to the same silo problem. This second solution is a more decentralized approach called enterprise application interface (EAI). ERP and EAI systems are sometimes referred to as *enterprise systems*.

### Enterprise Application Integration (EAI)

An **enterprise application integration (EAI)** system tackles the silo problem by providing layers of software that connect information systems together. EAI is software that enables information silos to communicate with each other and to share data. The layers of EAI software are shown in Figure 3-1. For example, when the accounting information system sends data to the human resources information system the EAI program intercepts the data, converts it to work in the format required by the human resources system, and then sends the converted data on to the human resources system. The reverse action is taken to send data back from the human resources system to the accounting system.

Although there is no centralized EAI database, EAI software keeps files of metadata that describe where all the organization's data are located and how the data must be transformed to work at each location. These details are hidden from users; the EAI system appears to be an integrated database to the user.

**FIGURE 3-1**

**EAI Architecture**

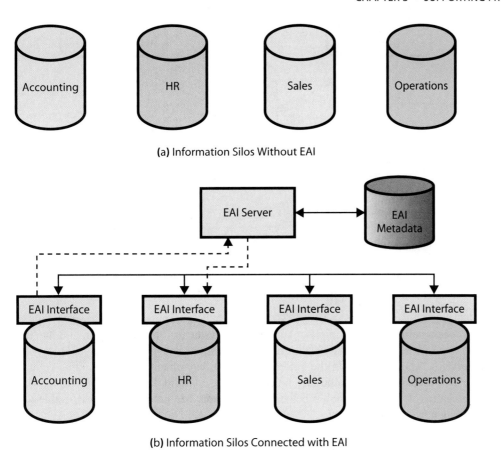

(a) Information Silos Without EAI

(b) Information Silos Connected with EAI

EAI does the following:

- It connects information silos via a new layer of software.
- It enables existing applications to communicate and share data.
- It provides integrated data.
- It leverages existing systems, leaving departmental information systems as is, but providing an integration layer over the top.
- It enables a gradual move to ERP.

The major benefit of the EAI connect-the-silos approach is that it enables organizations to use existing applications while eliminating many of the problems of information silos. Converting to an EAI system is not nearly as disruptive as converting to ERP, it can be less expensive, and it provides many of the benefits of ERP. Some organizations develop EAI applications as a stepping stone to complete ERP systems.

## Enterprise Resource Planning (ERP)

An **enterprise resource planning (ERP)** product is a suite of software, a database, procedures and a set of processes for supporting business operations with a single, consistent, information system. These systems integrate process data from departments such as accounting, human resources, sales, and operations into a single system, as shown in Figure 3-2. ERP is so named because it attempts to integrate all the resources of an enterprise into a single information system.

The primary purpose of an ERP system is integration; an ERP system allows the "left hand of the organization to know what the right hand is doing." *ERP systems standardize processes and bring the data from a company's processes into one place so that the data can go out to many places in real time.*

Properly implemented, an ERP system consolidates data about customers, products, people, equipment, machinery, facilities, production schedules, vendors, and finances in a single database. By consolidating the data in one place, the data are always up-to-date and available in real time to be used by any process in the organization.

**FIGURE 3-2**

**Data Integration with ERP of Processes in Four Example Departments**

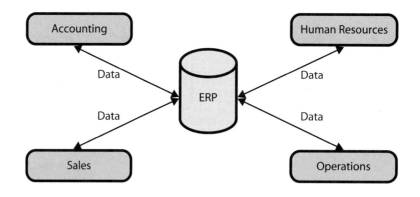

### ERP Implementation: Before and After Examples

To better understand the impact of an ERP system, we will examine processes in two organizations before and after an ERP system is implemented. The first organization is the university discussed in the opening vignette, the second is a company that assembles bicycles.

EXAMPLE 1: SINGLE PROCESS—UNIVERSITY PURCHASING Compare the university's procurement process before and after implementing an ERP system, as shown in Figure 3-3. On the top half of the figure, each university department works with its own purchasing agent to buy goods and services from suppliers. In the bottom half, each department works through a centralized university purchasing agent to buy from suppliers. By consolidating all the purchasing activity in one central office, the school is better able to standardize purchasing and it is able to gain bargaining power over suppliers.

**FIGURE 3-3**

**Procurement by University Departments Before and After ERP**

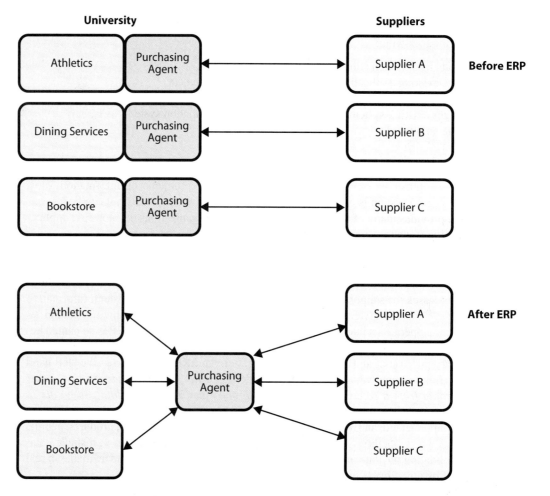

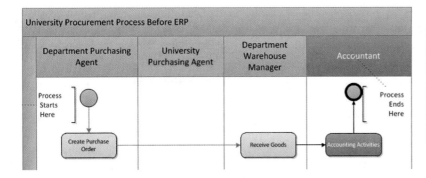

**Before ERP Implementation**

| Objectives | Measures |
|---|---|
| Use reliable suppliers | Not specified |
| Use boosters (unstated) | Not specified |

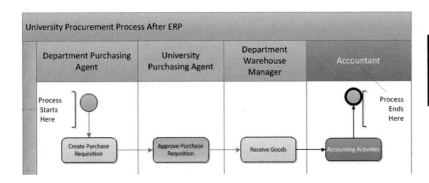

**After ERP Implementation**

| Objectives | Measures |
|---|---|
| Reduce cost | Cost |

**FIGURE 3-4**

**Procurement by University Before and After ERP**

Figure 3-3 shows the impact of an ERP system on the university. The impact of an ERP system on a department is shown in Figure 3-4. The top half shows the activities before implementing an ERP system, and the bottom half shows the activities after implementation. Before implementation, each department's procurement process had three main activities—Create Purchase Order, Receive Goods, and Accounting Activities, as shown in the top BPMN in Figure 3-4. The process was initiated by an actor in the Department Purchasing Agent role. Every department at the university had a Purchasing Agent; in the athletic department, this role was played by Jenna.

Jenna started the process by completing a Purchase Order (PO). An example PO might be an order for 500 T-shirts for summer camp. The second activity was Receive Goods. Goods were received when the T-shirts arrived on campus at the athletic warehouse where Joe, in the role of Warehouse Manager, signed for the delivery and put them on a shelf. Later, the university accounting office would get a bill from the T-shirt maker and pay it. The purchases by the athletic department were recorded in a department database (not shown for simplicity). The department databases are not shown in Figure 3-4 for simplicity. Each department on campus maintained its own purchasing database, creating information silos as a result.

The athletic department objectives for this process were to use reliable suppliers who would be able to deliver the goods on time and were reasonably priced. Jenna also had an unstated objective, which was to use suppliers who were also boosters of the athletic department. Measures for these objectives were never specified.

After implementing the ERP system, a new procurement process provided by the ERP vendor is used by every department. This new process is shown in the bottom of Figure 3-4. Now Jenna completes a Purchase Requisition. A Purchase Requisition is a PO awaiting approval. The Purchase Requisition is approved by a University Purchasing Agent as the second activity. The rest of the activities in this process remain the same. Rather than storing data in department databases, the new ERP process maintains all the procurement data in a central database. Now if any department wants to order T-shirts, all the data on T-shirt suppliers, delivery times, and prices are available in real time.

With the purchasing office now orchestrating the process, specific and clear objectives and measures have been developed for the process and shared with all purchasing agents. The university's objective with the new process is efficiency—lowering cost as measured by comparing this month's expenditures to last year's during the same month.

Although it is helpful to understand how an ERP system can improve a single process such as procurement at the university, it is perhaps more important to understand how an ERP system can improve the integration of processes for an entire organization. To see these larger-scale impacts, we shift gears to a bicycle assembly company.

EXAMPLE 2: PROCESSES AS A WHOLE—BICYCLE ASSEMBLY COMPANY Some of the main processes for the bicycle company before ERP implementation are shown in Figure 3-5. This figure illustrates how many of the bike company's processes work together, with the primary activities of the value chain across the top.

Notice the five databases shown as cylinders—Vendor, Raw Material, Manufacturing, Finished Goods, and CRM. CRM is customer relationship management; a CRM database keeps track of data about customers. These five databases are information silos, isolated from each other as they support different processes.

By not having data consolidated in one place, the bicycle company faces difficulty when data need to be shared in real time. For example, if the sales department has the unexpected opportunity to sell 1,000 bicycles, the sales manager must know if the company can produce these bikes in time to meet the delivery date. Unfortunately, the sales manager does not have all the data she needs, because the data are stored in isolated databases throughout the firm. She does not know the current data of finished bikes in the Finished Goods database or of bike parts in the Raw Materials database. With data scattered throughout the firm, the potential sale is in jeopardy.

Contrast this situation with the ERP system in Figure 3-6. Here, all the company's processes are supported by an ERP system, and the data are consolidated into a centralized ERP database. When the sales manager gets the opportunity to sell 1,000 bicycles, the data that the sales manager needs to confirm the order is readily available in the ERP system. From her desk, the sales manager can see how many bikes are finished and ready to sell and how many bikes will be

**FIGURE 3-5**

**Pre-ERP Information Systems for Bicycle Company**

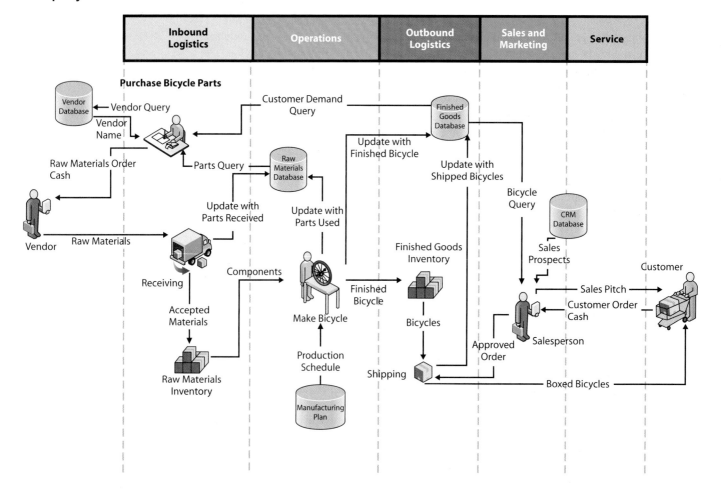

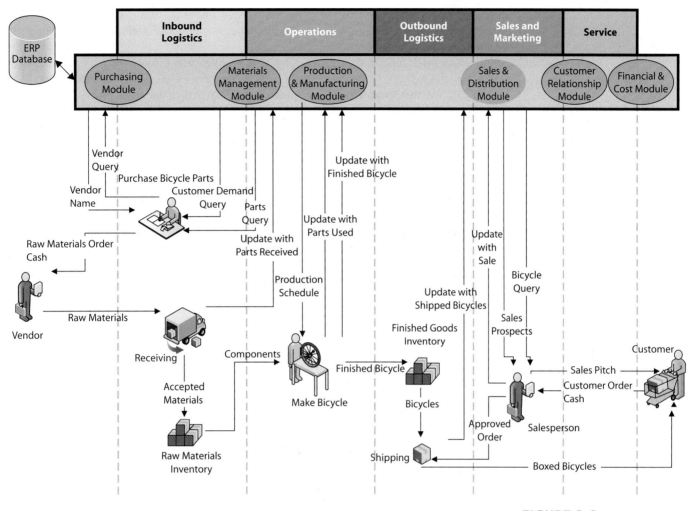

**FIGURE 3-6**

**ERP System for Bicycle Company**

produced in the coming days. Further, the ERP system can show the sales manager that if this current inventory is not quite enough the company can double production next week, but that the cost of the bikes will go up 40 percent.

If the sales manager decides to proceed with the sale and production must double, the ERP system notifies managers in inbound logistics, operations, and outbound logistics with supply and production schedules. By consolidating the data in one place, the impact of the sale can be shared in real time with all affected processes.

## Q2. What Are the Elements of an ERP System?

To better understand the components of current ERP systems, consider their evolution. Current ERP systems are particularly strong in the areas in which they were first developed, such as manufacturing and supply processes.

Although the term *ERP* is relatively new, businesses have been using IS to support their processes for 50 years, well before the Internet. In the 1960s, a business could use a dedicated phone line, a computer card reader, and punch cards to send inventory orders to a supplier. By the 1970s, businesses began to buy their own mainframe computers and manufacturing companies began to use software called **material requirements planning (MRP)** to efficiently manage inventory, production, and labor. As computing power became cheaper, **manufacturing resource planning (MRPII)** was developed that added financial-tracking capabilities as well as the opportunity to schedule equipment and facilities.

The business environment continued to evolve with the advent of **just in time (JIT)** delivery. JIT synchronizes manufacturing and supply—manufacturing occurs just as raw materials arrive. To execute JIT, tight supplier relationships were needed. These relationships depended on unimpeded flows of data between partners. Just as this business need was emerging, Internet technologies globalized supply chains and customer markets in the 1990s. Businesses began to see newly emerging ERP solutions as a comprehensive way to address their growing supply chain needs, ensure that the looming Y2K problem was solved, and overcome their information silo problem. A short time later, new federal laws such as the **Sarbanes-Oxley Act (SOX)** required companies to exercise greater control over their financial processes, and ERP systems addressed that new requirement. From this brief review, notice that businesses and IS coevolve; one makes progress and impacts the other, then the other way around.

As business changes, so must ERP systems. Today, for a product to be considered a true ERP product, it must include applications that integrate the processes in the following business functions:[1]

- Supply chain management (SCM; procurement, sales order processing, inventory management, supplier management, and related activities)
- Manufacturing (manufacturing scheduling, capacity planning, quality control, bill of materials, and related activities)
- Customer relationship management (CRM; sales prospecting, customer management, marketing, customer support, call center support)
- Human resources (payroll, time and attendance, HR management, commission calculations, benefits administration, and related activities)
- Accounting (general ledger, accounts receivable, accounts payable, cash management, fixed-asset accounting)

Although ERP solutions can integrate these processes, frequently an organization will purchase and implement just parts of the total ERP package. For example, a defense contractor might rely on just SCM and manufacturing, and a university may only install the human resources and purchasing functions. The most common partial implementations are CRM to support promotion, sales, and service processes or SCM to integrate supply chain processes and promote data sharing with supply chain partners.

### The Five Components of an ERP System: Software, Hardware, Data, Procedures, and People

As mentioned, an ERP product (like SAP) includes three of the five components of an IS. It includes software, databases, and procedures. To create an ERP product, an organization installs the software and databases on hardware and trains its people to use the procedures. Consider each component:

ERP SOFTWARE ERP software accomplishes interprocess data integration. The software typically resides on servers and on client machines in the company. The software can be customized to meet customer requirements without changing program code. This customization is called **configuration**.

This process of configuring the software is similar to the configuration you do when you install an e-mail system. During installation of an e-mail system, you might make 10 to 20 decisions, such as how long old e-mail is retained, what folders are available, and what names are used for address books. In the same way, a company will make over 8,000 configuration decisions to customize the ERP system to its needs. For example, an hourly payroll application is configured to specify the number of hours in the standard workweek, the hourly wages for different job categories, the wage adjustments for overtime and holiday work, and so forth. At the university, the software must be configured with spending limits for each department, warehouse addresses, bank accounts, and many other details.

Of course, there are limits to how much configuration can be done. If a new ERP customer has requirements that cannot be met via configuration, then the customer either needs to adapt its business to what the software can do or write application code to meet its requirements.

---

[1] ERP101, "The ERP Go To Guide." Available at *www.erpsoftware360.com/erp-101.htm*. Accessed June 2011.

For example, the athletics department has some of its own money given by boosters for particular items such as greens fees for the golf team. As it turns out, the university could not figure out how to configure the ERP system to display these funds appropriately. As a result, the university had to write its own code and add it to the ERP software.

Code can be added to any ERP implementation using specific application languages such as Java. The most common use of this application code is to create company-unique reports from ERP data.

The university could also pay another vendor to write this custom software for it. Custom software is expensive both initially and in long-term maintenance costs because it is not guaranteed to work with newer versions of ERP software. Thus, avoiding customization by choosing an ERP product that has applications that function close to the organization's requirements is critically important to success.

ERP DATABASES An ERP solution includes a gigantic, but largely unpopulated, database; a database design; and initial configuration data. It does not, of course, contain the company's actual operational data. Operational data are entered during development and use.

If your only experience with databases is creating a few tables in Microsoft Access, then you probably underestimate the value and importance of ERP database design. Good database design is essential, because an ERP database can contain over 25,000 tables. The design includes the metadata for those tables, as well as their relationships to each other, and rules and constraints about how the data in some tables must relate to data in other tables.

One of the key characteristics of relational databases is that they are modular. Being modular means that tables can be added or removed without significant impact on the overall structure. An ERP implementation may only use some of the 25,000 tables initially and then later seamlessly add new tables as more of the ERP database is used.

Databases used by ERP systems include IBM DB2, Oracle Database, and Microsoft SQL Server. There is a distinction between the DBMS that creates and maintains the database and the database itself. Figure 3-7 shows this relationship. An ERP system is the DBMS, and when the ERP system is installed, a database, often made by a different company than the ERP system, is also licensed and installed.

PROCEDURES IS procedures are instructions and methods for users to interact with the application. Training the employees of a business on how to interact with an ERP system can be a time-consuming and costly operation. To support this need, ERP vendors have developed extensive training classes and training curricula to enable users to learn the ERP system. ERP vendors typically conduct classes on site prior, during, and after implementation. To reduce expenses, the vendors sometimes train the organization's users to become in-house trainers in training sessions called **train the trainer**. Even with this approach, the training bill is very large; a firm will budget a third of the total cost of the implementation on training and consulting fees. ERP vendors also provide on-site consulting for implementing and using the ERP system. Additionally, a small industry of ERP consultants also support the training needs of new ERP customers.

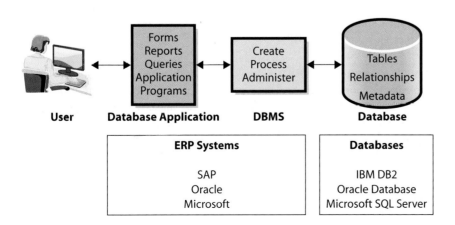

**FIGURE 3-7**

**DBMS and Database**

One other note on procedures is useful to students new to ERP systems. Each actor in a process only needs access to a limited set of ERP data and software. For example, Jenna only needs a few ERP menu options and on-screen forms to act as a Purchasing Agent. The University Purchasing Agent who approves Jenna's requisitions only needs a few other options and screens. When an ERP system is fully implemented, access to system functionality and data is limited by the role an employee plays. This important control feature of the system is often not apparent to new students who see the entire suite of functionality and data.

HARDWARE Each ERP implementation requires a wide variety of hardware, including disk storage, servers, clients, printers, scanners, network devices, and cables. To determine the necessary levels for each of these hardware devices, an organization first estimates the number of users, the processes supported, and the volume of data for the intended system. With these estimates, hardware sizing can be accomplished.

Currently, organizations are facing an ERP hardware dilemma. Employees are increasingly using smartphones to accomplish business activities and processes, including processes that interact with the company's ERP system. The dilemma: Should the firm allow individuals to use their private smartphones with installed company apps to interact with the ERP products or should they purchase company smartphones for its employees? With the latter option, employees would then have the opportunity to use their work phone for private use.

This smartphone issue is just the latest in a long list of hardware issues brought about by new hardware. Another is cloud computing. Currently, most ERP products are purchased and installed on company hardware. With the cloud, ERP systems may be rented with a much lower upfront cost, stored on cloud vendor hardware, and paid for by use. This move by ERP firms toward hosted implementations and away from on-premises solutions will continue. Ellison's NetSuite offers accounting and financial systems for large international organizations in the cloud. SAP's NetWeaver also provides a hosted solution, and SAP may be able to gradually move its large installed base to it.

All ERP solutions are designed and implemented on hardware that soon becomes dated. New hardware makes ERP systems more useful, but integrating the new hardware is often expensive and challenging.

PEOPLE The people involved with an ERP system fall into three roles. *Users* are the employees of the firm implementing the system. **Analysts**, also called *systems analysts* or *business analysts*, are also employees. Analysts have specialized training or education that enables them to support, maintain, and adapt the system after it has been implemented. Many analysts have a background or education in MIS or IT. A third role is *consultant*. A consultant works for the ERP vendor or a different company, called a *third party*, and helps budget, plan, train, configure, and implement the system. These consultants may work at the implementing firm for a period before, during, and after the implementation.

Although job titles and descriptions vary, a short list of the most common ERP positions is presented in Figure 3-8. Salary estimates are provided, although they vary widely by experience and location. Like an increasing number of IS jobs, success in these positions is based less on technical skill and more on process understanding and an ability to work with people. According to the Bureau of Labor Statistics, job opportunities in ERP and IS in general are expected to grow by 30 percent from 2008–2018.[2]

INHERENT BUSINESS PROCESSES ERP systems are more than an IS. They also specify processes for the implementing organization. These processes are called **inherent processes**. For the implementing organization, some of the changes it must make from existing processes to ERP processes are minor and hardly noticed, but some changes can be significant.

ERP systems include hundreds, or even thousands, of processes and activities. Some ERP vendors call these inherent processes **process blueprints**. Organizations implementing an ERP

---

[2] Bureau of Labor Statistics, "Career Guide to Industries, 2010–11 Edition: Software Publishers," December 17, 2009. Available at *www.bls.gov/oco/cg/cgs051.htm*.

| Title | Job Description | Salary (in U.S. dollars) |
|---|---|---|
| Consultant | Employed by firm other than implementing company or ERP vendor, can perform any of the following roles during implementation | 60,000–100,000 |
| Systems analyst | Understands technical aspects of ERP; helps plan, configure, and implement ERP system for company use | 70,000–90,000 |
| Developer | Writes additional code where necessary for implementing ERP systems | 76,000–92,000 |
| Project manager | Defines objectives; organizes, plans, and leads team that implements ERP solution | 70,000–110,000 |
| Business analyst | Understands process aspects; helps plan, configure, and implement ERP system for company use | 75,000–95,000 |
| Architect | High-level planner of IS at an organization; ensures compatibility of technology and directs technology toward strategic goals | 90,000–130,000 |
| Trainer | Trains end users on how ERP system operates, explains their roles, and trains trainers | 65,000–78,000 |

**FIGURE 3-8**

**ERP Job Titles, Descriptions, and Salary Estimates**

system must either adapt to the predefined inherent processes or design new ones. In the latter case, the design of a new process may necessitate changes to software and database structures, all of which mean great expense!

## Q3. What Are the Benefits of an ERP System?

In the previous chapter, we said that an IS can improve a process by improving activities, improving the links among activities, and improving the control of the process. Although improvements to a particular process are certainly beneficial, an ERP system also provides benefits to the organization as a whole. These organizational benefits are listed in Figure 3-9.

One benefit of an ERP system for the organization is converting its processes to the vendor's inherent, best-practice processes that are appropriate for that company's strategy. For example, at the university, best practices are now a part of the university procurement process. These practices include buying in bulk, negotiating prices prior to purchase, and a centralized procurement requisition approval activity. Prior to implementing the ERP system, the separate university departments purchased individually and not in bulk, they had little opportunity to negotiate price, and if a delivery was late or of poor quality the department had little training or expertise in making things right.

A second benefit is that real-time data sharing allows managers to see trends as they are occurring and to respond appropriately. For example, the purchasing office at the university can see up-to-the-minute totals for each department's purchases. As a result, if food prices rise

- Implements processes that are industry best practices.
- Data sharing occurs in real time.
- Management can be more insightful and provide better oversight.
- The information silo problem is solved.

**FIGURE 3-9**

**Benefits of Using an ERP Solution**

**FIGURE 3-10**

**Example Measures of the Benefits of ERP**

| Objective | Measure |
|---|---|
| Reduce inventory | Inventory costs were 25% of sales, now 15% |
| Reduce costs | Costs of raw materials 10% less than before |
| Reduce returns | Reduce number of returns by 10% |
| Reduce end-of-year closing time | Closing time in days was 14, now 4 |
| Volume of cross-selling | Cross-selling revenues double |

The cost of a new system can be determined in a number of ways. For a discussion of a few of the ethical issues relating to cost estimates, see the Ethics Guide on pages 76–77.

significantly, the purchasing office can help dining services reallocate funds from other dining services accounts or change upcoming orders. Similarly, if an academic department is approaching its enrollment limit on a class the ERP system can notify the department chair and if deliveries are running late a warehouse can be kept open late.

A third benefit for the organization is that an effective ERP system can lead to better management as more managers have visibility to more data. For example, if the athletics director wants to check on the status of an order before meeting with a coach, that data is only seconds away. Similarly, the university purchasing department can easily total all the purchases from a particular vendor and renegotiate prices.

Finally, as was discussed earlier, another significant benefit of an ERP system is solving the information silo problem. This means that at the university the different departments no longer create and maintain their own purchasing databases.

Although the general benefits are compelling, it is also useful to examine how these ERP benefits are measured. A sampling of these measures, along with typical objectives, is shown in Figure 3-10.

## Q4. What Are the Challenges of Implementing an ERP System?

The process of converting an organization like the one shown in Figure 3-5 to an ERP-supported organization like that in Figure 3-6 is daunting and expensive. In fact, the *Wall Street Journal* calls ERP implementation the "corporate equivalent of a root canal."[3] If not done well, the losses are often very significant. Well-known firms like Kmart and Hershey's lost over $100 million implementing ERP systems. In another debacle, the Los Angeles school district's ERP system issued 30,000 erroneous checks.[4]

Before implementation can even begin, users must be trained on the new processes, procedures, and use of the ERP system's features and function. Additionally, the company needs to conduct a simulation test of the new system to identify problems. Then, during implementation, the organization must convert its data, procedures, and personnel to the new ERP system. All of this happens while the business continues to run on the old system.

Implementing an ERP system is much easier for an organization that has implemented some type of enterprise system in the past. Often a firm will implement a full ERP using a pilot implementation strategy. Using this approach, the organization will first implement an ERP on a smaller scale, in one division or function. The most common initial processes are in the financial or human relations functions.

[3] *Wall Street Journal*, March 14, 1997, p. 1.

[4] Traci Barker and Mark N. Frolick, "ERP Implementation Failure: A Case Study," *Information Systems Management*, Volume 20, Issue 4, 2003, pp. 43–49.

# MIS InClass 3

## Building a Model

The purpose of this exercise is to better understand the impacts of an ERP on the organization. In this exercise, student teams will build replicas of a model that is hidden from their sight.

Before class, the instructor constructed a model that is now hidden from view. The goal of the student team is to build a model identical to that one. The model is concealed in the hallway immediately outside the classroom. The class is divided into teams, and each person on the team is assigned one of four roles. Each team is composed of between four and six students with the following roles:

*Source: Andresr/Shutterstock.*

- **Looker:** The looker looks at the instructor's model and remains in the hallway. The looker cannot write anything down. The looker explains to the messenger how to assemble the model.
- **Messenger:** The messenger listens to the looker's description. The messenger relays these verbal instructions to the builders in the room. The messenger cannot look at either the instructor's model or the team's model as it is being assembled.
- **Feedbacker:** The feedbacker can look at the instructor's model and the team's model. The feedbacker can say only "yes" or "no" to questions asked by any other team member.
- **Builders:** The rest of the team is made up of builders. Builders construct the replica of the instructor's model. They acquire the pieces from a supplier who supplies all the teams.

The game begins with the lookers in the hallway each giving their messenger an initial set of instructions. Play the game until the last team has built the replica.

After the game, discuss the following:

1. Do the roles in the game correspond to business roles?

2. Describe your team's building process and its objectives. Use the looker–messenger exchange as the first activity and assembling pieces as the last activity.
3. How did your process evolve from the first iteration of the process to the last? How did you learn to use the feedbacker? If the feedbacker is considered a simple IS, how does this IS lead to process improvement? If so, was that improvement to an activity, a linkage, or a control?
4. Communication standards enable effective communication. What are the communication standards your team needed to make progress?
5. There is no (computer) IS in this game. If your team had some money to spend on an IS, what would you buy?
6. Would the purchase of that IS improve an activity, a linkage, or a control?
7. After spending money on an IS, which player's job would change? In the real world, would this change create stress?
8. With the process used at the end of the game, how much time would it take to construct the next model?

## Implementation Decisions

For a successful implementation, the devil is in the details, and there are a lot of details. For a large organization, there can be tens of thousands of configuration details to decide. To make matters even more challenging, many of the most important decisions require a wide understanding of both the business and the ERP system. As a result, teams of experts are needed. With teamwork, additional challenges emerge, such as building effective collaboration, communication, commitment, and responsibility.

Earlier in this chapter, the configuration decisions about wages were introduced. Figure 3-11 lists a sample of the other kinds of configuration decisions implementation teams must make. One configuration challenge is item identifiers. Does the company want to identify or track every item in an incoming and outgoing shipment or just the shipment itself? Further, does it want to track material as it is being assembled or only when it is finished?

Another set of configuration decisions requires the company to specify resupply times. For each and every item in the company's supply chain, resupply times must be calculated.

| |
|---|
| What do we select as our item identifier? |
| How long are resupply times? |
| What will be our order sizes? |
| Which BOM format should we use? |
| Who approves customer credit (and how)? |
| Who approves production capacity (and how)? |
| Who approves schedule and terms (and how)? |
| What actions need to be taken if the customer modifies the order? |
| How does management obtain oversight on sales activity? |

These times are based on how long it takes to process the order, the time the supplier needs to ship it after an order is received, and the transportation times.

Another set of issues is order size. More specifically, the organization must specify the number of items in a standard order. At one extreme is to order continuously in small amounts to reduce inventory. However, using that approach, transportation and ordering costs become a problem. At the other extreme, order sizes that are larger require warehouse space and tie up substantial capital.

Another source of detail challenge is the structure of the **bill of material (BOM)**. The BOM is like a recipe, it specifies the raw materials, quantities, and subassemblies needed to create a final product. Most large organizations have a wide variety of BOM structures in place for making their products. Deciding on one BOM standard can be challenging, particularly when the organization makes different types of products in different divisions.

For each of these decisions, implementation teams must decide among choices offered by the ERP vendor. But there is another option in addition to the vendor's options for each choice. This is the option to purchase custom software, as mentioned on page 63. However, this choice presents yet another challenge. ERP vendors periodically update their software, and the custom software may not be compatible with the new ERP software. The custom software code would then have to be rewritten, retested, and reinstalled. A number of companies overcame the other implementation challenges only to fail at this one. They unwittingly created a monster of custom software that they must rewrite every time the ERP system changes.

### People Issues

In addition to the challenge of sorting through all these decisions, the actions and attitudes of the people in the implementing organization can make the situation even more challenging. This challenge is aptly summarized by the saying, "All our problems wear shoes." Although this may overlook the technical ERP challenges, the saying wisely indentifies the biggest challenge to successful implementation. These people-related issues are listed in Figure 3-12.

| |
|---|
| Work is changed |
| Top management involvement after initial decision to implement |
| Top management oversells capabilities |
| Perceived threat to department autonomy |
| Failure to specify objectives and measures for new processes |

ERP implementations change the way work is done in the organization. People tend to resist change even when the benefits of the change are well known. One reason is that the change often does not directly benefit the individual who has to change his or her work. The benefits occur for the organization. For example, Jenna's work doesn't get much easier at the athletics department after the ERP system is implemented, but the organization benefits by the change.

Another common problem is that top management believes that the hard part of the implementation process is the decision to implement. Once that decision is made, they believe that they can move on. Instead, they need to stay involved, monitor implementation progress, devote appropriate resources, and share a vision with their employees about why this system will be helpful.

A second top management problem is overselling the vision of what the system will do. Often management can be blinded by the benefits of the promised system and not look carefully at the assumptions behind the promises. This can lead top management to buy more features than they need or that the organization can implement successfully. Employees who may be more familiar with the assumptions and the necessary change quickly become jaded when the "grand solution" runs into inevitable implementation problems.

Another problem can arise when a manager views the ERP solution as a threat to his or her department's autonomy, to his or her way of doing things. For example, the athletics director at the university in the opening case was concerned that the new procurement system would limit his ability to do things to support the unique needs of the athletics department.

Finally, management may fail to specify how their grand vision of this ERP system translates into day-to-day operations. More specifically, they fail to specify objectives and measures for the new processes. Management must develop specific objectives and measures for processes appropriate to the company's strategy. For example, if the university strategy is to be the low-cost leader in higher education, then Jenna's procurement process should have objectives such as reducing time and cost of procurement and use measures such as labor hours saved and cost savings.

## Q5. What Types of Organizations Use ERP?

ERP systems are used by many organizations. Use depends on many factors. Two important factors—the organization's industry and the organization's size—are examined next.

### ERP by Industry Type

The first major ERP customers were large manufacturers in the aerospace, automotive, industrial equipment, and other industries. Given success in manufacturing, it was natural for ERP vendors to go up the supply chain and sell ERP solutions to those industries that supplied the manufacturers—distributors, raw materials extractors and processors, and the petroleum industry. At the same time, health care was becoming more complex, and hospitals were changing from a service to a profit orientation and began to adopt ERP solutions.

Over time, ERP use spread to companies and organizations in other industries, such as those listed in Figure 3-13. Today, ERP systems are used by governments and utilities, in the retail industry, and in education.

### ERP by Organization Size

ERP, as stated, was initially adopted by large manufacturing organizations that had complex process problems that needed ERP solutions. Those large organizations also had the resources and skilled personnel needed to accomplish and manage an ERP implementation. Over time, as ERP implementation improved, other smaller organizations were able to implement ERP. Today, ERP is used in organizations with yearly revenues as low as $5 million.

Value chains and basic business processes are not different in character between small and large organizations. To quote F. Scott Fitzgerald, "The rich are no different from you and me, they just have more money." The steps required to check credit, verify product availability, and

**FIGURE 3-13**
**ERP by Industry**

| Manufacturing |
| Distribution |
| Mining, materials extraction, petroleum |
| Medical care |
| Government and public service |
| Utilities |
| Retail |
| Education |

approve terms are no different for order processing at Amazon.com than they are at Phil's muffler shop. An excellent sales process for a multimillion-dollar company is very helpful to midsize companies. They differ in scale, but not in character.

However, companies of different sizes have one very important difference that has a major impact on ERP: the availability of skilled business and IT analysts. Small organizations employ only one or two IT analysts who not only manage the ERP system, but also manage the entire IS department. They are spread very thin and often are in over their heads during an ERP implementation. Smaller, simpler ERP solutions are common among these companies.

Midsize organizations expand IT from one person to a small staff, but frequently this staff is isolated from senior-level management. Such isolation can create misunderstandings and distrust. Because of the expense, organizational disruption, and length of ERP projects, senior management must be committed to the ERP solution. When IT management is isolated, such commitment is difficult to obtain and may not be strong. This issue is problematic enough that many ERP consultants say the first step for these firms in moving toward ERP is to obtain deep senior-level commitment to the project.

Large organizations have a full IT staff that is headed by the chief information officer (CIO), who is a business and IT professional who sits on the executive board and is an active participant in organizational strategic planning. ERP implementation will be part of that strategic process and, when begun, will have the full backing of the entire executive group.

### International ERP

One way that the needs of large organizations do differ in character from those of small organizations is international presence. Most billion-dollar companies operate in many countries, and the ERP application programs must be available in many languages and currencies. Some companies can declare a single "company language" and force all company transactions to use that language (usually English). Other companies must accommodate multiple languages in their ERP solution.

Once implemented, ERP brings huge benefits to multinational organizations. International ERP solutions are designed to work with multiple currencies, manage international transfers of goods in inventories, and work effectively with international supply chains. Even more important, ERP solutions provide a worldwide consolidation of financial statements on a timely basis. As a result, they can produce one set of financial reports, better analyze where costs could be saved, and identify where production can be optimized.

## Q6. Who Are the Major ERP Vendors?

Although over 100 companies advertise ERP products, not all of those products meet the minimal ERP criteria in Q2. Even of those that do, the bulk of the market is held by the five vendors shown in Figure 3-14.

| Company | ERP Market Rank | Remarks | Future |
|---|---|---|---|
| Epicor | 5 | Strong industry-specific solutions, especially retail. | Epicor 9 designed for flexibility (SOA). Highly configurable ERP. Lower cost. |
| Microsoft Dynamics | 4 | Four products acquired by acquisition: AX, Nav, GP, and Solomon. AX and Nav more comprehensive. Solomon on the way out? Large VAR channel. | Products not well integrated with Office. Not integrated at all with Microsoft development languages. Product direction uncertain. Watch for Microsoft ERP announcement on the cloud (Azure). |
| Infor | 3 | Privately held corporation that has acquired an ERP product named Baan, along with more than 20 others. | Span larger small companies to smaller large companies. Has many solutions. |
| Oracle | 2 | Combination of in-house and acquired (PeopleSoft, Siebel) products. | Intensely competitive company with strong technology base. Large customer base. Flexible SOA architecture. Expensive. Oracle CEO Ellison owns 70% of NetSuite. |
| SAP | 1 | Led ERP success. Largest vendor, most comprehensive solutions. Largest customers. | Technology older. Expensive and seriously challenged by less expensive alternatives. Huge customer base. Future growth uncertain. |

**FIGURE 3-14**

**Characteristics of Top Vendors**

## ERP Vendor Market Share

In 2011, SAP had the largest market share, with over 35 percent of the market. Oracle was second, Microsoft a distant third, and Infor and Epicor were fourth and fifth, respectively. Over the last several years, SAP's market share has decreased slightly as smaller vendors such as Infor and Epicor have gained market share. Most of these changes can be attributed to the growth in the small-to-medium market and the maturity of ERP systems in large organizations.

## ERP Products

Figure 3-15 shows how the ERP products from each of these companies relate to the size of their customers. Both Epicor and Microsoft Dynamics address the needs of small and midsize organizations. Infor has a product for almost everyone, as you will see. Oracle and SAP currently serve the largest organizations and are seeking to expand their offerings to medium and smaller-sized organizations.

EPICOR **Epicor** is known primarily for its retail-oriented ERP software, although it is broadening its penetration in other industry segments. Its lead ERP product, called Epicor 9, is based on a modern software development design pattern called service oriented architecture (SOA). SOA enables cost-effective application flexibility and allows organizations to connect their application programs with Epicor 9 in highly customizable ways. Epicor's products are lower in cost than products from other companies.

INFOR **Infor** has pursued an acquisition strategy to consolidate many product offerings under one sales and marketing organization. Infor has acquired more than 20 companies, and today it sells an ERP product for just about any type of firm in just about any industry. As you might imagine, the products vary in purpose, scope, and quality. They span the midrange as well as higher-end small companies and lower-end large companies.

MICROSOFT DYNAMICS **Microsoft Dynamics** is composed of four ERP products, all obtained via acquisition: AX, Nav, GP, and SL. AX and Nav have the most capabilities; GP is smaller and easier to use. Although Dynamics has over 80,000 installations, the future of SL

**FIGURE 3-15**

**Vendors and
Company Size**

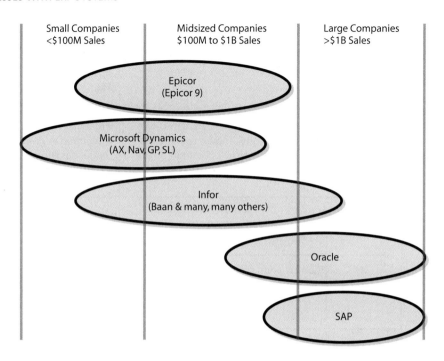

is particularly cloudy; Microsoft outsources the maintenance of the code to provide continuing support to existing customers. Each product is particularly capable in different business functions.

None of these products is well integrated with Microsoft Office, none of them uses SOA, and none of them is integrated at all with Microsoft's development languages. In fact, Microsoft's ERP direction is difficult to determine. It seems to have four horses headed in different directions, and none of them is attached to the primary Microsoft coach. Possibly, it will make an ERP announcement for a new ERP product in the cloud. Or maybe, as long as these products meet most of the needs of its customers, Microsoft executives are just too busy to care.

ORACLE Oracle is an intensely competitive company with a deep base of technology and high-quality technical staff. Oracle developed some of its ERP products in-house and has complemented those products with others obtained through its acquisition of PeopleSoft (high-quality HR products) and Siebel (high-quality CRM products).

Because they are designed according to SOA principles, Oracle's ERP is adaptable and customizable. Beginning with its first DBMS product release, Oracle has never been known to create easy-to-use products. It is known, however, for producing fully featured products with superior performance. They are also expensive.

Oracle CEO Larry Ellison owns 70 percent of NetSuite, a company that offers a cloud-based solution for integrated financial reporting for large, international organizations. It would not be unusual for Oracle to acquire that company as part of a future ERP product in the cloud.

SAP SAP is the gold standard of ERP products. SAP is used by midsized and large companies and offers the most expensive of the ERP products. In Q7, we elaborate more on SAP than the other ERP products, because we will use it in the next two chapters to explain the procurement and sales processes and how an ERP system improves those processes.

## Q7. What Makes SAP Different from Other ERP Products?

SAP is a product of **SAP AG**, a German firm. The core business of SAP AG is selling licenses for software solutions and related services. In addition, it offers consulting, training, and other services for its software solutions. Founded in 1972 by 5 former IBM employees, SAP AG has grown to become the third largest software company in the world, with about 50,000 employees, 100,000 customers, and 10 million users in over 100 countries.

The stated goal of SAP software is to help companies make their business processes more efficient and agile. To do this, it relies on a database of over 25,000 tables. It is pronounced as three letters, S-A-P, not as the word *sap*. The letters are an abbreviation for "Systems, Applications, Products," which in German is "*Systeme, Anwendungen, Produkte.*" Detractors humorously claim it might also stand for "Stop All Progress" or "Start And Pray," titles that hint at the challenges of using SAP and of its importance to the company.

Over 80 percent of *Fortune* 500 companies use SAP, including Coke, Caterpillar, Exxon Mobile, Procter & Gamble, IBM, Marathon Oil, General Motors, Nike, and General Electric. To install SAP today, those companies might spend $100 million or more. Of this total cost, hardware may account for 20 to 25 percent, software 20 to 25 percent, and "human ware" (training, consulting, and implementation) 50 to 60 percent. Training, consulting, and implementation of SAP products has become a career for many in IT, and it is easy to see why—companies need technical people who understand the business and business processes and can make SAP work for them.

The prices mentioned above vary, because getting SAP up and running in a company varies—in some cases the process can take years. One time-consuming process is answering the over 8,000 configuration decisions mentioned earlier. To speed up the configuration process, SAP produces and sells **industry-specific platforms**. An industry-specific platform is like a suit before it is tailored; it is a preconfiguration platform that is appropriate for a particular industry, such as retail, manufacturing, or health care. All SAP implementations start with an SAP industry-specific platform and are further configured to a particular company with the configuration choices mentioned earlier. A second lengthy and expensive process is training employees of all levels how to use the system.

A common way to view SAP is as a collection of interconnected and interdependent modules, some of which are listed in Figure 3-16. A **module** is a distinct and logical grouping of processes. For example, SD, the Sales and Distribution module, is a collection of processes supervised by the marketing department. These processes record customer data, sales data, and pricing data. Not every module is implemented in every installation of SAP. Companies that install SAP choose modules for their implementation.

## SAP Inputs and Outputs

An example SAP screen is shown in Figure 3-17. When the screen first loads, it is largely empty. On a screen like this, Jenna enters a vendor number in the box numbered 1 and the material in box number 2. After clicking the check icon, marked as 3, SAP populates the screen as shown with data about the company, payment options, and pricing choices for Jenna.

The screen shown in Figure 3-17 is called the Create Purchase Order: Overview screen. When SAP is implemented and configured at a particular organization, this screen is made available only to approved purchasing agents in each department. Different roles in the organization give people access to different screens and different data; accountants would have access to their screens, warehouse people their screens, and so on.

| | | | |
|---|---|---|---|
| QM | Quality Management | PP | Production Planning |
| FI | Financial Accounting | CO | Controlling |
| PM | Plant Maintenance | SD* | Sales and Distribution |
| HR | Human Resource | MM** | Materials Management |
| PS | Project Systems | BI | Business Intelligence |

**FIGURE 3-16**
**SAP Modules**

*SD    includes sales processes, the topic of Chapter 5.
**MM  includes procurement processes, the topic of Chapter 4.

**FIGURE 3-17**

**Procurement Example Screen**

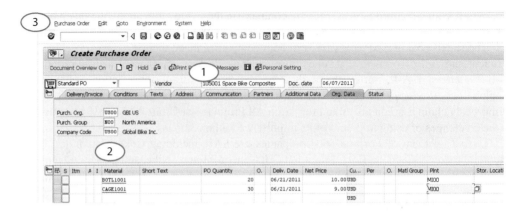

Although it is difficult to tell from this example, Jenna does not have the option to permanently delete a purchase order once it has been saved. SAP is designed to preclude deleting saved records. This control makes auditing and supervision of the transactions more complete and reduces the risk of fraud. Other controls limit the data the salesperson can enter. For example, items sold must already be in inventory, zip codes must match cities, and delivery locations to a warehouse must be specified.

### SAP Software

SAP was the first ERP software designed to work at different companies. Prior to SAP, early ERP programs were customized products—companies wrote their own programs to support their own processes. When SAP was launched, its first effort was to consolidate data for financial, accounting, inventory, and production-planning processes. Personnel and plant management modules were developed in the 1980s.

One of the more well-known versions of SAP is called **R/3**. The R/3 program (where R means "real time") was the first truly integrated system that was able to support most of an organization's major operational processes. Built in the 1990s, the R/3 platform uses client-server architecture. It experienced runaway growth in the 1990s and was installed in 17,000 organizations. Ironically, this past success creates a problem today. SAP R/3 uses classic, thick-client, client-server architecture, rather than a browser-based approach that would be easier to use on a wide range of devices, such as smartphones and other thin clients.

Because of this large installed base, SAP has lagged the competitions' rapid move to thin-client, SOA, cloud-based solutions. Instead, it must focus resources and attention on the needs of its current customers (and the attendant, large revenue stream from their maintenance contracts). SAP has the twin challenge of building a stable single platform that makes company processes efficient today, but at the same time providing a platform that will adapt to take advantage of new IT developments. SAP overcame its early dependence on mainframe architecture, now it must do so again to overcome its dependence on client-server architecture.

To this end, SAP has rebranded its R/3 software as the **SAP Business Suite**. The SAP Business Suite runs on a program called an *application platform*. The SAP application platform is NetWeaver. NetWeaver is like the operating system in your computer. An operating system helps connect programs, printers, and other devices. Similarly, **NetWeaver** connects SAP to hardware, third-party software, and output devices. NetWeaver also has SOA capabilities that help it integrate SAP with non-SAP applications. These features enable the Business Suite/NetWeaver approach to be more adaptive to new IT developments compared to R/3. **ABAP** is SAP's high-level application language that is used to enhance the functionality of an SAP implementation.

Helping your future company, whether large or small, make wise use of ERP systems will be one of the challenges you will face during your business career. You will be hired initially into a department based on your experience and education, but all businesses want integrated processes. As a result, you will be asked to think about how your department's processes can be improved with the ERP system and how they can be integrated with other processes in the firm.

Employers seek new hires who have mastered some of the aspects of ERP systems. So take time to command the vocabulary in these next several chapters. Learn how the procurement and sales processes work in Chapters 4 and 5 and how an ERP system supports those processes. If you have access to SAP, accomplish the SAP exercises at the end of the next two chapters and, once complete, start over and deliberately make mistakes, try new things, and see how SAP acts. Learn beyond the book; later you'll be glad you did.

# Ethics Guide

## ERP Estimation

Todd Douglas Jones was the director of IT at Central Colorado State when the ERP system was implemented. He was a big advocate of the ERP system because he had seen such systems work elsewhere and was convinced it would work well at the university.

Todd was charged with the task of determining the costs and benefits for the new system. After some preliminary research on the topic he decided that cost should primarily be measured in the price of the product and the number of hours of training for the users of the system. Benefits will be determined by the reduction in operating costs.

In order to help the university's president and staff see that the benefits of purchasing and implementing an ERP solution outweighed the costs, Todd shaded the facts in order to make the ERP choice look more promising. Todd did a number of questionable things:

a.  He researched 10 schools that had implemented a similar system. He could have used the cost and labor of all 10 schools as estimates for his school. However, in his opinion, three of the schools mismanaged the implementation, and he chose not to include those schools in his estimate, resulting in a lower cost estimate for his university.

b.  He estimated that end-user training would be 750 hours, although he expected at least 1,000 hours would be needed. He planned to fund the other 250 hours from his IT training budget for next year.

c.  To calculate cost savings, Todd used a different set of 10 schools than he used in item a. He believed that these 10 schools were closer in size to his own school and were more representative of his university, and they made the cost savings look better than the 10 other schools.

Six months after the very successful implementation, Todd was hailed as a visionary. The university is saving thousands of dollars a month. Seven months after the implementation, an auditor discovered the three questionable activities listed above.

You are Todd. Your boss knows what you did. You look into your own motivations and with a clear conscience you tell yourself:

> I did not tell a lie. I knew that the system would be a tremendous success, and if I did not help the boss come to see that I would have let a great opportunity pass us by. I did what was best for the most people. I did not directly profit from this. If I were the boss, I would want my IT manager to help me reach the right conclusion, too. And look how it turned out—that alone shows I did the right thing.

## DISCUSSION QUESTIONS

1. Of the ethical lapses listed, which one was the most serious?
2. What would you do if you were Todd's boss? How does this change your management of Todd in the future?
3. What is the difference between inappropriate rationalization and justification?
4. How do you know when you are rationalizing inappropriately?
5. Do you agree with Todd's last statement? Does a good result always indicate a good process or a good decision?

# Active Review

Use this Active Review to verify that you understand the material in the chapter. You can read the entire chapter and then perform the tasks in this review, or you can read the text material for just one question and perform the tasks in this review for that question before moving on to the next one.

## Q1. What problem does an ERP system solve?

Explain how businesses used IS before ERP systems. Identify the problem solved by an enterprise system. Explain information silos. State the differences between the two enterprise systems—EAI and ERP. Define *EAI* and describe how EAI works. Explain how metadata is used by EAI. Give several reasons why a firm might want to use an EAI rather than ERP. Name the components of an ERP. Describe the primary purpose of an ERP.

## Q2. What are the elements of an ERP system?

Explain how businesses used computers for inventory purposes before the Internet. Explain the difference between MRP and MRPII. Explain how business and IS have coevolved. Name several of the business functions integrated by ERP. Explain why an ERP implementation might not install all these functions. Describe why a company might create a custom program for its ERP implementation. Define *configuration*. Describe the relationship between ERP systems and databases. Describe a new hardware dilemma and how it impacts ERP. Explain several ERP jobs. Describe inherent processes and explain why they are a part of ERP.

## Q3. What are the benefits of an ERP system?

Explain why it is not accurate to say that ERP improves existing processes. Describe the advantages of the real-time data benefit of ERP systems. Explain how ERP benefits management. Give examples of how the benefits of an ERP implementation could be measured.

## Q4. What are the challenges of implementing an ERP system?

Why is implementing an ERP solution easier for some organizations? Describe the challenges common to all teams, not just implementation teams. Give several examples of the types of decisions a firm must make to implement an ERP system. Explain the general options the implementation team has for each decision. Explain the disadvantages of using custom software with ERP. Describe how management can make implementation more difficult than necessary.

## Q5. What types of organizations use ERP?

Explain how the type of firm that uses ERP has changed over time. How can the size of the organization impact ERP success? What ERP needs are unique to large organizations?

## Q6. Who are the major ERP vendors?

How do the top ERP vendors differ? Name four or five of the top vendors and explain how they are unique. Identify the relative market share of each. Explain which ERP vendors serve small and midsized organizations and which serve large organizations.

## Q7. What makes SAP different from other ERP products?

Describe SAP AG. Break down the expenses for implementing SAP. Define *module* and give examples of SAP modules. Explain how access to SAP screens can be controlled and how SAP limits or controls data inputs. Describe SAP's NetWeaver. Explain the important characteristics of R/3.

## Key Terms and Concepts

ABAP  *74*

Analysts  *64*

Bill of material (BOM)  *68*

Configuration  *62*

Enterprise application integration
(EAI)  *56*

Enterprise resource planning
(ERP)  *57*

Epicor  *71*

Industry-specific platform  *73*

Infor  *71*

Inherent processes  *64*

Just in time (JIT)  *61*

Manufacturing resource planning
(MRPII)  *61*

Material requirements planning
(MRP)  *61*

Microsoft Dynamics  *71*

Module  *73*

NetWeaver  *74*

Process blueprints  *64*

R/3  *74*

SAP AG  *72*

SAP Business Suite  *74*

Sarbanes-Oxley Act (SOX)  *62*

Train the trainer  *63*

## Using Your Knowledge

1. Give two examples of organizations you know that have information silos. Would either of these organizations choose an EAI solution over an ERP solution? Explain. Using Figure 3-15, what size category are these organizations and which vendors have a possible ERP solution to offer?

2. What would happen next fall if the freshman class is unexpectedly 20 percent larger than this year's class? Which campus organizations need to know that data early? Do you think your university has a way to share this data efficiently?

3. An ERP can create a digital dashboard of important statistics and measures. What data would you like on your dashboard if you were the athletics director? Are they all measures of process objectives? What data would you like if you were the president of the university? Who else at the university could use a dashboard to do their work more effectively?

4. What does this MIS class do differently than other classes? Maybe the assignments are a bit different, maybe the instructor does some things a little differently. What if a university instructional ERP system was invented that featured inherent processes that removed these unique elements? Would that make the school's teaching process more efficient and effective? How could you measure that improvement. Would it be worth it?

5. The athletics director buys sports equipment from a supplier with a well-implemented ERP. What advantages are there for your school to buy from a supplier with an ERP system? You might expect to see an advertising claim from that company like, "We can meet customer orders in 20 percent less time than the industry average." Create a list of two or three measures you would expect to hear from a supplier with an effective ERP system and two or three measures that an ERP system might not improve.

6. To have a successful ERP system, a sports equipment supplier will have made a variety of good configuration decisions. Give examples of what you think might be the company's item identifiers, resupply times, and order sizes. Also, who do you think approves customer credit and production capacity increases? What actions need to be taken if a customer modifies an order?

7. Assume that a sports equipment supplier chose SAP and is an equipment wholesaler and does not produce the equipment that it sells to universities. As a wholesaler, which module in Figure 3-16 might the supplier not purchase from SAP?

8. Figure 3-4 shows the procurement process now used at the university and the objectives and measures used by the athletics department. If you worked as the purchasing agent for food services, buying all the food served in campus dining halls, what would be the objectives and measures of your procurement process?

# Collaboration Exercise 3

Collaborate with a group of fellow students to answer the following questions. For this exercise do not meet face to face. Your task will be easier if you coordinate your work with SharePoint, Office 365, Google Docs with Google+ or equivalent collaboration tools. Your answers should reflect the thinking of the entire group, and not just that of one or two individuals.

1. Using your local hospital as an example, answer the following questions:
   a. Where might information silos exist if an ERP system is not being used?
   b. Should the hospital pursue more efficient processes or more effective ones? Does it matter if you are a patient?
   c. Using your answer to item b, what measures might be used to assess the benefits of an ERP system at the hospital? (See Figure 3-10 on page 66 for example measures).
   d. Of the implementation decisions listed in Figure 3-11, which ones apply to the hospital?
   e. Which ERP vendor would you suggest for the hospital? Explain your selection.
   f. Assign each person on your team the task of diagramming a different hospital process using BPMN. Then merge your diagrams and reduce the detail in each of the individual processes so that the overall process diagram has about the same number of activities as the individual processes did before merging.

2. Using your university or college as an example, answer the following questions:
   a. Where might information silos exist if an ERP system is not being used?
   b. Will using an ERP system improve the efficiency or effectiveness of processes? What are the objectives of the process(es) being improved?
   c. Using your answer to item b, what measures might be used to assess the benefits of an ERP system at the university? (See Figure 3-10 on page 66 for example measures.)
   d. Of the implementation decisions listed in Figure 3-11, which ones apply to the university?
   e. Which ERP vendor would you suggest for the university? Explain your selection.

3. The exercise in MIS InClass 6 was designed to help you see important aspects of processes and enterprise systems:
   a. What lessons from the chapter did you learn by playing the game?
   b. What other lessons from the chapter could have been learned but seemed to have been missed by your class?
   c. Rewrite the instructions to improve the game.
   d. Could this game be used in other business school classes? What learning objectives could this game deliver?

# CASE STUDY 3

## The Sudden End of the U.S. Air Force[5]

"Why does the country need an independent Air Force?" This question is now being asked by the top brass and the civilian leadership at the Pentagon. Many other agencies—local, state, and federal—are asking similar types of questions. New enterprise systems available to government agencies are making them question old ways of doing things and old processes. The need for intelligence agencies to overcome their information silos and share data on potential terrorist threats is constantly in the news. The same information silo problem exists with your local police and fire departments and with many other government agencies at all levels. The Air Force issue is a classic case of what happens when a new IS and information silos meet.

The military still needs airplanes, but what it needs more are integrated end-to-end processes that connect soldiers fighting on the ground with airplanes supporting them. Military airplanes provide two important services—they collect data about the war zone and they drop ordinance on targets. In both cases, these are just activities within larger processes, processes that until now had to be done by different departments using their own isolated databases.

[5] Based on: Greg Jaffe, "Combat Generation: Drone Operators Climb on Winds of Change in the Air Force," *Washington Post,* February 28, 2010.

One process is the Collect Battlefield Intelligence (BI) process. Troops currently fighting and managers planning the fighting both need BI. In both cases, the process starts as a Department of the Army request for intelligence. This request is passed to the Department of the Air Force, which then schedules the flight, assigns pilots, specifies locations, and collects the data. After the flight, the data is then sent back to the Army. The delivery of ordinance goes through exactly the same interdepartmental process; the only difference is that when the trigger is pulled in the airplane a bomb goes out rather than data comes in.

These processes have worked this way for about 50 years. Recently, pilotless drones have been developed that do the work that manned airplanes did in the past. These drones have much in common with information systems. The plane, the hardware, is controlled by the software that flies the plane. Data is collected by the drone, and the drone has a database of GPS coordinates and data on the height of every obstacle near it. People operate the drone to drop ordinance and collect BI using well-established procedures.

These flying information systems, these drones, have changed many of the old processes used by the organization in much the same way ERP changes processes. Because they can be much smaller than manned airplanes, and much cheaper, drones can be assigned to the Army units doing the fighting. As a result, the process to drop ordinance or gather BI is accomplished much more quickly. Instead of information silos that separated Air Force and Army data, now the drone can quickly respond to the request and the data can be made available in real time to the Army units that need it. If these new processes are completely adopted, there may be no need for an independent Air Force.

## Questions

1. Using BPMN documentation, diagram the Collect Battlefield Intelligence process before and after the use of drones. Some activities are Request for Intelligence, Schedule Airplane, and Transmit Data. Resources include the Army database and the Air Force database. Roles include Warfighter, Planner, and Airplane Scheduler. Actors can be Airplane and Drone.
2. Will the new process have the same objectives as the old process? Are the new objectives focused on effectiveness or efficiency, or both? What measures should be used to prove efficiency and effectiveness?
3. Beyond the two processes mentioned here, if the Department of Defense implemented an ERP system, which of the benefits in Figure 3-9 could it expect to attain?
4. Again, if one ERP system is used in the future, what are the most significant challenges the Department of Defense will encounter?
5. Pick another government agency that you understand well. Explain what existing processes would be replaced, what the benefits of an ERP system would be, and the challenges faced.

"Tell me, Wally, what was the hardest part of your job as a warehouse manager?" asks Jerry Pizzi. The two are huddled around a small table in a warehouse at Chuck's Bikes, Inc. (CBI),[1] a small bicycle company that buys frames, tires, and accessories and then assembles bikes that it then sells to retailers. They are discussing Wally's pending retirement.

"It was probably dealing with people. Suppliers would only tell me half the story when my orders were going to be late, and our salespeople seem to think I should be able to read their minds," says Wally.

"And, by the way, this job description doesn't describe what I do," says Wally, pointing to an updated version of his job description.

"Wally, you are one of a kind. We can't replace you, but we can be specific about the skills we need," Jerry replies. Jerry, the head of human resources at CBI, and Wally are tweaking a draft job description to hire Wally's replacement.

"Wally, do you see anything we missed?"

"Nothing is missing, but this description makes my job sound like you need to be a statistics and computer whiz just to apply. I never thought the job was that complicated—just figure out what you need to order, what you have, what is available, and when you need everything. This year's orders are like last year's orders. You keep a little of everything."

"Wally, you made that work. I wish we could hire you. But since we can't, we'll change the job and make sure the new person can use the new SAP system well."

"You know that system is not as easy to use as was advertised."

"That's an understatement. I'm still getting used to it. Some days I wish I were the one retiring."

After they work on some details, Jerry thanks Wally for his help and sees him out. Later, Jerry and Wally's boss, Tim, discuss the job description.

"Wally was the best warehouse manager Chuck's Bikes ever had," Tim says.

---

[1] At the request of the SAP University Alliance, we did not make any changes or extensions to the Global Bike, Inc. (GBI) case. Instead, we have created a company that is different, a competitor, for which we can add characters without compromising the GBI SAP materials but that is close enough to enable students to be able to use the GBI SAP simulation, if appropriate.

"But, he's also one reason the new system doesn't run well," adds Jerry. "His skill set was well matched to that job as it was about 15 years ago."

"I know, but I'm still glad he took our offer to retire early. You're right, he hasn't adapted to the SAP system very well."

"I don't think it was just the new system. His job was already becoming more complex. Wally was great until we expanded the product line a couple of years ago."

"Wally did mention that he thought this new description overemphasizes math and computer skills."

"I see his point. I think we should balance those with team skills and communication. The new position will require more communication with the other warehouses and departments here."

"I'll add those. But look at this description now. Doesn't it seem odd that someone who we both think was terrific at one time couldn't win his own job today."

"It does seem like a new day."

**Q1.** What are the fundamentals of a Procurement process?

**Q2.** How did the Procurement process at CBI work before SAP?

**Q3.** What were the problems with the Procurement process before SAP?

**Q4.** How does CBI implement SAP?

**Q5.** How does the Procurement process work at CBI after SAP?

**Q6.** How can SAP improve the integration of supply chain processes at CBI?

**Q7.** How does the use of SAP change CBI?

## Chapter Preview

In this chapter, we look into the Procurement process that Wally supervised before and after the implementation of SAP. We are interested in how SAP made that process and other processes at his company better.

In the previous two chapters, we introduced processes and ERP systems. Here and in the next chapter we show how the general ideas about processes and ERP systems from those two chapters can be applied to two common business processes. We will see the benefits of standardizing processes and bringing the data from CBI's processes into one place so that the data can be used throughout the company in real time. In this chapter, we examine the Procurement process. In Chapter 5, we examine the Sales process.

We begin by considering how CBI accomplished procurement before implementing SAP. We then examine how SAP improved CBI's Procurement process. Although most of the chapter concerns the Procurement process, toward the end of the chapter we will broaden our discussion to other processes in CBI's supply chain. Certainly the Procurement process can be made more effective with SAP, but the impacts of SAP on a firm's supply chain are even more significant.

## Q1. What Are the Fundamentals of a Procurement Process?

Before discussing the Procurement process at CBI, a short review of procurement will set the stage for understanding this process at CBI. **Procurement** is the process of obtaining goods and services. Examples of these goods are raw materials, machine spare parts, and cafeteria services. Procurement is an operational process executed hundreds or thousands of times a day in a large organization. The three main procurement activities are Order, Receive, and Pay, as shown in Figure 4-1. These three activities are performed by actors in different departments and were briefly introduced in Chapter 3 with the example of procurement at a university.

Procurement is the most common organizational process. Every organization, from single-employee startups to Walmart, from county to federal governments, relies on its Procurement process. Even college students have to procure items: You order books and movies online, and you buy clothes and food. Everything you own, you procured in some way. And, like procurement at an organization, your process has objectives—you do not want to buy inferior goods and you do not want to waste time or money.

Many organizations have similar procurement objectives, the most common of which are saving time and money. According to some estimates, a well-managed procurement process can spend half as much as a poorly managed procurement process to acquire the same goods.[2]

**FIGURE 4-1**

**Main Procurement Process Activities and Roles**

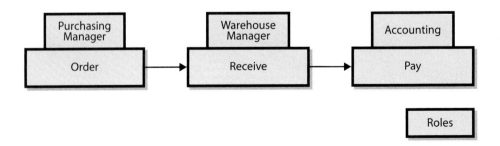

[2] High performance through procurement Accenture 2007. *https://microsite.accenture.com/supplychainmastery/ Insights/Documents/Achieving%20High%20Performance%20through%20Procurement%20Mastery.pdf*

| Primary Activity | Description | Process and Chapter |
|---|---|---|
| Inbound logistics | Receiving, storing, and disseminating inputs to products | Procurement, Chapter 4 |
| Operations | Transforming inputs into final products | |
| Outbound logistics | Collecting, storing, and physically distributing products to buyers | |
| Sales and marketing | Inducing buyers to purchase products and providing the means for them to do so | Sales, Chapter 5 |
| Customer service | Assisting customers use of products and thus maintaining and enhancing the products' value | |

**FIGURE 4-2**

**Procurement Process Within the Value Chain of CBI**

The state of Pennsylvania has saved $360 million a year by restructuring its procurement process; other states have saved 10 to 25 percent of their purchasing budgets.[3] Another reason why procurement is an important process is that when firms grow by acquisition, procurement is one of the only processes that spans the entire new organization. By combining procurement into one process, the new larger firm can leverage the quantity of the items ordered to gain lower prices. Many states are combining the procurement processes at their various universities and prisons to obtain lower prices from suppliers.

In this chapter, we consider the portion of procurement that supports the inbound logistics process in the value chain. In this role, procurement obtains the raw material needed for subsequent assembly in the production process of the operations activity in the value chain, as shown in Figure 4-2. Other value chain activities also develop and execute procurement processes to obtain things other than raw materials, such as legal services, machine parts, and transportation services.

The activities in the Procurement process at CBI are shown in Figure 4-3. To better understand the activities in Figure 4-3, consider how CBI acquires tires for its bikes. The first activity is to find qualified suppliers who make tires. Once these firms have been identified as potential suppliers, CBI asks each supplier to specify the price it would charge for each type of tire and order quantity. Using this price data, CBI creates a **purchase order (PO)**, a written document requesting delivery of a specified quantity of a product or service in return for payment. At CBI the

**FIGURE 4-3**

**Main Procurement Process Activities, Subactivities, and Actors at CBI**

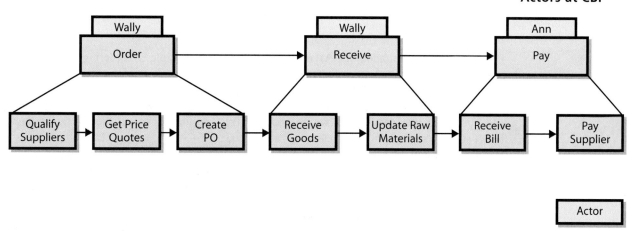

[3] David Yarkin, "Saving States the Sam's Club Way," *New York Times*, February 28, 2011, p. A23.

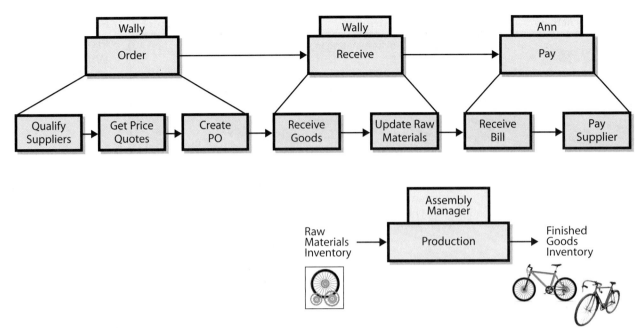

**FIGURE 4-4**

**Main Procurement Process Activities, Subactivities, Production Process, and Inventories**

Purchase Order specifies a supplier, the tire part number, quantities of tires, and delivery dates. The tires are then received from the supplier in one of CBI's warehouses. Once the tires are received, CBI updates its Raw Materials Inventory database. Soon after, a bill arrives from the supplier and the supplier is paid.

A key term in the Procurement process is inventory. CBI maintains two types of inventory, as shown in Figure 4-4. At the top of Figure 4-4, the Procurement process acquires raw materials, whereas the Production process, shown on the bottom, converts the raw materials into finished goods. **Raw materials inventory** stores components like bicycle tires and other goods procured from suppliers. These raw materials must be on hand for assembly operations to occur in the Production process. At CBI, raw materials inventory includes bike frames, wheels, and seats. **Finished goods inventory** is the completed products awaiting delivery to customers. At CBI, finished goods inventory is the assembled bikes and accessories. Before SAP was implemented, CBI stored records of both inventories in its Inventory database.

## Q2. How Did the Procurement Process at CBI Work Before SAP?

Prior to the implementation of SAP at CBI, Wally was responsible for ordering and receiving raw materials. He issued orders when the raw materials inventory was low, stored parts when they arrived, kept track of where he put them, and planned and managed the people and equipment to accomplish those tasks. His objectives were to avoid running out of a raw materials, to use reliable suppliers, and to stay within a budget. The measures for these objectives were number of stockouts, number of late deliveries, and price.

The Procurement process at CBI before SAP is shown in Figure 4-5. As shown in Figure 4-5, the process has six roles. Two of these, Warehouse Manager and Accountant, are performed by people; the other four are done by computers. As you will see, each of the computer roles uses its own database, creating four information silos.

The first activity in the process shown in Figure 4-5 is Pre-Order Actions. In this step, Wally, in his role as Warehouse Manager, would notice that an item was below its reorder point, look over previous purchases for these items to discover a good supplier, and determine his order quantity. He would often log in to the Sales database to see if that item would be needed in the

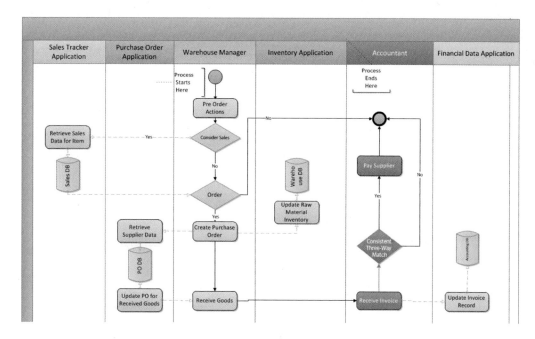

**FIGURE 4-5**

**Procurement Process at CBI Before SAP**

next few days to fulfill recent sales. If he decided to order at the Order decision node, he would start the Create Purchase Order activity and log in to his Purchase Order database to obtain supplier data needed to complete the Purchase Order. Wally would use the purchase order form shown in Figure 4-6. In this example, he ordered 15 Deluxe Road Bike frames from Space Bike Composites of Houston, Texas.

Later, when the items arrive at the warehouse, the Receive Goods activity occurs. In this activity, a warehouse worker unpacks the box, counts the items, and updates the raw material inventory quantity in the Warehouse database. At the end of the day, Wally updates the Purchase Order database to reflect all the purchase orders that were received that day.

Several days later, an **invoice**, or itemized bill, is received from the supplier. The data on the invoice—the amount due and the purchase order number for that invoice—are entered into the Accounting database. Before the accountants pay the bill, they make sure that the data on the invoice matches the data in the purchase order and the goods receipt (see Figure 4-7). If the data in this **three-way match** are consistent, a payment is made and the payment data are posted to the Accounting database. In the entire Procurement process at CBI, four databases are used—one in sales, two in the warehouse, and one in accounting. Each of these databases was constructed to serve the needs of different departments; over the years, they have resulted in information silos.

## CBI BICYCLES

PURCHASE ORDER

**FIGURE 4-6**

**Wally's Purchase Order in Paper Form**

TO:                    SHIP TO:                 P.O. NUMBER:
Space Bike Composites  Chuck's Bikes Inc        **15432**

| P.O DATE | REQUISITIONER | SHIPPED VIA | F.O.B. POINT | TERMS | |
|----------|---------------|-------------|--------------|-------|---|
| 1/14/2012 | Wally Jones | Truck | Midpoint | | |

| QTY | UNIT | DESCRIPTION | | UNIT PRICE | TOTAL |
|-----|------|-------------|---|------------|-------|
| 15 | PQ131 | Deluxe Road Bikes | | $120 | 1800 |

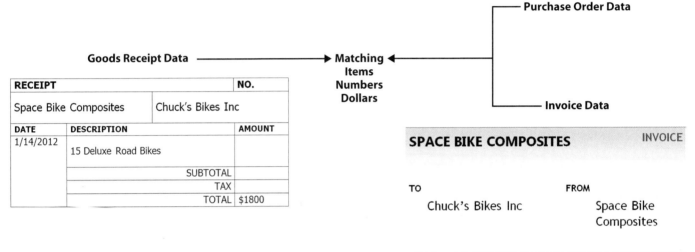

**FIGURE 4-7**

**Three-Way Match**

## Q3. What Were the Problems with the Procurement Process Before SAP?

The problems with the Procurement process before SAP were well known at CBI. They are listed in Figure 4-8.

### Warehouse Problems

In the years preceding SAP implementation, CBI had expanded its sales and product line. It had also adopted a strategy of quick response to changes in customer demand. It wanted to be the

**FIGURE 4-8**

**Problems at CBI with Procurement Before SAP**

| Role | Problems |
|---|---|
| Warehouse | Growth in finished goods inventory reduces warehouse space for raw material inventory. <br> Warehouse manager does not have data on sales price discounts. |
| Accounting | Three-way match discrepancies take time to correct. <br> Accounting data are not real time. |
| Purchasing | Purchasing agents not centralized; training experience and motivation difference. <br> Weak internal controls lead to limited scrutiny of purchases. |

company that bike retailers could count on to supply popular new bike models and accessories. As a result, CBI wanted to hold a wide variety of finished goods so that it could quickly respond to changes in customer demands. As it turns out, the finished goods inventory and the raw material inventory share the same warehouse, so more finished goods meant that there was less room for raw materials. Less room for raw materials and more types of raw materials for the wider variety of finished goods created a perfect storm in Wally's warehouse. He was increasingly running out of raw materials.

Another problem was that Wally was blind to sales price data. Wally could log into the Sales database to see what bikes and accessories CBI sold each day, but that database did not include price discounts. He did not know if a sudden increase in sales of one bike was due to a deep price discount or whether the product was being bundled with something else that was selling well. The sudden increase might be due to these marketing campaigns, or it might be the first sign of a big spike in popularity for that bicycle. Wally was always the last to find out. As a result, Wally frequently ordered too few or too many bike components.

## Accounting Problems

In accounting, Ann supervised the payment activities. Most of Ann's challenges occurred at the end of the Procurement process. One of her activities was to ensure that the three-way match was correct. When discrepancies occurred, the accounting department had to begin a costly and labor-intensive process that required several e-mails to the warehouse and the supplier to resolve. For example, if the warehouse miscounted or if the supplier shipped the wrong components, Ann would have to access various databases, compare results, and e-mail suppliers to confirm the results of her inquiry.

The other accounting problem was that accounting reports always lagged; they were never up-to-the-minute. Actually, they were never up-to-the-day. This was a result of not sharing real-time accounting data throughout the organization. Instead, accounting reports were produced at the end of the month. It took the accountants several days to **roll up**, or compile and summarize, the accounting transactions into balance sheets and income statements. This was a problem, because other firms that competed with CBI had begun to rely on ERP systems to produce real-time accounting data. With more current data, managers at these other firms could notice problems sooner and respond to customers more quickly.

## Purchasing Problems

CBI had no purchasing department, a fact that created numerous problems. First, the purchasing agents, like Wally, were scattered throughout the firm. They had diverse training, experience, and motivation. As a result, they produced a variety of mistakes on the purchase orders. Further, they had little knowledge about what was happening in other parts of the organization. For example, CBI's repair shop had recently found several very good suppliers of bike parts that Wally in the warehouse would have used, too, but he was not aware of them. These suppliers would have granted CBI lower prices if both Wally and the repair shop combined their purchases. The old Procurement process at CBI required each of its purchasing agents to be meticulous record keepers. However, Wally and other purchasing agents sometimes forgot to transcribe data from the handwritten purchase order to the database, used wrong addresses for suppliers, or entered incorrect totals. Doing their primary jobs was their passion; the procurement paperwork was a much lower priority. Further, it was hard to train these dispersed purchasing agents because they were scattered throughout the organization and had great differences in training needs and expectations from their bosses.

A final problem with the old process was that the upper management at CBI was under pressure from the board of directors to exercise more control over financial processes. A lack of financial control was at the root of Enron and WorldCom's financial meltdowns, which led to new federal government financial requirements, such as the Sarbanes-Oxley Act. The Sarbanes-Oxley Act of 2002 imposed new regulations on how corporations govern themselves, requiring them to set higher standards for the control of their financial operations. Wally and his colleagues could make costly mistakes, favor suppliers for the wrong reasons, or succumb to the temptation to procure items based on their own interests and not the firm's. By bringing all the purchasing to one office in the company, CBI could exercise much better oversight.

The true cost of a system is rarely known before full implementation. Read the Ethics Guide on pages 104–105 to examine the ethical dilemmas in procuring a system.

This improved oversight is an example of **internal control**. Internal controls systematically limit the actions and behaviors of employees, processes, and systems within the organization to safeguard assets and to achieve objectives. One of the key benefits of ERP systems and IS in general are improved internal controls of financial data.

## Q4. How Does CBI Implement SAP?

CBI wanted to use SAP not only to overcome these problems but also to better achieve its competitive strategy. Thus, CBI began the SAP project by examining and focusing its strategy. They could then use the revised strategy to guide its managers when making various SAP configuration decisions. For CBI, the strategy examination process has three activities:

- Determine industry structure.
- Commit to a specific competitive strategy.
- Develop objectives and measures for processes to support the competitive strategy.

CBI initiated its planning process by using Porter's Five Forces model to determine the structure of its industry, as shown in Figure 4-9. CBI determined that the bike wholesale industry has strong rivalry and that customers have low switching costs. Because of low switching costs, a bike retailer could easily switch from one bike maker to another.

To survive and flourish in such an industry, CBI decided to pursue a competitive strategy that focused on high-end bikes and a differentiation strategy of responsiveness to retailers. This competitive strategy is shown in the bottom-right quadrant of Figure 4-10. The high-end bike industry segment includes very lightweight racing bikes and touring bikes with composite frames and sophisticated gear-shifting systems. Responsiveness means that orders from retailers are fulfilled rapidly; a retailer could order a wide range of products, and new hot-selling items would be available. While CBI pursues this competitive strategy, it also seeks to reduce its own internal costs, particularly in procurement and sales.

As stated, CBI wanted to use SAP to help it achieve this strategy. In particular, CBI believed that SAP would help focus its processes on responsiveness to customers while holding costs down. To help it implement SAP to support this strategy, CBI hired an IS consulting firm that specialized in SAP implementation. Matt, the lead consultant, organized managers into teams to create objectives and measures for each of CBI's processes. Matt's firm also provided each team a project manager and a systems analyst to help create the objectives and measures. Wally participated on the team that created the objectives and measures for the Procurement process. This team decided on the four objectives as shown in Figure 4-11.

Wally's team decided on two efficiency objectives—smaller finished goods inventory and fewer errors. To assess the less inventory objective, the team chose to keep track of **inventory turnover**, which is the number of times inventory is sold over a given period, most commonly a year. CBI also decided to measure the total cost of the inventory on hand. To assess the fewer errors objective, CBI decided to record three-way match errors.

On the effectiveness side, the team decided on two measures for better financial controls and three for responsiveness to customers. Financial controls will be better if the rollup time at the end of the month is shorter and if more managers make requests for financial reports. To evaluate responsiveness, the team picked order fulfillment time; number of products to sell; and stockouts of new, hot-selling products.

**FIGURE 4-9**

**Determine Industry Structure with Five Forces Model**

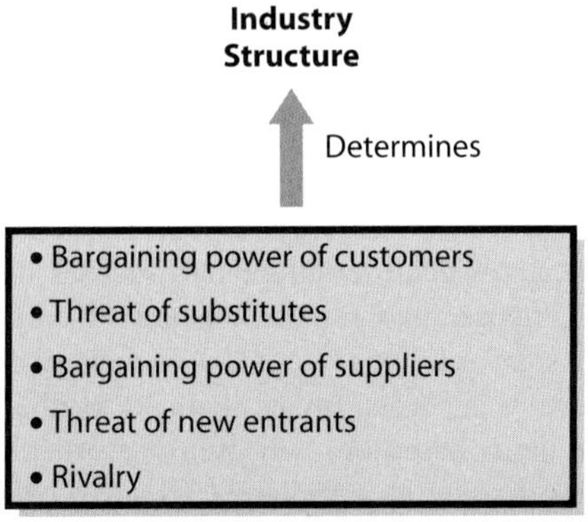

Industry Structure

Determines

- Bargaining power of customers
- Threat of substitutes
- Bargaining power of suppliers
- Threat of new entrants
- Rivalry

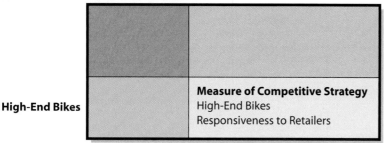

**Cost    Differentiation**

**Industry-wide**

| Lowest cost across the industry | Better product/service across the industry |

**Focus**

| Lowest cost within an industry segment | Better product/service within an industry segment |

**(a) Competitive Strategies**

**Responsiveness**

**High-End Bikes**

**Measure of Competitive Strategy**
High-End Bikes
Responsiveness to Retailers

**(b) Competitive Strategy Chosen by CBI of High-End Bikes; Customer Responsiveness Differentiation**

**FIGURE 4-10**

**Four Competitive Strategy Options and CBI's Competitive Strategy**

| Objective | Measure |
|---|---|
| **Efficiency** | |
| Smaller finished goods inventory | Inventory turnover<br>Total cost of inventory on hand |
| Fewer errors | Number of three-way match errors |
| **Effectiveness** | |
| Better financial control | Time required for end of period rollup<br>Number of managers requesting financial reports |
| More responsive to customers | Order fulfillment time<br>Number of products to sell<br>Stockouts of new, hot-selling products |

**FIGURE 4-11**

**Objectives and Measures for the New Procurement Process**

As you read this, understand that these details at CBI are not the major point. The major point is that *before implementing any ERP system, an organization must first use its strategy to set objectives and measures for major business processes.*

## Q5. How Does the Procurement Process Work at CBI After SAP?

Let's fast-forward 2 years. CBI has now fully implemented SAP, and Wally, as first introduced in the opening vignette to this chapter, is approaching retirement. The SAP inherent Procurement process has replaced CBI's previous Procurement process. Although the new process has the

**FIGURE 4-12**

**Procurement Process at CBI After SAP**

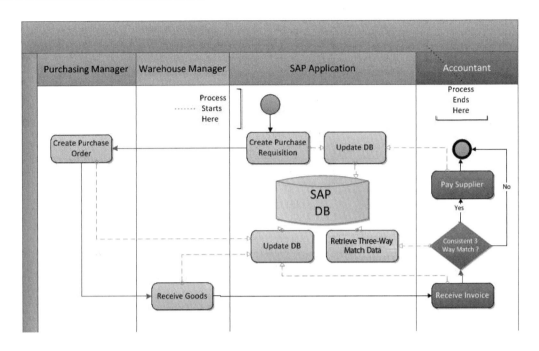

same major activities—Order, Receive, and Pay—the Order activity has changed significantly. See Figure 4-12 for a BPMN diagram of the new SAP-based Procurement process.

The Order activity in the new Procurement process begins with the Create Purchase Requisition activity. A **purchase requisition (PR)** is an internal company document that issues a request for a purchase. This activity is automated at CBI; a computer is the actor, not a human. For example, a PR is automatically generated when the amount of raw material inventory goes below the reorder point. In the example that follows, the PR is for 20 water bottles and 30 water bottle cages.

### Purchasing

In the new purchasing department, if Maria, the purchasing manager, approves of the purchase, she converts the PR into a purchase order (PO). Whereas the automatically generated PR is a CBI document, the PO is a document that CBI shares with its suppliers and, if accepted, is a legally binding contract. In this example, when the PO is completed and accepted, the supplier, Space Bike Composites, has agreed to deliver the goods.

Maria logs into SAP and navigates to one of her screens, the Create Purchase Order screen, which is shown in Figure 4-13. We will return to Maria in a moment, but first a few words about the SAP screens you will see here and in the next chapter. Tens of thousands of such screens exist

**FIGURE 4-13**

**Purchase Order Screen in SAP**

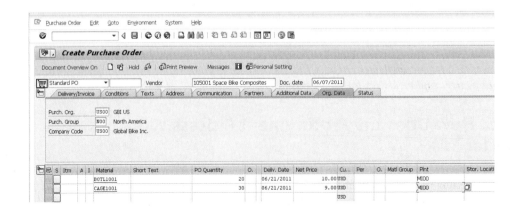

in SAP, so learning the particulars of a few of them is not of great value. Rather, we want you to learn the reoccurring features of an SAP screen, the data typed in by employees, and how the Procurement activity flows from one screen to the next. These skills will be useful for you no matter which ERP screens or process you work with.

Every screen has a title. Here, that title is Create Purchase Order and is shown on the top left. Immediately above the screen title is a drop-down menu (Purchase Order, Edit, GoTo, etc.) and a series of icons for navigating, saving, and getting help. Most of these menu items and icons are the same for almost all SAP screens. Below the title is a header section where Maria must input some data. We pick up her story again at this point.

In this example, the header includes three identifying data items that Maria must input. The header's three boxes—Purch. Org., Purch. Group, and Company Code—are used to identify a particular CBI warehouse.[4] Other inputs would identify CBI's other divisions and warehouse locations. Below the header is the items section that allows Maria to specify for this PO the Material (bottles and cages), PO Quantity (20 and 30), Delivery Date (06/21/2011), Net Price (10.00 and 9.00), and Plant (MI00 for Miami). Each PO can have many of these item lines. Maria finishes the PO by specifying Space Bike Composites (105001) as the vendor in the box in the center of the screen above the header section.

Once Maria saves this PO, SAP records the data in the database. At that point, Maria might move on to entering another PO or log out. After each PO is saved, SAP accomplishes several other tasks. SAP creates a unique PO number and displays this number on Maria's screen. SAP notifies Space Bike Composites via e-mail, a Web service, or an electronic message of the PO details. SAP also calculates the shipment's total weight and total cost and updates the inbound raw material inventory table in the database.

## Warehouse

Once the PO is saved and transmitted to Space Bike Composites, the next activity at CBI is Receive Goods when the shipment arrives. Let's move the clock forward 7 days from when the PO was sent. The bottles and cages have arrived in a box delivered to Wally's warehouse. On the outside of the box, Space Bike Composites has printed the PO number and the contents of the box. Wally notes the PO number, opens the box, and counts and inspects the contents. He then goes to his computer and logs into SAP and the Goods Receipt screen. This screen is shown in Figure 4-14.

The title of this screen, near the top, is Goods Receipt Purchase Order. The header includes a Document Date of 06/07/2011, the Vendor (Space Bike Composites), and other data that Wally types in. He counts the quantity of bottles and cages in the box and discovers that 20 bottles and 30 cages were shipped. He moves to the item section and checks the two OK boxes (the OK column is shortened in the Figure to O) in the item area to confirm that the material arrived in acceptable condition. Wally then enters 20 and 30 for the quantities that arrived. For larger orders, several shipments may be required. Here one PO has one goods receipt. He clicks Save and exits SAP.

**FIGURE 4-14**

**Goods Receipt Screen in SAP**

---

[4] Note that the figures refer to Global Bike, Inc. (GBI), not CBI. Again, CBI is used in this textbook; GBI is the dataset provided by SAP to University Alliance members.

Once Wally saves the goods receipt, SAP creates a document number for this particular goods receipt. In addition, it updates records in the Raw Material Inventory table in the database to reflect the addition of these new bottles and cages. Because CBI now owns the goods, SAP posts a debit to the raw materials inventory account. Finally, an entry is made in the PO record to show that a goods receipt occurred that corresponds to that PO.

### Accounting

The next activity, Receive Invoice, occurs when Space Bike Composites sends CBI an invoice for the material. Ann in accounting receives the invoice the day after the material arrives. To record the arrival of the invoice, she opens the Enter Incoming Invoice screen, shown in Figure 4-15.

In the header section, she enters the date of the invoice (06/07/2011), the Amount ($470.00), and the Purchase Order number (4500000172). After she enters this data, the system finds other data about the PO and displays it on the screen. This data includes the vendor name and address and the two items that were ordered, each on its own row in the items section. When Ann saves this data, SAP records the invoice, displays a new document number for the invoice, and updates the accounting data records to reflect the arrival of the invoice.

The final activity, Pay Supplier, posts an outgoing payment to Space Bike Composites. This is the electronic equivalent of writing a check. Before she posts the payment, Ann performs a three-way check. She compares the data on the PO, the goods receipt, and the invoice to make sure that all three agree on items, numbers, and dollar amounts.

Once payment is made, Ann opens the final SAP screen, Post Outgoing Payment, shown in Figure 4-16. Here she specifies the date of the payment (06/07/2011), the bank Account (100000), and the Amount (470.00). She also must specify an existing vendor in the Account box at the bottom of the screen (the vendor number for Space Bike Composites is 105001). She clicks the Process Open Items icon in the upper-left side of the screen and then saves the transaction. A document number is again created, and an accounting update is made to reflect the outgoing payment.

As you can see, each actor—Maria, Wally, and Ann—interacts with SAP using different screens. Each actor has access to only a limited number of SAP screens. This access is based on each actor's role in the process.

### The Benefits of SAP for the CBI Procurement Process

By bringing all the data into one place for use in real time, SAP helps overcome the problems of the old Procurement process listed in Figure 4-8. For example, in the warehouse, Wally now knows prices charged to customers. In accounting, there are fewer three-way mismatches, because SAP reduces errors made by the purchasing agents and the financial data are now always current. By centralizing purchasing, the new process improves the scrutiny of purchases, because all the procurement data for the organization is in one central database.

**FIGURE 4-15**

**Enter Incoming Invoice Screen in SAP**

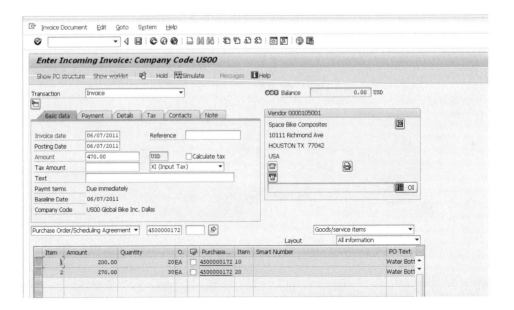

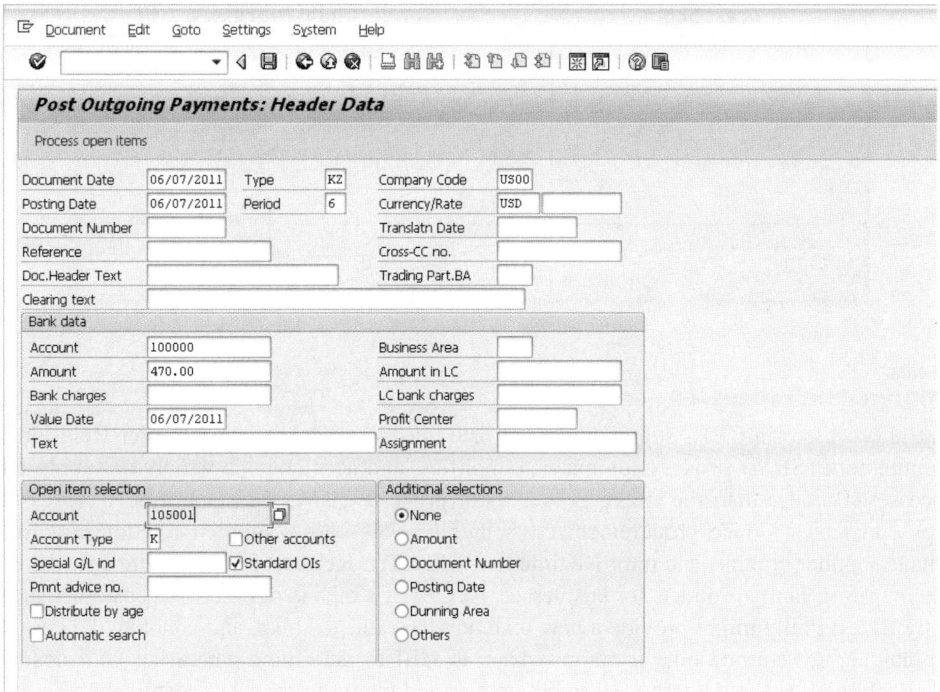

**FIGURE 4-16**

**Post Outgoing Payments Screen in SAP**

As stated, CBI implemented SAP to not only overcome problems, but to pursue its particular strategy. This strategy and the Procurement process objectives that support it were listed earlier in Figure 4-11. The new Procurement process is more efficient than before, because SAP reduces inventory. By implementing SAP, CBI has automated several of the Procurement activities and subactivities. Because the process is now faster, resupply times have been reduced; as a result, less raw material inventory for every item can be held. With less inventory, the time raw materials sit in inventory before it is used in production is reduced.

A second objective of the new process was to reduce errors. Fewer errors now occur because the data are entered into only one database, and controls on inputs reduce input mistakes. For example, before SAP Wally had to enter supplier data in both the PO database and the Inventory database. If he mistyped data in either system, that error would not be caught. The number of three-way mismatches is less with the new process.

The new process is also more effective because financial controls have been improved. The objective of improved financial control can be seen by the faster rollup times at the end of the month now that the data are consolidated. With more current data, CBI managers now request more financial reports and use them more frequently.

Finally, SAP helped CBI's Procurement process become more responsive to customer demands. CBI uses SAP to share sales and sale forecast data with its suppliers. As a result of having more data, forecasts for each supplier in the chain are more accurate. The improved supply chain helps CBI reduce order fulfillment times, increase product variety, and improve sales of new products.

## Q6. How Can SAP Improve the Integration of Supply Chain Processes at CBI?

Clearly, SAP can help improve the Procurement process for CBI. However, procurement is just one of many processes SAP can support within the company's supply chain. The real benefit of SAP is integration of many individual processes.

Many companies have a well-run procurement process before implementing ERP. However, the SAP Procurement process is just one of a family of inherent processes that SAP designed to run well together. As a result, process integration is much more easily achieved with SAP than by attempting to cobble together processes designed independently.

**FIGURE 4-17**

**Sample of Supply Chain Processes**

| Process Scope | Supply Chain Processes |
|---|---|
| Operational | Procurement |
| Managerial | Supplier Relationship Management (SRM) Returns Management |
| Strategic | Supplier Evaluation |

## Supply Chain Processes

Several processes in CBI's supply chain are listed in Figure 4-17. The **Supplier Relationship Management (SRM) process** automates, simplifies, and accelerates a variety of supply chain processes. Broader than the single Procurement process, SRM is a management process that helps companies reduce procurement costs, build collaborative supplier relationships, better manage supplier options, and improve time to market. The **Returns Management process** manages returns of faulty products for businesses. At CBI, if a bike is returned to a customer such as Philly Bikes, Philly might provide a new bike, tag the returned bike, and annotate the customer complaint. The returned bike is shipped back to CBI to determine where the fault occurred. Efficiently getting the defect to the right supplier and charging the right cost to each company in the supply chain are the goals of the Returns Management process. The **Supplier Evaluation process** determines the criteria for supplier selection and adds and removes suppliers from the list of approved suppliers.

## Supply Chain Process Integration

Although CBI would like to improve each of these processes, CBI would also like to integrate them. The integration of supply chain processes is called **supply chain management (SCM)**. More specifically, SCM is the design, planning, execution, and integration of all supply chain processes.[5] SCM uses a collection of tools, techniques, and management activities to help businesses develop integrated supply chains that support organizational strategy. SAP offers SCM capabilities and can help CBI to integrate these processes.

The integration of processes is improved by sharing data between processes and increasing process synergy. Integration of processes is the same idea as linkages among activities that was introduced in Chapter 2. There we said that linkages occur when one activity impacts another. Here, process integration occurs when one process impacts another. In the following paragraphs, we will see how sharing data and increasing process synergy, two techniques for integrating processes, can lead to benefits for CBI and its supply chain partners.

## Improving Supply Chain Process Integration by Sharing Data

Process integration is improved when processes share data. Figure 4-18 shows two examples where processes are improved by sharing data. For example, data from the Returns Management process about defective bicycle parts should be shared with the Supplier Evaluation process to ensure that suppliers with high defect rates are removed from the list of approved suppliers.

Not only can SAP help integrate CBI's supply processes, it can also help integrate CBI's processes with its supply partners by sharing data. Before CBI and its suppliers shared data, CBI's raw material inventories were quite large. For example, CBI maintained a large quantity of tires and other raw materials to feed its production lines. In those days, procuring raw materials could take weeks, so running out of a raw material could shut down production for days. One reason that procurement was a slow process was that CBI's suppliers only produced raw materials when orders arrived. Today, CBI shares its sales data with its suppliers in real time. As a result, suppliers can anticipate CBI's orders and make raw

[5] Association for Operations Management, *APICS Dictionary*, 13th ed. (Chicago: 2011).

**Integrating Processes—Processes Sharing Data**

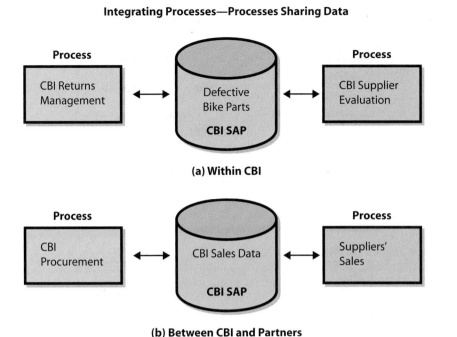

(a) Within CBI

(b) Between CBI and Partners

**FIGURE 4-18**

**Examples of Process Integration by Sharing Data**

materials in anticipation of orders. By sharing more data and sharing this data rapidly, raw material inventory at CBI could shrink as suppliers become better informed of and more responsive to changes in CBI's sales. Inventories shrink and customer responsiveness improves as more and more data are shared.

Integrating supply chain processes not only reduces raw material inventory at CBI, it helps to reduce the bullwhip effect in the supply chain. The **bullwhip effect** occurs when companies order more supplies than are needed due to a sudden change in demand. For example, if a spike in sales occurred in the old days, CBI would increase its orders to its suppliers. However, in the old days it might be several days after the initial spike for the order to arrive at the supplier. By this time, if sales keep up, CBI could be facing a critical shortage and its order would increase. This type of delay in ordering would also occur for CBI's supplier, the frame manufacturer. While the middle man, the frame maker, was waiting for parts from its supplier, CBI might increase its demand still more as it sees even stronger retailer demand and grow increasingly impatient. If the frame manufacturer was pressed by CBI and others it sells to, the frame manufacturer may raise its order to its suppliers, too. By the time upstream suppliers crank up supply for parts for the new bike frame, demand from customers may recede, leaving the frame manufacturer or CBI holding extra inventory that cannot be sold. This effect can be diminished by real-time sharing of sales order data among collaborating firms in the supply chain.

### Improving Supply Chain Process Integration by Increasing Process Synergy

As mentioned previously, a second way to improve process integration is to increase process synergy. Process synergy occurs when processes are mutually supportive; that is, when one process is done well, the objectives of another process are supported. Examples of synergy among processes are shown in Figure 4-19. You synergize your dating and studying processes when you study with your significant other. You synergize your shopping and your banking by doing both on one trip.

One example of process synergy occurs at CBI between the Returns Management process and the Production process. One of the objectives of production is to reduce defective bikes. The Returns Management process collects data on defective returns from retailers of CBI bikes and accessories. The final step of the Returns Management process is to analyze how to improve the Production process to create fewer defects and thus fewer returns. When the Returns Management process is done well, an objective of the Production process is supported.

FIGURE 4-19

**Examples of Process Integration by Process Synergy**

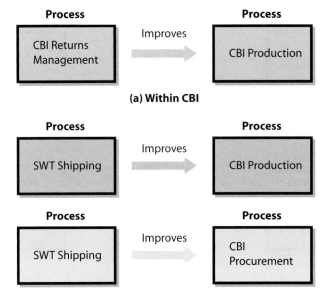

**Integrating Processes—Process Synergy**

**(a) Within CBI**

**(b) Between CBI and Partners**

Increasing process synergy can also be seen in CBI's supply chain. If retailer demand shifts suddenly, CBI and its suppliers can quickly shift production lines to meet the new demand. CBI and its suppliers rely on the SW Trucking Company to deliver raw materials. In the old days without process synergy, SW Trucking had no excess capacity to support the extra shipping needed to move the bike parts from suppliers to CBI to retailers. SW Trucking was a bottleneck. A **bottleneck** occurs when a limited resource greatly reduces the output of an integrated series of activities or processes. SW Trucking decided to improve its Shipping process by keeping excess capacity available. As a result, the Production process at CBI was improved, because one of its objectives was being responsive to customer demand. Not only did this improve production at CBI, it also improved procurement, because the additional shipping capacity meant that CBI's Procurement process could better achieve its objective of reducing raw material inventory.

## SAP Integration Problems with Emerging Technologies

Before we wrap up this question, you should understand that SAP is just one way to improve procurement processes and integration. Some companies want to use other, newer information systems technologies like those listed in Figure 4-20. If they do so, they will need to integrate those new capabilities with SAP. Such integration may be expensive, but to preserve the benefits of SAP, it must be done.

FIGURE 4-20

**IS That Impact Supply Chain Processes**

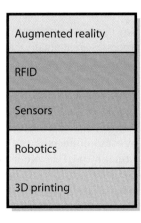

Source: Kazuhiro Nogi/Getty Images, Inc. AFP.

**FIGURE 4-21**
**Augmented Reality**

With **augmented reality (AR)**, computer data or graphics are overlaid onto the physical environment. An example of augmented reality is shown in Figure 4-21. Using AR, warehouse workers at CBI can look at video images of the warehouse and see overlaid on top of the image data about the location of a product they are looking for, the arrival date of the next shipment of a particular item, or the weight of a container. By augmenting reality with procurement data, CBI can save time looking for items and make other procurement and production activities more efficient.

**Radio-frequency identification (RFID)** technology, as shown in Figure 4-22, can be used to identify and track items in the supply chain. As small and as cheap as a grain of rice, RFID chips broadcast data to receivers that can display and record the data. In the supply chain domain, suppliers put RFID chips on the outside of boxes and shipping pallets so that when those boxes get to their destination the receiving company can know the contents of the box without opening it. This makes tracking inventory faster and cheaper for all collaborating companies in a supply chain.

CBI and its supplier partners can outfit their trucks with sensors and tracking devices to make the Transportation activity of the Procurement process more efficient. Transportation is one of the highest-cost activities in the Procurement process, and equipping every truck with two-way data exchange can lower costs by optimizing routes to avoid traffic jams, using on-board sensors to better plan vehicle maintenance, and alerting warehouse personnel when delivery trucks are approaching a warehouse.

**FIGURE 4-22**
**RFID Chip**

Source: © Noah Addis/Star-Ledger/Corbis

# MIS InClass 4

## The Bicycle Supply Game[6]

The purpose of this exercise is to better understand how supply chains are affected by information systems. In this game, the class will form supply chains and attempt to be the most efficient supplier.

The four links in each chain are retailer, distributor, whole-saler, and frame maker. The game is played for a period of 50 weeks. Each week each of the four teams in the supply chain orders bikes from its supplier and each team fulfils the orders from its customer. Pennies represent bicycles as the sole item in the supply chain, drinking cups are used to transport pennies between stations, and Post-it notes are used to make orders.

The goal is for each supplier in the chain to have the most efficient procurement process; that is, minimizing inventory and back orders.

Set up as many identical supply chains as needed, as shown in Figure 4-23. Notice that the supply chains are constructed with delays between the ordering of bicycles and their arrival. Each supplier is comprised of a team of one to three students. Each

Source: Dmitry Yashkin/Shutterstock.

supplier records its orders, inventory, and backlog on a form like the one shown in Figure 4-24.

The retailers perform the same actions as the other groups, except their orders come from a stack of 3 × 5 cards that contain

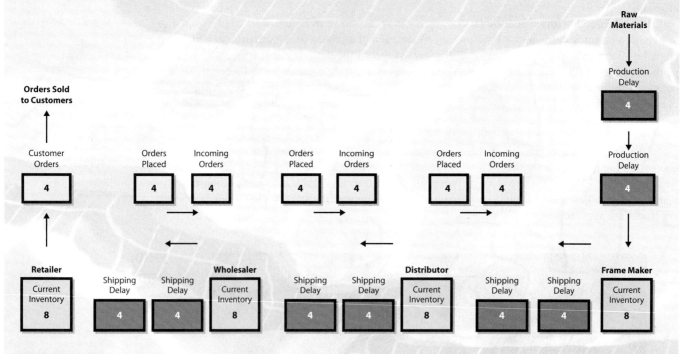

## FIGURE 4-23

## Supply Chain Game Setup

(continued)

[6] See the "MIT Beer Game" in Chapter 3 of Peter Senge's *The Fifth Discipline: The Art & Practice of The Learning Organization*, rev. ed. (New York: Random House, 2006). Also see Wikipedia, "Beer Distribution Game," *http://en.wikipedia.org/wiki/MIT_Beer_Game*.

**Game Record**

Position: _____          Team Member Names: _____

**FIGURE 4-24**

**Supply Chain Game Form**

| Week | Inventory | Backlog | Total Cost for Week |
|------|-----------|---------|---------------------|
| 1. | 4 | 0 | $ 2.00 |
| 2. | | | |
| 3. | | | |
| 4. | | | |
| 5. | | | |

prerecorded orders that specify customer demand for the 50 weeks. Students are not to look at incoming orders, prerecorded orders, or supplies until that activity and then they may look at only that week's order and supply.

Each week follows the same process with these five activities:

1. Receive inventory and advance the shipping delay.
2. Receive incoming orders and advance the order delay.
3. Fill the order.
4. Record inventory or backlog.
5. Place and record orders.

When the game is played, follow these activities as the instructor directs so that every team has accomplished each activity before any team moves on to the next. The game begins with a balanced condition in the supply chain; that is, every existing order is for four pennies, every delivery cup is filled with four pennies, and every supplier begins with eight pennies in inventory.

At the end of the game each supplier calculates its overall costs.

$$\text{Cost} = .50 \text{ (inventory)} + 1.00 \text{ (backlog)}$$

A backlog occurs when an order is made that cannot be fulfilled. This backlog accumulates from week to week until it is paid off completely. The supplier with the lowest value is the winner.

At the end of the game discuss the following:

1. Describe the order pattern from the customers to the retailer every week.
2. Why did the ordering pattern between the suppliers in the supply chain evolve the way it did?
3. What are the objectives and measures for each team's procurement process?
4. Where is the IS? What would more data allow? What data are most needed?
5. If you spent money on an IS, would it improve an activity, a linkage, or a control?
6. Create a BPMN diagram of your team's weekly procurement process.

Advances in robotics are leading to more widespread use of robotic forklifts in warehouses. At CBI and other warehouses, pallets of raw material inventory are moved from inbound delivery trucks to storage locations and then to outbound trucks using robotic forklifts. These forklifts rely on RFID chips on pallets to locate the pallet in the warehouse and to be directed to where the pallet is to go. Although the initial costs are significant, robots can reduce inventory costs markedly for CBI and other firms.

Three-dimensional (3D) printing technologies will also impact CBI's Procurement process. With **3D printing**, also called *additive manufacturing*, objects are manufactured through the deposition of successive layers of material, as shown in Figure 4-25. Just as two-dimensional printers deposit ink in two dimensions, 3D printers deposit material in three dimensions, layering material in the third dimension as it dries. Rather than rely on suppliers for all its raw materials, CBI may choose to "print" some raw materials in house. This will impact several supply chain processes and is an example of improving process synergy.

These IS are impacting procurement now, and other, new IS technologies are on the way. As companies continue to pursue their strategies, new technologies will be absorbed into

**FIGURE 4-25**

**3D Printing**

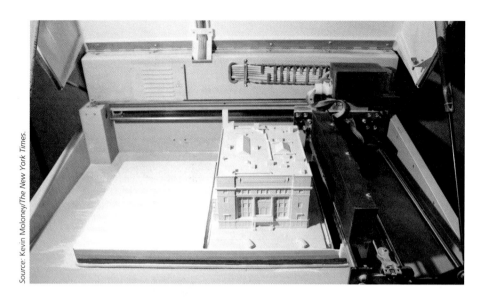

Source: Kevin Moloney/The New York Times.

the companies' processes. SAP will chose to adapt its applications to some of these new technologies, but for the rest, organizations will need to develop their own patches of the new technology into SAP. The bottom line: SAP and other new IS can significantly improve the Procurement process but they will need to work together.

## Q7. How Does the Use of SAP Change CBI?

While pursuing a better Procurement process with SAP, companies like CBI are inevitably changed. Some of these changes are listed in Figure 4-26, and a few of them are quite significant. Some changes can be anticipated and are clear from the beginning. For example, CBI employees knew that SAP would require a new purchasing department to accomplish the Procurement process.

Other changes are more subtle, such as the new sets of skills necessary to optimize a supply chain. For example, with more data being produced and saved, CBI will hire more people with abstract reasoning and analytical skills to look for patterns in the data that will lead to new ways to improve processes. Another change that can be expected is that CBI will become more process focused; that is, it will increasingly focus on the inputs and outputs of its processes to connect with partner firms. Pressures from suppliers and customers to share more and more data will lead CBI to be more open with company data than in the past. Finally, the adoption of SAP may lead CBI to use more outsourcing. Many firms outsource parts of their production to take advantage of other firms that can produce a subassembly or service cheaper than they can.

In the CBI warehouse, Wally has seen these organizational and technological changes in the past few years. One result is that CBI is doing less production of bicycles and instead is purchasing more finished bicycles. CBI believes this will help it reduce costs by shifting production to suppliers who can do the work at a lower cost. CBI is also lowering costs by using more full truck shipments rather than partial loads. Because of these large shipments, storage of the finished goods is optimized across CBI's worldwide system and is not done locally. The inventory system dictates where in the warehouse each item is stored; in fact, at Wally's warehouse the SAP system now dictates an item's location to the robot forklifts. Another recent change is that much more data are produced by the new system and shared with CBI customers and suppliers than was ever done in the past. This willingness to share inventory and pricing data gives CBI customers the opportunity to compare prices.

Finally, one more change is significant for Wally and the other warehouse managers at other locations. Before SAP, they were the ones who decided what was purchased. They would notice low raw material levels and then use their experience to decide if, when, and how many parts or

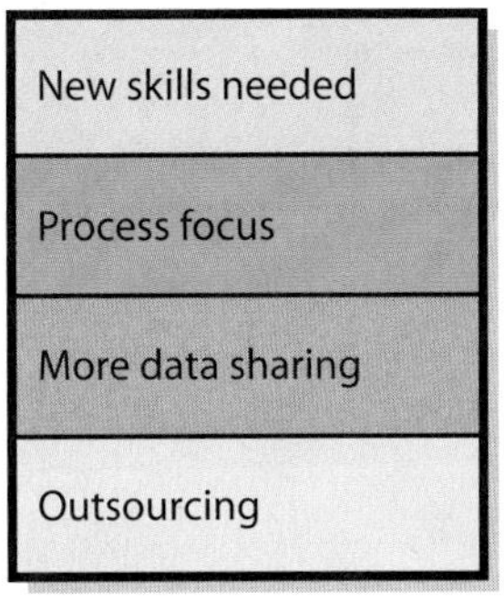

**FIGURE 4-26**

**Impacts of SAP on Organizations**

| |
|---|
| New skills needed |
| Process focus |
| More data sharing |
| Outsourcing |

bikes were ordered. Now, the system automatically tracks raw material inventory and generates purchase requisitions when reorder levels are reached.

## Wally's Job Change

These changes have taken a toll on Wally. Before the installation of SAP, Wally's job was to manage the inventory levels in the warehouse. And he was good at it. Using Excel spreadsheets, some freeware programs he found on the Internet, and his fax machine, Wally did the job well. When the new company-wide SAP system was announced, he could see that it was a good idea, and the only way for the firm to stay in business. Although helping to implement the system in the warehouse was a time-consuming challenge, Wally looked forward to seeing the project through. He took on the responsibility of scheduling training classes for everyone at the warehouse. However, he encountered his first disappointment when he noticed that the budget for these classes was much less than was planned for earlier, apparently a victim of cost overruns in other parts of the implementation.

As the system went online he helped sell the system to frustrated and disgruntled workers. Some of his people were not able to see the big picture and resisted the changes the new processes brought about. He could understand their frustration with this new technology. Data that was easy to find now seemed needlessly hidden, reports were different and not as informative as before, and the error messages were very confusing. Data was spread out and not as easy to cobble together as before. Wally faithfully helped triage the complaints for upper management and for the IT staff, who appreciated his support and ability to keep things working during a difficult implementation.

As time went on, other problems left him wondering about his future. Most of the jobs in the warehouse were redesigned. A few people had to be let go, others found work elsewhere in the company. Overall, a third of the staff was quickly gone. The substitution of robots for forklift drivers was the most obvious job change. But other changes were also noticeable. Much more of everyone's time was spent entering data into the system, checking and producing reports, or responding to questions from the system or from other offices in the company he had never heard of. His particular job changed quite a lot. He was no longer the purchasing agent, instead he monitored the purchase requisitions the system kicked out every day. At first he thought the system was making purchase requisitions erratically, but as he raised doubts he noticed that management was satisfied with most of the requisitions and he was told the system was operating correctly. Recently, he came to realize that he missed being more involved. He wanted to use his wits and experience rather than watch numbers on a screen. He decided to take an early retirement, and go find his old job.

Wally's experiences are not uncommon. They are included here to present some of the human challenges when ERP systems are implemented. ERP implementations change the type of work many people do. Change, a constant in IT and in business, can be hard on the people experiencing it. And although change is hard on people, it is necessary for businesses to stay competitive. Jack Welch, the CEO of General Electric once said that if change is happening on the outside of a company faster than on the inside, the end of that company is in sight.

# Ethics Guide

## Procurement Ethics

**Buy-in** is a term that refers to selling a product or system for less than its true price. An example for CBI would be if a consultant proposed $15,000 to provide some software code when good estimating techniques indicate that the price should be at least $35,000. If the contract for the system or product is written for "time and materials," CBI will ultimately pay the $35,000 for the code or it will cancel the acquisition once the true cost is known. However, if the contract for the system or product is written for a fixed cost, then the developer will absorb those extra costs. The latter strategy is used if the contract opens up other business opportunities that are worth the $20,000 loss.

Buy-ins always involve deceit. Most would agree that it is unethical or wrong for the consultant in this case to offer a time-and-materials project with the intent of sticking CBI with the full cost later. Opinions vary on buying in on a fixed-priced contract. Some would say that buying in is always deceitful and should be avoided. Others say that it is just one of many different business strategies.

What about in-house projects? Do the ethics change if an in-house development team is building a system for use in-house? If team members know that there is only $50,000 in the budget for the new system, should they start the project if they think its true cost is $75,000? If they do start, at some point senior management will either have to admit a mistake and cancel the project or find the additional $25,000.

These issues become even stickier if the team members disagree about how much the project will cost. Suppose one faction of the team believes the new system will cost $35,000, another faction estimates $50,000, and a third thinks $65,000. Can the project sponsors justify taking the average? Or, should they describe the cost as the range of estimates to senior management?

Other buy-ins are more subtle. Suppose you are a project manager of an exciting new project that is possibly a career-maker for you. You are incredibly busy, working 6 days a week and long hours each day. Your team has developed an estimate for $50,000 for your project. A little voice in the back of your mind says that maybe not all the costs for every aspect of the project are included in that estimate. You mean to follow up on that thought, but more pressing matters in your schedule take precedence. Soon you find yourself in front of management presenting the $50,000 estimate. You probably should have found the time to investigate the estimate, but you didn't. Is your behavior unethical?

Or, suppose you approach a more senior manager with your dilemma: "I think there may be other costs, but I know that $50,000 is all we've got. What should I do?" Suppose the senior manager says something like, "Well, let's go forward. You don't know of anything else, and we can always find more money in the budget elsewhere if we have to." How do you respond?

You can buy in on schedule as well as cost. If the marketing department says, "We have to have the new product for the trade show," do you agree, even if you know it's highly unlikely? What if marketing says, "If we don't have it by then, we should just cancel the project." Suppose it's not impossible to make that schedule, it's just highly unlikely. How do you respond?

## DISCUSSION QUESTIONS

1. Do you agree that buying in on a time-and-materials project is always unethical? Explain your reasoning. Are there circumstances in which it could be illegal?

2. Suppose you learn through the grapevine that your opponents in a competitive bid are buying in on a time-and-materials contract. Does this change your answer to question 1?

3. Suppose you are a project manager who is preparing a request for proposal on a time-and-materials systems development project. What can you do to prevent buy-ins?

4. Under what circumstances do you think buying in on a fixed-price contract is ethical? What are the dangers of this strategy?

5. Explain why in-house development projects are always time-and-materials projects.

6. Given your answer to question 5, is buying in on an in-house project always unethical? Under what circumstances do you think it is ethical? Under what circumstances do you think it is justifiable, even if it is unethical?

7. Suppose you ask a senior manager for advice, as described in the guide. Does the manager's response absolve you of guilt? Suppose you ask the manager and then do not follow her guidance. What problems result?

8. Explain how you can buy in on schedule as well as costs.

9. For an in-house project, how do you respond to the marketing manager who says that the project should be cancelled if it will not be ready for the trade show? In your answer, suppose that you disagree with this opinion—suppose you know the system has value regardless of whether it is done by the trade show.

Source: Shutterstock

# Active Review

Use this Active Review to verify that you understand the material in the chapter. You can read the entire chapter and then perform the tasks in this review, or you can read the text material for just one question and perform the tasks in this review for that question before moving on to the next one.

## Q1. What are the fundamentals of a Procurement process?

Define *procurement* and explain its three main activities. Name the value chain activity in which the Procurement process, as addressed in this chapter, operates. Explain the common subactivities in the Procurement process. Explain how raw material and finished goods inventories differ.

## Q2. How did the Procurement process at CBI work before SAP?

Explain the Procurement process at CBI before SAP. Describe the Pre-Order Actions activity, particularly with regards to the Sales database. Describe what data are stored in the four different databases. Explain what an invoice is, who sends it, and what happens when it arrives. Describe which data must match for a three-way match.

## Q3. What were the problems with the Procurement process before SAP?

Explain the problems at CBI in the warehouse, in accounting, and in purchasing prior to the implementation of SAP. Describe the conflict between raw material inventory and finished goods inventory at CBI. Explain how not having price data impacts the Procurement process. Describe why a company might want to restrict purchasing to just one department and not scatter it throughout the organization. Explain what the Sarbanes-Oxley Act requires and how ERP systems address that requirement.

## Q4. How does CBI implement SAP?

Describe the activities in CBI's strategy process. Explain the competitive strategy chosen by CBI. Explain the objectives and measures selected by CBI for the Procurement process.

## Q5. How does the Procurement process work at CBI after SAP?

Describe the Procurement process after the implementation of SAP. Explain the difference between a purchase requisition and a purchase order. Describe the main sections of an SAP screen. Explain the actions that automatically occur after a purchase order is saved and after a goods receipt is saved. Describe how the new Procurement process with SAP is both more efficient and effective.

## Q6. How can SAP improve the integration of supply chain processes at CBI?

Describe the processes of Supplier Relationship Management, Returns Management, and Supplier Evaluation. Define supply chain management (SCM) and explain the benefits of effective SCM. Explain the two ways processes can be integrated and give an example of each. Explain the bullwhip effect and bottlenecks and explain how they occur. Also describe how integrated processes can alleviate these situations. Explain how AR, RFID, and 3D printing can impact supply chain processes.

## Q7. How does the use of SAP change CBI?

Explain some of the new skills needed at CBI after SAP is implemented. Describe why CBI is becoming more process focused after implementing SAP. How does the adoption of SAP lead CBI to share more data with suppliers and customers? Explain the advantages of outsourcing. Explain some of the changes at CBI due to SAP. Explain how Wally accomplished his Procurement process before SAP. Describe some of the actions Wally took to support a smooth transition to SAP. Describe how Wally's job changed.

## Key Terms and Concepts

3D printing  *101*

Augmented reality (AR)  *99*

Bottleneck  *98*

Bullwhip effect  *97*

Buy-in  *104*

Finished goods inventory  *86*

Internal control  *90*

Inventory turnover  *90*

Invoice  *87*

Procurement  *84*

Purchase order (PO)  *85*

Purchase requisition (PR)  *92*

Radio-frequency identification (RFID)  *99*

Raw materials inventory  *86*

Returns Management process  *96*

Roll up  *89*

Supplier Evaluation process  *96*

Supplier Relationship Management (SRM) process  *96*

Supply chain management (SCM)  *96*

Three-way match  *87*

## Using Your Knowledge

1. Two supply chain processes introduced in this chapter are Returns Management and Supplier Evaluation.
   a. Create a BPMN diagram of each of these processes.
   b. Specify efficiency and effectiveness objectives for each process and identify measures appropriate for CBI.
   c. What new information system technologies could be used by CBI to improve these processes, as specified by your measures in part b? Can AR, RFID, or 3D printing be used to improve these processes?
2. Which of the four nonroutine cognitive skills (i.e., abstract reasoning, systems thinking, collaboration, and experimentation) did you use to answer the previous question?
3. Which of the four skills in Exercise 2 would be most important for Wally's replacement?
4. The Procurement process in this chapter is an inbound logistics operational process. Name two other operational processes at CBI. Describe two inbound logistics managerial processes and two strategic processes.
5. If a warehouse worker opens a box and the contents are broken, those items will be returned to the supplier. Add this activity to the BPMN diagram of the Procurement process (Figure 4-12).

6. SAP generates a document number for many of the activities in the Procurement process to aid in order tracking and auditing. Which activities generate a document number?
7. For the Procurement process after SAP implementation, what are the triggers for each activity to start? For example, what action (trigger) initiates the Create PO activity?
8. What kinds of errors can Wally, Maria, and Ann make that are not captured by SAP? One example is that Wally might count 20 bottles and 30 cages but mistakenly enter 20 cages and 30 bottles. Describe a particularly harmful mistake that each can make and how the process could be changed to prevent that error.
9. How does a pizza shop's Procurement process differ from CBI's? What do you believe is the corporate strategy of your favorite pizza franchise? What are the objectives and measures of its Procurement process to support this strategy?

# Collaboration Exercise 4

Collaborate with a group of fellow students to answer the following questions. For this exercise do not meet face to face. Your task will be easier if you coordinate your work with SharePoint, Office 365, Google Docs with Google+ or equivalent collaboration tools. Your answers should reflect the thinking of the entire group, and not just that of one or two individuals.

In Chapter 3, a university implemented an SAP system. One of the changes is that most purchases must now be approved by a new university purchasing office. The athletics director is concerned that centralizing the purchasing at the university will impose difficulties on the athletics department.

1. Figure 4-8 lists problems with the Procurement process at CBI. Which of these would apply to the university?

Which would not? What are some procurement problems that might be unique to an athletics department?
2. Figure 4-11 lists objectives and measures that the managers at CBI determined for the Procurement process. What objectives and measures would you suggest for the university? What objectives and measures would you expect the athletics director to suggest?
3. Figure 4-26 lists the impacts of SAP on an organization. Which of these impacts would affect the athletics department?
4. Four important nonroutine cognitive skills are abstract reasoning, systems thinking, collaboration, and ability to experiment. Explain how implementing the new Procurement process at CBI will require each of these skills from the members of the SAP implementation team.

# ACTIVE CASE 4: SAP PROCUREMENT PROCESS TUTORIAL

A tutorial for a Procurement process using SAP is located in the appendix to this chapter. That tutorial leads the student through a Procurement process that orders, receives, and pays for 20 bicycle water bottles and 30 water bottle cages. Once the tutorial is complete, students should answer the following questions.

**Questions**

1. Describe your first impressions of SAP.
2. What types of skills seem to be necessary to use this system?
3. Create a screen capture of an SAP screen. Underneath the image, provide an answer to each of the following questions:
   a. In which of the activities does this screen occur?
   b. What is the name of this screen?
   c. What is the name of the screen that precedes it? What screen comes after it?
   d. What actor accomplishes this activity?
   e. Describe an error that this actor may do on this screen that SAP will prevent.
4. Make an informal diagram of the four main actors: Supplier (Composite Bikes), Purchasing (Maria), Warehouse (Wally), and Accounting (Ann). Draw arrows that show the data that flows among the actors during this process. Number the arrows and include on each arrow what data are included in the message.
5. Using the same four main actors as in question 4, this time show with the arrows how the material (the water bottles and cages) moves.
6. One concern of a business is fraud. One fraud technique is to create suppliers who are not suppliers but are coconspirators. The conspirator inside the business accepts invoices for non-existent deliveries. For this fraud scheme to work, who at CBI has to take part? How can SAP processes decrease the chance of this type of fraud?
7. Select any of the main activities or subactivities in the Procurement process.
   a. What event triggers this activity?
   b. What activity follows this activity?
   c. For one data entry item for this activity, describe what would happen in the rest of the process if that entry was erroneous.
   d. For one data entry item for this activity, describe what limits (controls) you would put in place on the data to prevent the type of error described in item c.

# APPENDIX 4—SAP PROCUREMENT TUTORIAL

This tutorial follows the Procurement process shown in Figure 4A-1. The top of Figure 4A-1 appears in Chapter 4 as Figure 4-3. This top figure shows the three main Procurement activities—Order, Receive, and Pay, and the subactivities (Qualify Suppliers, etc.). At the bottom of Figure 4A-1, we have added the six SAP steps included in this tutorial. These six steps were chosen to keep this tutorial simple. To further simplify the process we begin with step 3, Create Purchase Order. As shown in Figure 4A-1, you will play the roles of Wally and Ann.

**FIGURE 4A-1**

**Procurement Process and SAP Steps**

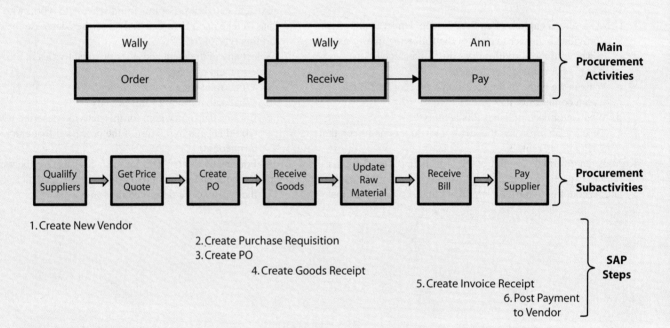

Navigate to the SAP Welcome screen (Figure 4A-2).

**FIGURE 4A-2**

**Welcome Screen**

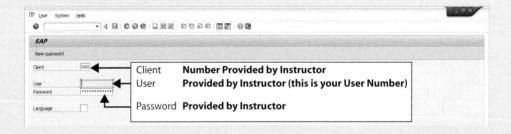

In this first exercise, we will purchase 20 water bottles and 30 water bottle cages from an existing vendor called Space Bike Composites. The bottles cost $10.00 and the cages $9.00. While our company in this tutorial is Global Bike, Inc., our actors—Wally and Ann—and our Procurement process are from Chuck's Bikes.[1] The three digits at the end of your User ID will be used throughout this tutorial. For example if your User ID is GBI-123, then 123 is your User Number. In this tutorial 001 is used as the User Number.

## 1 Create New Vendor

Skipped—does not apply to this first exercise, it is introduced later.

---

[1] All tutorials in this text use Global Bike 2 (6.04), IS8 System ID, and IDES SAP ERP ECC 6.04 SAPGUI Description.

## 2   Create Purchase Requisition

Skipped—does not apply to this first exercise, it is introduced later.

## 3   Create Purchase Order

As a warehouse manager like Wally, your first step is to create a Purchase Order. From the SAP
Easy Access screen (Figure 4A-3), navigate to the Purchase Order screen by selecting:

*Logistics > Materials Management > Purchasing > Purchase Order > Create >*
*Vendor/Supplying Plant Known*

**FIGURE 4A-3**
**SAP Easy Access Screen**

A purchase order, when received and accepted by a vendor, creates a legally binding contract between two parties. The first screen is the Create Purchase Order screen (Figure 4A-4).

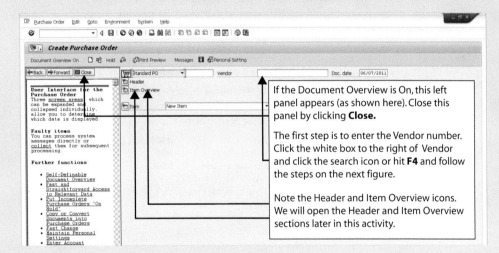

**FIGURE 4A-4**
**Create Purchase Order Screen**

If the Document Overview is On, this left panel appears (as shown here). Close this panel by clicking **Close.**

The first step is to enter the Vendor number. Click the white box to the right of Vendor and click the search icon or hit **F4** and follow the steps on the next figure.

Note the Header and Item Overview icons. We will open the Header and Item Overview sections later in this activity.

The next screen is the Vendor Search screen (Figure 4A-5). We need to find the vendor
number for Space Bike Composites to complete the Purchase Order. While Wally might have
this number memorized, we want to search in order to demonstrate how searching is done within
SAP. Please note that where 001 appears in Figure 4A-5 you will type in your User Number.

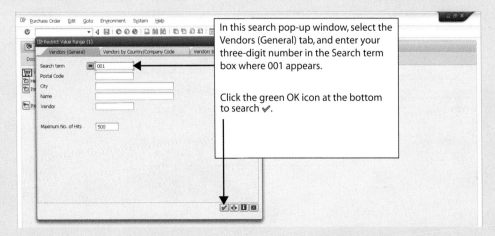

**FIGURE 4A-5**
**Vendor Search Screen**

In this search pop-up window, select the Vendors (General) tab, and enter your three-digit number in the Search term box where 001 appears.

Click the green OK icon at the bottom to search ✓.

The Vendor List screen (Figure 4A-6) now loads.

**FIGURE 4A-6**

**Vendor List Screen**

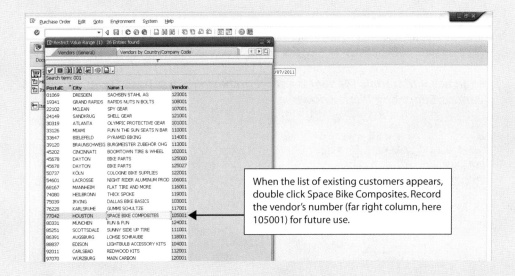

After double-clicking on Space Bike Composites, the system returns to the Create Purchase Order screen. On the next screen (Figure 4A-7), you will enter three inputs for Purch. Org., Purch. Group, and Company Code, the last two digits of each of the inputs is a zero, not the letter "O." These three inputs specify which office at Global Bikes is making the order.

**FIGURE 4A-7**

**Create Purchase Order with Vendor Screen**

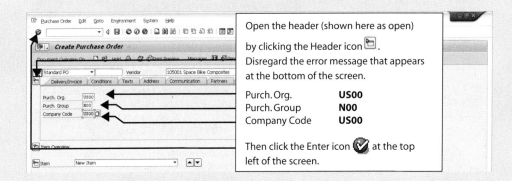

After clicking Enter, the system loads more data on the screen. Next we will enter data about the Material (the water bottles and cages) we are purchasing (Figures 4A-8 through 4A-11).

**FIGURE 4A-8**

**Create Purchase Order with Item Overview On Screen**

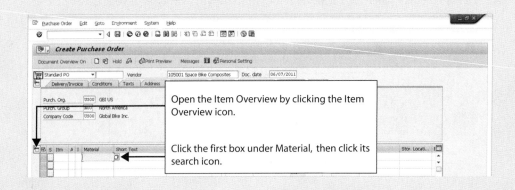

This will load the Material Search screen (Figure 4A-9) that will help us find the Material numbers we need for the Purchase Order.

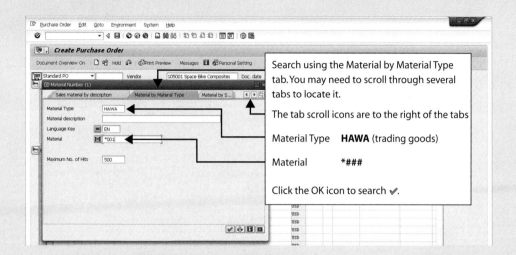

**FIGURE 4A-9**

**Material Search Screen**

HAWA is the code used by SAP to identify trading goods. The next screen (Figure 4A-10) will show the trading goods you can order.

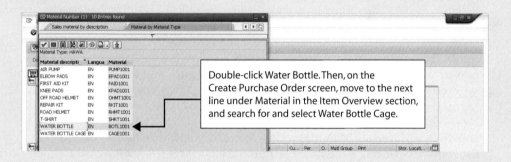

**FIGURE 4A-10**

**Material List Screen**

When you return to the Create Purchase Order screen after selecting Water Bottle, complete the following inputs (as shown in Figure 4A-11). Then to complete the second line, you can search for *Water Bottle Cages* or simply type in *Cage1###* (where ### is your User Number). On the following screen (Figure 4A-11), you will enter a date (for the delivery date). To enter date data, use the convenient Search button located to the right of the date input box. Also note, the plant (Plnt on the screen) is MI00, not M100 .

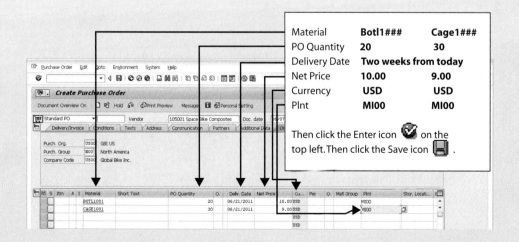

**FIGURE 4A-11**

**Create Purchase Order with Material Screen**

A pop up box appears (Figure 4A-12), click the Save button.

**FIGURE 4A-12**

**Create Purchase Order Save Screen**

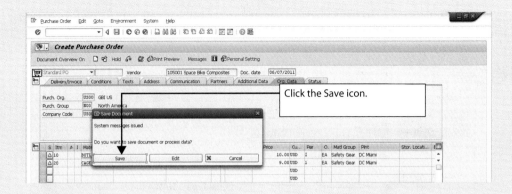

The SAP database now updates and when complete, the Purchase Order screen reappears, the bottom of the screen is shown in Figure 4A-13.

**FIGURE 4A-13**

**Purchase Order Number Screen**

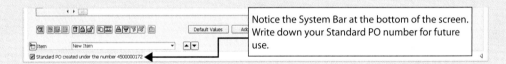

Return to the SAP Easy Access menu by clicking the yellow circle Exit icon near the top of the screen. This icon is located on the same ribbon as the Enter and Save icons.

### 4   Create Goods Receipt for Purchase Order

The next step for Wally and for you is to create a Goods Receipt for this Purchase Order. This step will occur after the water bottles and cages arrive at Wally's warehouse. From the SAP Easy Access screen, navigate to the Goods Receipt Purchase Order screen by selecting:

> *Logistics > Materials Management > Inventory Management > Goods Movement > Goods Receipt > For Purchase Order > GR for Purchase Order (MIGO)*

A goods receipt is recognition that the goods ordered in the PO have arrived. Once the goods receipt has been created, inventory for these items is increased and accounts payable is increased (Figure 4A-14).

**FIGURE 4A-14**

**Goods Receipt Screen**

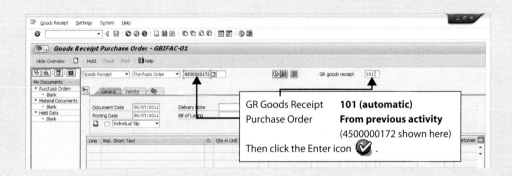

The system loads data from the PO, as shown in Figure 4A-15.

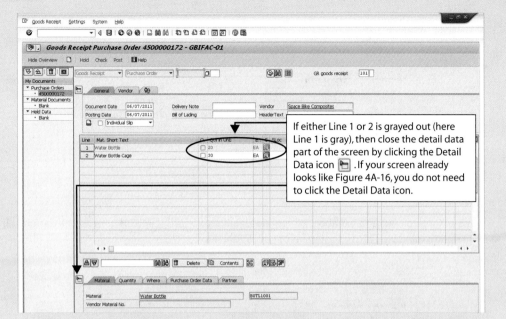

**FIGURE 4A-15**

**Goods Receipt with Detail On Screen**

By closing the detail data part of the screen, your screen will look like Figure 4A-16. The reason the Water Bottle line was grayed out in 4A-15 is that the Detail Data section was open at the bottom of the screen. Notice in 4A-16 the Detail Data section is closed.

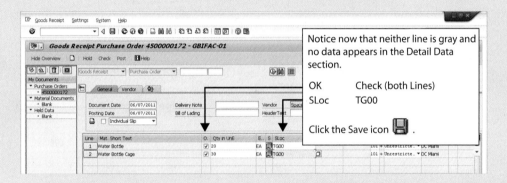

**FIGURE 4A-16**

**Goods Receipt with Detail Off Screen**

By checking OK, you are verifying that 20 water bottles and 30 cages were delivered (Figure 4A-17). If not, you would not check OK and would instead enter the quantity that did arrive. Figure 4A-16 shows this column header as O. instead of O.K., which can be shown by adjusting the column width.

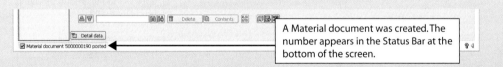

**FIGURE 4A-17**

**Goods Receipt Material Document Screen**

Return to the SAP Easy Access menu by clicking the Exit icon.

## 5  Create Invoice Receipt from Vendor

An accountant, like Ann, would accomplish the final two steps—Creating an Invoice and Paying the Vendor. From the SAP Easy Access screen, navigate to the Enter Incoming Invoice screen by selecting:

*Logistics > Materials Management > Logistics Invoice Verification > Document Entry > Enter Invoice*

Shortly after the goods arrived, the vendor has sent us a bill for $470 for the bottles and cages, and here we record this bill in our system (Figure 4A-18). Note, in Figure 4A-18 that the Tax Amount is entered via a drop-down box, which is the rightmost input box for Tax Amount.

**FIGURE 4A-18**

**Create Invoice Screen**

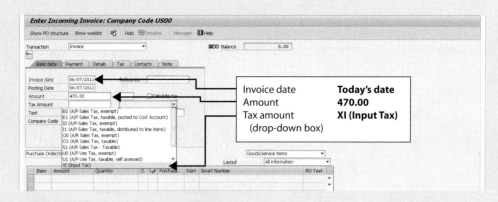

We also enter our PO number, which was generated earlier in this process at the end of step 3 (Figure 4A-13). This is shown below in Figure 4A-19.

**FIGURE 4A-19**

**Create Invoice with PO Number Screen**

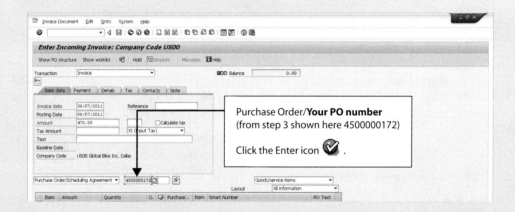

The system loads vendor data and displays the updated Incoming Invoice screen (Figure 4A-20).

**FIGURE 4A-20**

**Create Invoice Final Screen**

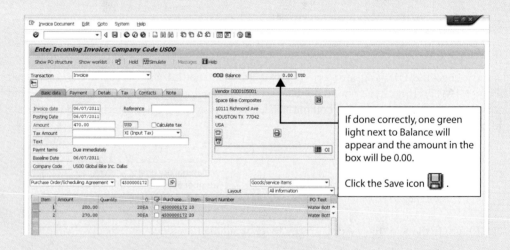

If there are no errors, a document number is produced on the bottom of the next screen (Figure 4A-21).

**FIGURE 4A-21**

**Create Invoice Document Number Screen**

Return to the SAP Easy Access menu by clicking the Exit icon.

## 6  Post Payment to the Vendor

The final step occurs when you or Ann pays the vendor. This payment may be made immediately upon receipt of the invoice or shortly thereafter. From the SAP Easy Access screen, navigate to the Post Outgoing Payments screen by selecting:

### *Accounting > Financial Accounting > Accounts Payable > Document Entry > Outgoing Payment > Post*

In this activity, we record our payment to the vendor for $470.00 (Figure 4A-22). A journal entry is made to decrease accounts payable.

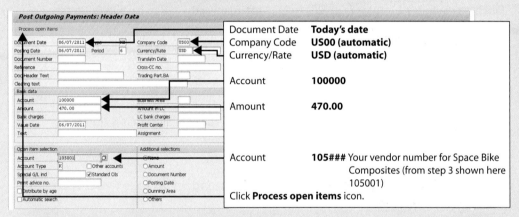

**FIGURE 4A-22**

**Post Outgoing Payments Screen**

If you have to search for your vendor number in the bottom Account text box, select the Vendors (General) tab in the search pop-up window and use ### as the search term. Once you click on Process open items, the Post Outgoing Payments Process open items screen appears (Figure 4A-23).

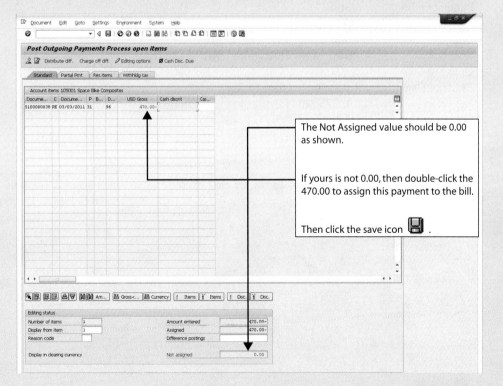

**FIGURE 4A-23**

**Post Outgoing Payments Final Screen**

The SAP database is again updated and the Post Payment Document Number screen (Figure 4A-24) appears.

**FIGURE 4A-24**

**Post Payment Document Number Screen**

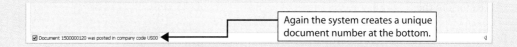

Record the document number that once again appears on the Status bar. Return to the SAP Easy Access screen by clicking the Exit icon. This will generate a pop-up window that is misleading. There is no data to be lost at this point, so click Yes.

You have finished the first exercise.

## You Try It 1

Purchase the following three materials from a different vendor—Rapids Nuts N Bolts:

| | | |
|---|---|---|
| 5 | Air Pumps | $14 each |
| 10 | Elbow Pads | $375 each |
| 15 | First Aid Kits | $20 each |

Request delivery in 2 weeks. Use Miami for the plant. The total amount is $4120.00.

**3   Create Purchase Order**

*Logistics > Materials Management > Purchasing > Purchase Order > Create > Vendor/Supplying Plant Known*

Data needed:

| | |
|---|---|
| Vendor | **108### (Your Rapids Nuts N Bolts vendor number based on your User Number)** |
| Purch. Org. | **US00** |
| Purch. Group | **N00** |
| Company Code | **US00** |
| Material | **PUMP1###, EPAD1###, FAID1### (These are Trading Goods)** |
| Quantity | **5, 10, 15** |
| Delivery Date | **Two weeks from today** |
| Net Price | **14, 375, 20** |
| Currency | **USD** |
| Plnt | **MI00** |

Not every screen is shown here. Refer to the first exercise to see each screen. The completed Create Purchase Order screen as it appears at the *end* of step 3 is shown in Figure 4A-25.

**FIGURE 4A-25**

**Completed Create Purchase Order**

Click the Save icon. Record the PO number at the bottom of the screen. Return to the SAP Easy Access menu by clicking the Exit icon.

## 4   Create Goods Receipt for Purchase Order

*Logistics > Materials Management > Inventory Management > Goods Movement > Goods Receipt > For Purchase Order > GR for Purchase Order (MIGO)*

Data needed:

| | |
|---|---|
| Gr Goods Receipt | **101** |
| Purchase Order | **From previous step (4500000173 shown here)** |
| OK | **Three check marks** |
| SLoc | **TG00 (Trading Goods)** |

The completed Goods Receipt screen is shown in Figure 4A-26.

**FIGURE 4A-26**

**Goods Receipt Final Screen**

Click the Save icon. Return to the SAP Easy Access menu by clicking the Exit icon.

## 5   Create Invoice Receipt from Vendor

*Logistics > Materials Management > Logistics Invoice Verification > Document Entry > Enter Invoice*

Data needed:

| | |
|---|---|
| Invoice Date | **Today's date** |
| Amount | **4120.00** |
| Tax Amount | **XI (Input Tax)** |
| Purchase Order | **Your PO number (4500000173 shown here)** |

Once these four items have been entered and the Enter icon has been clicked, the Enter Incoming Invoice screen will appear, as shown in Figure 4A-27. If done correctly, the Balance box in the upper right-hand corner should indicate 0.00.

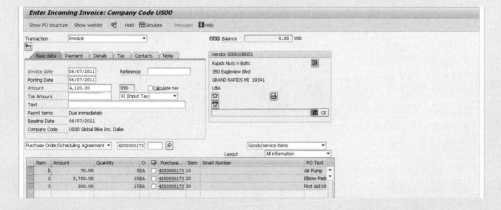

**FIGURE 4A-27**

**Create Invoice Final Screen**

Click the Save icon. Return to the SAP Easy Access menu by clicking the Exit icon.

### 6  Post Payment to the Vendor

*Accounting > Financial Accounting > Accounts Payable > Document Entry > Outgoing Payment > Post*

Data needed:

| | |
|---|---|
| Document Date | **Today's date** |
| Company Code | **US00 (automatic)** |
| Currency/Rate | **USD (automatic)** |
| Account | **100000** |
| Amount | **4120.00** |
| Account | **108### (Rapids Nuts N Bolts vendor number based on your User Number)** |

Before clicking Process Open Items, the Post Outgoing Payments screen appears as shown in Figure 4A-28:

**FIGURE 4A-28**

**Post Outgoing Payments Header Screen**

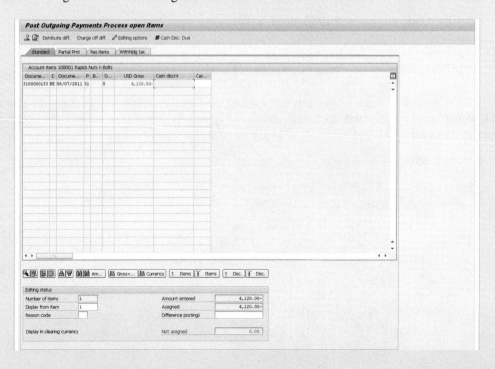

After clicking Process Open Items, the screen appears as shown in Figure 4A-29. If correct, the Not Assigned at the bottom-right corner will be 0.00. Then click the Save icon.

**FIGURE 4A-29**

**Post Outgoing Payments Final Screen**

You are now finished with You Try It 1. Return to the SAP Easy Access menu by clicking the Exit icon.

## You Try It 2

In step 1 of You Try It 2, you will create a new vendor called Bike Parts. Then, in step 2, Creating a Purchase Requisition, you will request a price quote for 10 repair kits. In step 3, you will once again create a PO; however, this time the PO is based on the purchase requisition you created in step 2.

### 1  Create New Vendor

*Logistics > Materials Management > Purchasing > Master Data > Vendor > Central > Create*

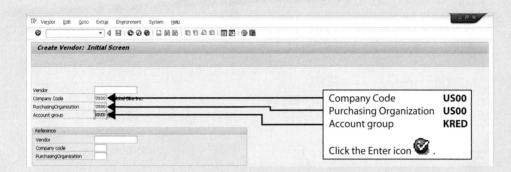

**FIGURE 4A-30**

**Create Vendor Initial Screen**

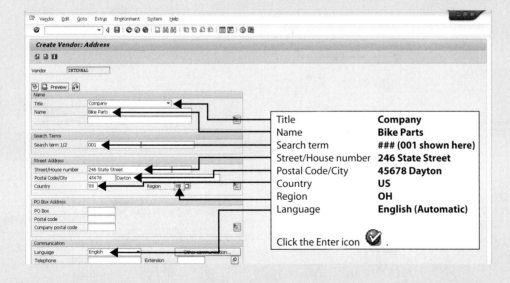

**FIGURE 4A-31**

**Create Vendor Address Screen**

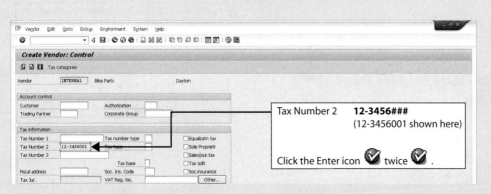

**FIGURE 4A-32**

**Create Vendor Tax Screen**

**FIGURE 4A-33**

**Create Vendor
Accounting Screen**

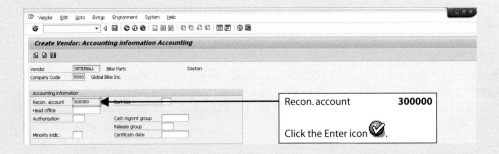

**FIGURE 4A-34**

**Create Vendor Payment
Screen**

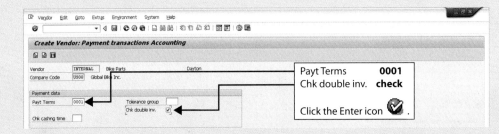

**FIGURE 4A-35**

**Create Vendor
Correspondence Screen**

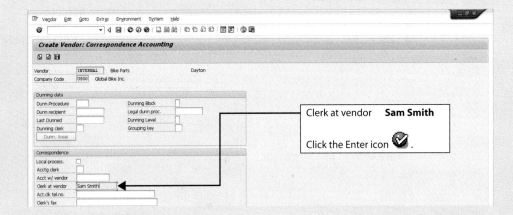

**FIGURE 4A-36**

**Create Vendor
Purchasing Screen**

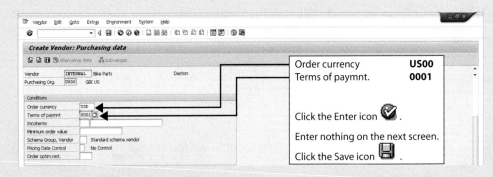

**FIGURE 4A-37**

**Create Vendor Number
Screen**

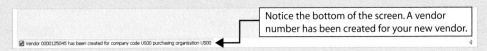

2    **Create Purchase Requisition**

*Logistics > Materials Management > Purchasing > Purchase Requisition >
Create*

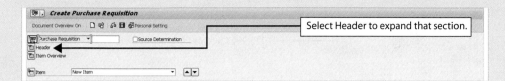

**FIGURE 4A-38**

**Purchase Requisition Screen**

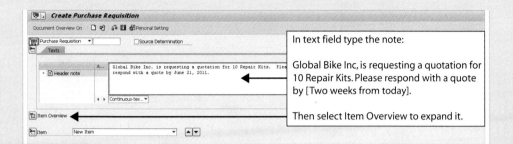

**FIGURE 4A-39**

**Purchase Requisition Text Screen**

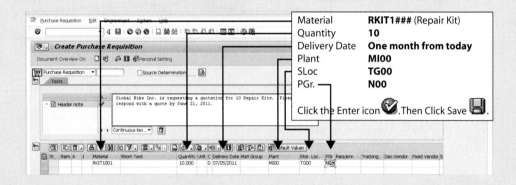

**FIGURE 4A-40**

**Purchase Requisition Item Screen**

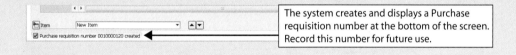

**FIGURE 4A-41**

**Purchase Requisition Number Screen**

## 3 Create Purchase Order (now from Requisition)

***Logistics > Materials Management > Purchasing > Purchase Order > Create > Vendor/Supplying Plant Known***

Step 3 was completed in the first exercise and in You Try It 1. This time you are creating the PO from the purchase requisition you created in step 2.

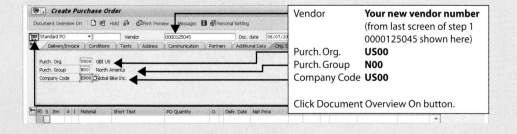

**FIGURE 4A-42**

**Purchase Order Screen**

**FIGURE 4A-43**

**Purchase Order from Purchase Requisition Screen**

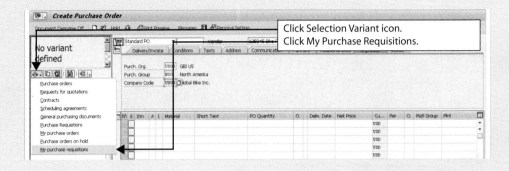

Click Selection Variant icon.
Click My Purchase Requisitions.

**FIGURE 4A-44**

**Purchase Order from Purchase Requisition Selection Screen**

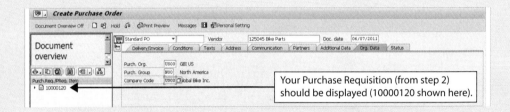

Your Purchase Requisition (from step 2) should be displayed (10000120 shown here).

**FIGURE 4A-45**

**Purchase Order Adopt from Purchase Requisition Screen**

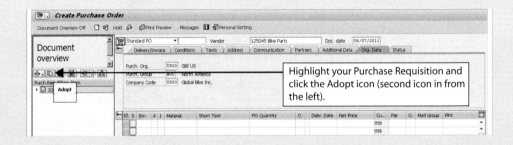

Highlight your Purchase Requisition and click the Adopt icon (second icon in from the left).

**FIGURE 4A-46**

**Purchase Order Price Screen**

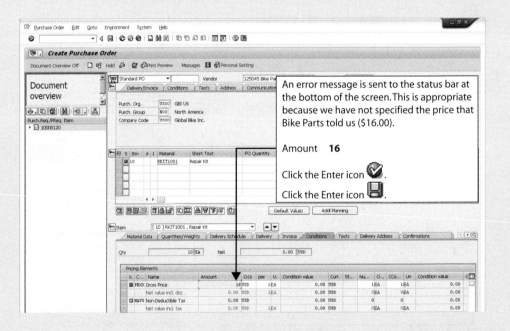

An error message is sent to the status bar at the bottom of the screen. This is appropriate because we have not specified the price that Bike Parts told us ($16.00).

Amount   **16**

Click the Enter icon.
Click the Enter icon.

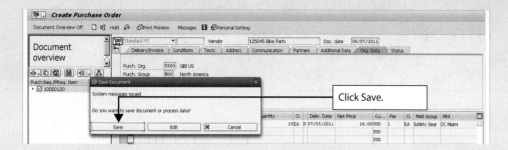

**Purchase Order Save Screen**

**Purchase Order Number Screen**

You have finished You Try It 2.

"Our best client! And we lost the sale!" Sue's exasperated as she talks to Doug in sales.

"Nothing you could have done, Sue. You can't sell bikes that we don't have and couldn't get."

"But Doug, why, why, why does this keep happening??? Don't they know we're losing sales left and right? And now Heartland, our biggest customer!"

"I guess this won't happen with the new SAP system. It will give us up-to-the-minute inventory figures."

"I hope CBI is still in business by the time we get the system."

Sue later hears the full story from Ann in accounting.

"Ann, when I looked at the inventory I saw that we had 55 of the bikes they wanted, and I only needed 50 for the sale."

"Yeah, it did show that. But what it didn't show is that Doug had sold 10 of them earlier that day."

"So, when I thought we had 55, which is what the computer showed, we actually had 45?"

"Right."

"But, Ann, Doug sold those bikes to that little outfit in Kansas City. Those guys are small potatoes compared to Heartland. Why didn't we cancel their order instead of Heartland's?"

"That makes sense, but we've never done that."

"Even worse, Ann, Heartland didn't want the bikes until next month. Couldn't we order the frames and parts and put them together in the next 2 weeks or so? We've done that before to save sales."

"Wouldn't work. Space Bike Composites is our only supplier of that frame and they've discontinued it."

"Why wasn't the sales department told?"

"We thought another supplier was going to come through with the frame, but that was a dead end."

"We've got to find a way to keep the sales reps in the loop. We're going to lose Heartland if I have to cancel more orders."

"I agree, but how? There are hundreds of items we sell and hundreds of suppliers, and the suppliers have suppliers. Would sales reps read hundreds of e-mails about possible problems? Nobody reads that security stuff the IT people send out every day, and that's just one paragraph."

"Fine. That doesn't do anything about Heartland, though … or my commission check."

| | |
|---|---|
| **Q1.** | **What are the fundamentals of a Sales process?** |
| **Q2.** | **How did the Sales process at CBI work before SAP?** |
| **Q3.** | **What were the problems with the Sales process before SAP?** |
| **Q4.** | **How does CBI implement SAP?** |
| **Q5.** | **How does the Sales process work at CBI after SAP?** |
| **Q6.** | **How can SAP improve the integration of customer-facing processes at CBI?** |
| **Q7.** | **How does e-commerce integrate firms in an industry?** |

## Chapter Preview

In this chapter, we examine sales. More specifically, the Sales process at a small bicycle company called Chuck's Bikes, Inc. before and after the implementation of SAP. To accomplish this, we will examine the same questions we used in Chapter 4 when we discussed the Procurement process. It is not coincidence that our approach here is the same as in Chapter 4. One of the most valuable aspects of a process perspective is that once its lessons are learned, they apply to all business processes.

We begin by examining the Sales process at CBI before SAP and learning how SAP ultimately improved it. We conclude the chapter by considering other processes that involve customers and how SAP and IS can be used to improve and integrate them.

As with the procurement discussion, it is easy to get lost in the details. Keep in mind that sales is all about building relationships with customers. As you will see, SAP can help.

## Q1. What Are the Fundamentals of a Sales Process?

Sue made, and lost, a large sale to CBI's best customer. CBI is a bicycle company that buys frames, tires, and accessories and assembles bikes that are then sold to retailers. Before we rush to find fault at CBI, let's make sure we understand the activities involved in a sale. The business definition of a **sale** is an exchange of goods or services for money. More precisely, a sale is revenue from delivery of merchandise or a service where payment may be made in cash or other compensation. The Sales process is an operational process with three main activities—Sell, Ship, and Payment—as shown in Figure 5-1.

The sales activities—Sell, Ship, and Payment—are accomplished by actors playing the Sales Agent, Warehouse Manager, and Accountant roles. The Sales process is located within the value chain in the sales and marketing primary activity shown in Figure 5-2.

**FIGURE 5-1**

**Main Sales Process Activities and Roles**

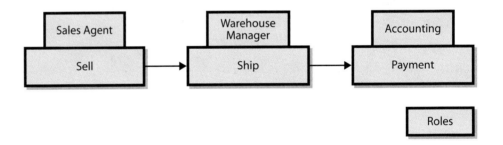

**FIGURE 5-2**

**Sales Process Within the Value Chain of CBI**

| Primary Activity | Description | Process & Chapter |
|---|---|---|
| Inbound logistics | Receiving, storing, and disseminating inputs to products | Procurement, Chapter 4 |
| Operations | Transforming inputs into final products | |
| Outbound logistics | Collecting, storing, and physically distributing products to buyers | |
| Sales and marketing | Inducing buyers to purchase products and providing the means for them to do so | Sales, Chapter 5 |
| Customer service | Assisting customers' use of products thus maintaining and enhancing the products' value | |

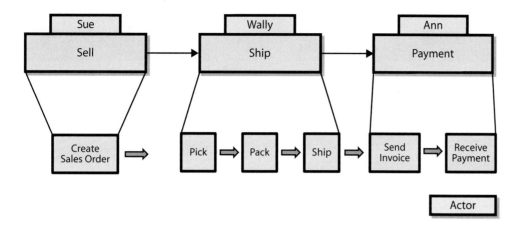

**FIGURE 5-3**

**Main Sales Process Activities, Subactivities, and Actors**

For a business, sales is the most important process. Without sales, no one gets paid and buildings go dark. Although sales is a complex and difficult process, it is also governed by a simple overriding principle: Satisfy the customer. Peter Drucker, one of the fathers of modern management theory, once said that there are no results that matter inside the company, the only result that matters is a satisfied customer.[1]

The online sale of flowers provides a good example of the Sales process. Online florists use effective sales processes to build long-term, mutually beneficial relationships with customers. For example, when you send flowers to your mother for her birthday and include a birthday greeting, the flower company keeps track of this transaction and will send you a reminder e-mail a few days before her birthday. If you regularly send flowers to a particular person and then lapse, the company may again send a reminder: "It's been two months since you last sent Debbie flowers." The florist may also suggest a particular arrangement or offer you a discounted price to retain you as a frequent customer.

The florist would like to retain good customers. Acquiring new customers can cost 5 to 10 times as much as retaining existing ones. To retain customers, the florist needs to know things about its customers, like buying preferences and important dates. The more the company knows about its customers and their needs, the better the chance it has to sell them flowers in the future.

Let's consider the Sales process at CBI in the chapter opening scenario. Figure 5-3 shows the main sales activities and subactivities. The first subactivity is to create a sales order that specifies that Heartland wants 50 bikes in 2 weeks. Later, on the planned shipping date, Wally, the warehouse manager, ensures that the bicycles from finished goods inventory are picked, packed in a box, and shipped to Heartland. Shortly thereafter, Ann in accounting sends Heartland an invoice. When Heartland's payment arrives, Ann posts the payment to a bank account.

We make two simplifications to the Sales process in this chapter. First, we address sales from one business to another rather than from a business to its consumers. These **business-to-business (B2B)** sales are much more common than **business-to-consumer (B2C)** sales like the florist example just given. This is because each B2C sale typically requires many B2B sales within the supply chain to acquire and assemble the product. A second simplification is that this chapter primarily addresses the sale of products, not services.

## Q2. How Did the Sales Process at CBI Work Before SAP?

Before we can appreciate the benefits of using SAP, we will start with the lost sale described earlier. To understand why Sue's sale was cancelled, consider the Sales process for CBI. The significant activities in this process are shown in Figure 5-4. This process has six roles, three performed by human actors—Sue, Wally, and Ann—and three by computer. Each computer actor is served by its own database, creating three information silos.

The Ethics Guide on pages 146–147 demonstrates how one person's actions can affect a process and an entire company.

[1] *Forbes ASAP,* August 29, 1994, p. 104.

FIGURE 5-4

**Sales Process at CBI
Before SAP**

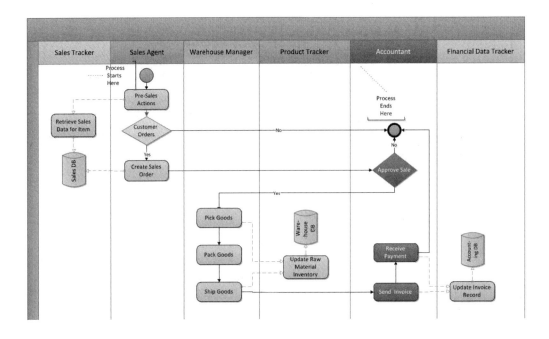

The first activity in Figure 5-4 is Pre-Sales Actions. In this activity, Sue and other sales reps contact customers, give price quotes, verify that products are available, check on special terms, and confirm delivery options.

If the customer decides to order, the next activity is Create Sales Order. An example of a sales order (SO) is shown in Figure 5-5. On the example shown, Sue is selling Heartland Bikes 50 Stream bikes at $300 each for a total price of $15,000.

Once complete, the SO is sent to accounting for approval. To approve the SO, Ann in accounting gets price data from the Sales database, customer data from the Accounting database, and inventory data from the Warehouse database. These data flows to Ann are not shown in Figure 5-4 for sake of simplicity. For existing customers, Ann uses data in the Accounting database to determine the history of payments by the customer, Heartland, in this case, before approving the sale. If this sale is for a new customer, there would be no customer data in the Accounting database, and Ann would add the new customer to that database and determine the risk of selling to this customer.

FIGURE 5-5

**Sue's Sales Order in
Paper Form**

## Sales Order

03/21/2012

| TO | **Heartland
Bike** | SHIP
TO | **Heartland
Bike** |
|---|---|---|---|

| Salesperson | Job | Shipping Method | Shipping Terms | Delivery Date | Payment Terms | Due Date |
|---|---|---|---|---|---|---|
| Sue | | | | | Due on receipt | |

| Qty | Item # | Description | Unit Price | Discount | Line Total |
|---|---|---|---|---|---|
| 50 | TXTR1001 | Stream N3 28 | $300 | | $15,000 |

During this activity, Ann also accesses data in the Warehouse database to make sure there is sufficient inventory to sell. If there is not enough inventory, the sale is usually disapproved. However, as in the case of Sue's sale to Heartland, if the delivery for the sale is delayed at the customer's request, Ann will call the warehouse to ask if future deliveries are expected that will replenish the inventory in time.

If approved by accounting, the SO is passed onto the warehouse where Wally and his staff will collect (or "pick") and ship the bicycles on the correct day. These activities in the Sales process diagram are labeled Pick Goods, Pack Goods, and Ship Goods. Once the bikes are shipped by the warehouse, Wally sends a notice to accounting that the goods have shipped so that accounting can send Heartland the invoice. The final activity, Receive Payment, occurs when Heartland sends a payment to CBI for the sale.

This process rejected Sue's sale for two reasons. Recall that the inventory data in the Warehouse database lags by a day. When Sue made the sale, the database indicated the inventory at the beginning of the day—55 Stream bikes. However, 10 of those bikes were sold before Sue's sale to a little retailer in Kansas City. When the SO of 50 bikes arrived at accounting, there were only 45 Streams available to sell. As mentioned in the introduction, Ann in accounting will coordinate to get an additional shipment of bike frames if the delivery of the sale provides enough time. However, in this case, Ann discovers that the supplier is discontinuing the frame. She contacted Heartland to ask if they would change their order and accept the 45 bikes instead of the desired 50, but when Heartland declined she had to cancel the sale.

## Q3. What Were the Problems with the Sales Process Before SAP?

The pre-SAP Sales process has led to a number of problems that have plagued CBI over the years. These problems are shown in Figure 5-6.

### Sales Problems

Starting with the Sales role, the inventory data visible to salespeople in the Warehouse database lags by one day. Currently, Wally updates his finished goods inventory data in the Warehouse database at the end of the day. The updated inventory data are sent to the salespeople overnight so that when CBI opens in the morning the salespeople know which bikes are available in inventory. At times, as in the opening scenario, this has led to the sale of bicycles no longer in inventory. Although the bicycles are in the inventory at the warehouse at the beginning of the day, those bicycles have already been sold. As a result, salespeople promise bikes and delivery dates to customers that cannot be met.

Input errors can also occur. Sue and other salespeople have at times written down the wrong address for a customer, incorrectly calculated a price discount, or created multiple versions of the same customer or same order. These errors take time to discover and correct.

### Warehouse Problems

In the warehouse, Wally and his crew also have their share of problems. When a sale is made to a new customer, the warehouse picks and packs the order before receiving final permission to ship. The New Customer Order process is set up this way to reduce the time from order to delivery for

| Role | Problems |
|------|----------|
| Sales | No current inventory data<br>Input errors |
| Warehouse | Pick and pack for new customers is inefficient if sale is cancelled<br>No way to share production or supply issues and delays |
| Accounting | Time spent on invoice and other errors<br>New customer delays |

**FIGURE 5-6**

**Problems at CBI with Sales Before SAP**

new customers. If the warehouse waited until accounting approved the sale to start the pick-and-pack activities, many of the promised delivery times would not be met and some of the new customer order inventory might be shipped in other orders. Because of this process, when new customers are disapproved by accounting, Wally and his crew must unpack and return the products to the shelves and update the inventory data in the Warehouse database.

A second issue is that Wally does not have any way to communicate with salespeople about upcoming supply disruptions. Wally knew that the Stream bike frame supplier had decided not to produce any additional frames for the Stream bikes Sue wanted to sell to Heartland.

### Accounting Problems

Things are not much better in accounting. Ann supervises a staff of very careful accountants who make the occasional data entry and arithmetic errors. Some problems are unique to the Accounting role. Her office occasionally receives payments from customers with incorrect or missing invoices. The staff may also credit the wrong account or make other update errors. These infrequent errors can take hours to sort out and damage customer relations.

Delays also occur in checking the credit of new customers. This step has created a number of unwarranted shipment delays when credit checks run long or when ambiguous credit scores are found.

These problems have cost CBI sales and customers over the years, and as industry competition increased CBI had to change or it would go out of business. CBI believed that SAP would help correct these Sales process deficiencies.

## Q4. How Does CBI Implement SAP?

Many of these problems with the current Sales process can be overcome with an effective ERP system like SAP. However, as mentioned in Chapter 4, ERP systems are implemented not only to overcome problems, but also to achieve strategy. To implement SAP successfully, top management reexamined CBI's strategy and committed to a competitive strategy that focused on a particular industry segment—high-end bikes—and a differentiation on responsiveness to retailers.

CBI then selected the SAP Sales process most appropriate for this strategy. SAP provides a variety of Sales processes to its customers. CBI, like other SAP customers, selected the Sales process it believed was best suited to its strategy. CBI then configured this process to its sales objectives. Sales managers decided on one efficiency objective and two effectiveness objectives, which are shown in Figure 5-7.

The efficiency objective—fewer cancelled sales—will be measured by the percentage of sales that are cancelled. A cancelled sale is one that is made but subsequently disapproved, as in the example at the beginning of the chapter.

The first effectiveness objective—faster customer response—will be measured by the time from sales order agreement to the arrival of ordered products. A second measure will be the percentage of sales of first-year products. CBI offers new bikes and accessories based on customer input. If these new products are being purchased by retailers, this is a sign that CBI is

**FIGURE 5-7**

**Objectives and Measures for the New Sales Process**

| Objective | Measure |
|---|---|
| **Efficiency** | |
| Fewer cancelled sales | Percentage of cancelled sales |
| **Effectiveness** | |
| Faster customer response | Elapsed time for order to arrival<br>Percentage of sales of first-year products |
| Reduce cancelled sales to top customers | Cancelled sales to top 20 retailers |

responding well to customer wants. A second effectiveness objective is to reduce lost revenue from cancelled sales to their best customers. CBI wants to be able to cancel lower revenue sales when they conflict with higher revenue sales.

## Q5. How Does the Sales Process Work at CBI After SAP?

Now consider the situation two years later. CBI has implemented the SAP system, and every employee knows how to use it. Figure 5-8 shows the SAP inherent Sales process implemented at CBI.

### Sales

The new Sales process features the same three actors as the previous Sales process—Sue, Wally, and Ann. However the three computer actors are reduced to the single SAP system that tracks all the sales data. For comparative purposes, we will trace the same Sales process as before. This is the sale of 50 Stream bikes to Heartland when only 45 are available.

The Pre-Sales Actions activity is the same with one exception. The inventory and price data are now current. Sue can see that 55 bikes are available and that 10 of the 55 have been sold. She can see that the 10 bikes have not been shipped, and that her customer will have priority. As we pick up Sue's story, she has just made the sale and is sitting down in her office to input the sales data into SAP in the Create Sales Order activity. As she logs into the system, her Sales Order screen looks like Figure 5-9 before data have been added to it.

The Sales Order screen has many of the same features as the Procurement process screens in Chapter 4. The title, at the top left in this case, is Create Standard Order: Overview. In the header section, Sue enters Heartland's customer number (25056), the date of the transaction (PO date of 06/20/2011), and the transaction number (PO Number 05432). The PO Number is determined by Heartland's numbering system. The PO date for Heartland is the sales date for

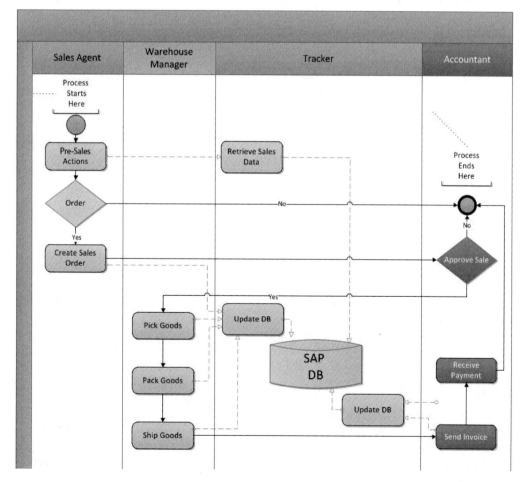

**FIGURE 5-8**

**Sales Process at CBI After SAP**

**FIGURE 5-9**

**Sales Order Screen in SAP of 50 Stream Bikes to Heartland**

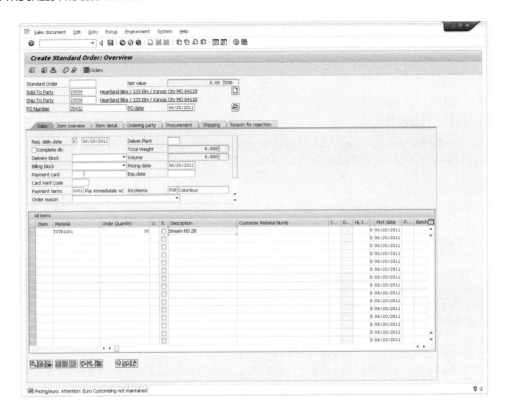

CBI—the date the sale was made. Once Sue enters these three data elements, SAP retrieves the customer's name and address. In the detail section below the header, Sue inputs the material number for Stream bikes (TXTR1001) and the number ordered (50). Her screen now looks like Figure 5-9. If the sale had more than one item, these additional items would be included on lines below the Stream bikes. Sue then saves the information and enters another sale or exits the system.

Once Sue saves the SO, SAP creates an SO number and updates the inventory table in the database to reflect the sale of 50 Streams. In addition, a new SO record is created that will subsequently be updated when the warehouse picks, packs, and ships the bikes.

In addition to updating data, several other actions are triggered. First, a message is sent to the accounting department requesting credit approval and a decision to approve or disapprove the sale. A second action updates the assembly schedule for CBI. SAP recognizes that the warehouse only has 45 Stream bikes, and attempts to acquire from suppliers the additional bike frames and parts to assemble. When automated responses in the supply chain indicate no opportunity to acquire these frames, Ann in accounting receives a message. She sees Sue's pending sale to a preferred customer, the 45 bikes in inventory, and the 10 bikes sold earlier that day to another customer. Because Heartland is a preferred customer, Ann is able to cancel the sale of 10 bikes and move 5 of these bikes to Heartland.

### Warehouse

Once this sale is approved, SAP sends a message to Wally in the warehouse to create an outbound document for this sales order.

Wally navigates to the Create Outbound Delivery screen, as shown in Figure 5-10. On this screen he enters the Shipping point as Miami (MI00), the Selection date (6/27/2011), and the Order number (185), which is the SO number. On a subsequent screen that is not shown, he specifies more details about the sale and saves the document.

Later, on the appointed day, Wally removes the bikes from finished goods inventory, packs them into a crate, and places the crate in the truck loading bay.

Once the bikes are picked and packed, Wally logs into SAP. After he enters the SO number, he sees the Outbound Delivery screen shown in Figure 5-11. He confirms that the data provided by SAP in the header and detail sections are correct. If he did not pick the entire quantity

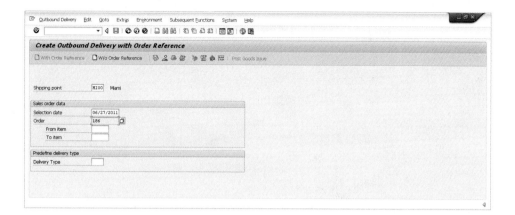

**FIGURE 5-10**

**Outbound Delivery Screen in SAP**

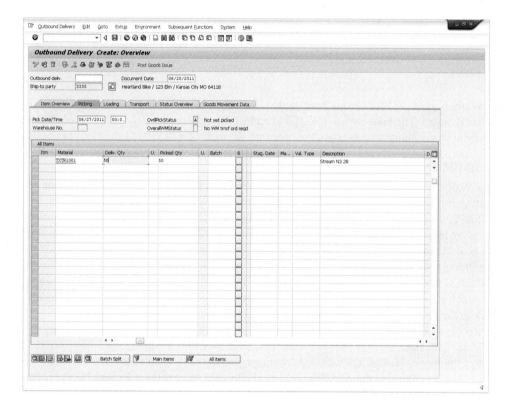

**FIGURE 5-11**

**Picking Screen in SAP**

specified in the sale, 50 in this case, he would overwrite the defaulted value of 50 that appears in the Deliv. Qty column. Once he saves this data, the inventory table is updated and the sales record is edited to reflect that the Stream bikes have now been picked and packed.

The Ship Goods activity occurs when the delivery truck leaves the warehouse with the shipment. Again, Wally navigates to the Outbound Delivery screen shown in Figure 5-12. Because this sales order has been picked and packed, the screen is now labeled Change Outbound Delivery

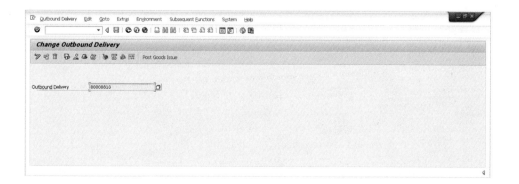

**FIGURE 5-12**

**Posting Screen in SAP**

**FIGURE 5-13**

**Maintain Billing Due List Screen in SAP**

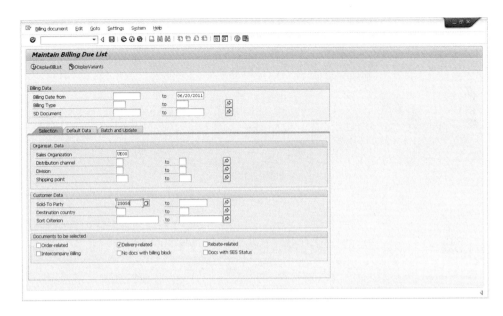

and Wally selects the Post Goods Issue button. **Posting** means that legal ownership of the material has changed. The bikes are no longer owned by CBI; they are now the property of Heartland. Posting in this example occurs when the bikes are shipped.

### Accounting

After Wally has posted the goods issue and the bicycles have changed ownership, Ann in accounting receives a message that she can bill Heartland for the 50 Streams.

She logs into SAP and navigates to the Billing Due List screen that is shown in Figure 5-13. She enters Heartland's number in the Sold-To Party field (25056) and selects the DisplayBillList icon near the top of the screen. On the following screen (not shown), Ann selects from a list of sales orders to Heartland, adds the sales order for the 50 Stream bikes, and clicks the Save icon. This action triggers SAP to send a message to Heartland Bike Company. The message is the bill, which is also called an invoice, for the 50 bikes. A week later, Ann in accounting receives a check in the mail for the 50 Streams.

To credit Heartland's account, she navigates to the Post Incoming Payments screen shown in Figure 5-14. Here she specifies that Heartland, with Account number 25056, has paid $15,000 and that the money has been placed in Account number 100000. On a following screen that is not shown, Ann specifies that this $15,000 payment is allocated to the sales order with 50 Stream bikes.

Once Ann saves the documents, SAP updates the sales record and makes the appropriate accounting entries.

**FIGURE 5-14**

**Post Incoming Payments Screen in SAP**

## The Benefits of SAP for the CBI Sales Process

Several general benefits of the new SAP system at CBI are immediately evident. Sales reps have access to the most current data in the one SAP database. The New Customer Approval activity is quicker, and, as a result, the warehouse no longer packs new customer orders before approval. Data on significant supply chain disruptions is made available to all in the organization.

Although these are very helpful improvements, CBI implemented SAP to help it achieve a specific strategy. Earlier in the chapter the objectives and measures for the Sales process appropriate for this strategy were specified in Figure 5-7.

The implementation of SAP helps CBI achieve its efficiency objective. With more accurate and up-to-date pricing and inventory data, there are fewer cancelled sales.

One of the effectiveness objectives was faster customer response. With SAP, more of the sales activities and subactivities are automated, so the process is faster. The measurement used at CBI, time from sale until arrival, is reduced. Also, the sale of first-year products has increased with SAP. With SAP, sales reps have more accurate data on inventory levels of the new products throughout the supply chain. Prior to SAP, these new products would not appear as inventory in the Warehouse database for potential sale until the day they arrived. Now sales reps can see when these new products will be available and have accurate data on pending sales of these new items.

The second effectiveness objective of reducing cancelled sales to the best customers is also achieved. SAP helps achieve this by allowing the accounting department to give priority to its better customers when products are limited.

Having considered the benefits of SAP on the Sales process, we now broaden the processes under consideration. These other processes, such as the Customer Service process and the Promotion process, involve CBI's customers. These processes are called customer-facing processes.

# MIS InClass 5

## Phones and Processes

Divide the class into small groups according to each student's cell phone platform (Android, iPhone, etc.). Some popular platforms may have multiple groups. Each group should address the following questions. A team spokesperson should then explain the group's answers to the class or the team can submit its answers to the instructor.

Source: Robert Kneschke/Shutterstock.

1. Why did you pick the cell phone that you have? Are you a satisfied customer? Why or why not? What positive and negative experiences have you had with your phone?
2. What features about your phone are most important to you? Which of your personal processes do these features support? (Socializing, coordinating, scheduling, etc.)
3. Pretend to be your parents or someone their age. Answer items 1 and 2 from their perspective.
4. Where do you interact with your platform provider, and what data does it collect? What data should it collect?
5. Which processes of your platform's provider (Apple, Samsung, etc.) does data from your phone help to improve?
6. Now consider your phone's carrier (AT&T, Verizon, etc.). Which processes of your cell phone carrier does data from your phone help to improve?
7. Are you a customer your phone company would want to retain on the next contract? Explain why or why not.
8. Assume that you are working at a company in the area of your choice. Which business processes do professionals in that job use their cell phones to support? What are the objectives and measures of that process? How does using a cell phone improve that process?

**FIGURE 5-15**

**Sample of Customer-Facing Processes**

| Process Scope | Customer-Facing Processes |
|---|---|
| Operational | Promotion<br>Sales<br>Service |
| Managerial | Promotional Discounting<br>Service Trends |
| Strategic | New Product Launch<br>Promotion Evaluation |

## Q6. How Can SAP Improve the Integration of Customer-Facing Processes at CBI?

We have examined how SAP can improve CBI's Sales process. However, the Sales process is just one of many customer-facing processes that SAP can support. These processes are listed in Figure 5-15. The Promotion process is designed to increase sales, stimulate demand, or improve product availability over a predetermined limited time. The Sales process, defined earlier, is the exchange of goods or services for money. The Service process, first defined in Chapter 2, provides after-sales support to enhance or maintain the value of a product.

### Integration of Customer-Facing Processes

Although supporting each of these processes is helpful, the real value of SAP is integrating these processes. Integrating these customer-facing processes and managing all the interactions with customers is called **customer relationship management (CRM)**. The relationship of the Sales process to other customer-facing processes and CRM is the same as the Procurement process, other supply chain processes, and supply chain management (SCM), as shown in Figure 5-16. Like integration of processes across the supply chain, the integration of customer-facing processes is improved by sharing data and increasing process synergy.

### Improving Customer-Facing Process Integration by Sharing Data

Process integration is improved when processes share data. To see how this works, consider your process of returning merchandise to a retailer. It is easier for you to return your merchandise if you have a receipt. If this receipt was e-mailed to you, it may be easier to find than a printed receipt. By using electronic receipts, your retailer's Sales process has made your returns process easier. Rather than issue paper receipts, which are more costly and more frequently lost, many retailers are sharing receipt data with customers electronically by sending an e-mail or a message to a customer's smartphone. Not only does this reduce sales costs, an objective of the retailer's Sales process, it also improves the customer's Returns process, because customers can find their receipts more frequently.

**FIGURE 5-16**

**CRM and SCM Processes**

| CRM Processes—Chapter 5 | SCM Processes—Chapter 4 |
|---|---|
| **Front Office-Customer Facing** | **Back Office-Supply Chain** |
| Sales | Procurement |
| Service | Demand Management |
| Promotion | Returns Management |
| Other Processes | Other Processes |

**Integrating Processes—Processes Sharing Data**

FIGURE 5-17

**Examples of Data Sharing**

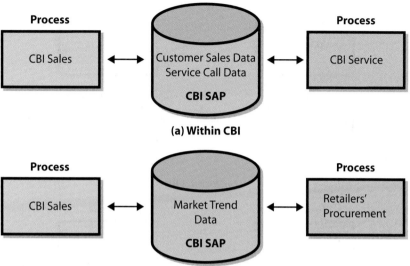

(a) Within CBI

(b) Between CBI and Partners

Examples of integration of processes by data sharing at CBI are shown in Figure 5-17. Both sales and service are improved when they share customer data. By having access to customer sales data, CBI service is improved. For example, when a customer calls for service about a problem with a particular shipment, the service agent at CBI knows the sales data for that shipment and all shipments to that customer. By having the sales data, the agent is better informed about the customer's situation. Likewise, the Sales process is improved with customer service call data. A sales representative can review service data from a customer before initiating a sales call. That way the sales representative can offer to the customer products that were not the subject of a service call.

By sharing data, the Sales process of CBI can be integrated with the Procurement processes of its customer retailers. For example, CBI sells to many small outlets. These small retailers do not have the resources to collect data on market trends. CBI does. CBI can share its market trend data with retailers, who can then make better procurement decisions about what bikes to buy from CBI. Both firms win when CBI's Sales process and the small retailer's Procurement process share this market trend data, because they both sell more bikes.

These are not isolated examples. SAP helps CBI integrate all its processes by consolidating data in one database. This standardizes the data, overcomes information silos, and enables sharing data in real time with all processes.

## Improving Customer-Facing Process Integration by Increasing Process Synergy

The second way to improve process integration is to increase process synergy. Process synergy occurs when processes are mutually supportive—when one process is done well, then the objectives of another process are supported. Synergy between sales and procurement is evident in your personal life. Amazon.com recognizes the synergy between its Sales process and your personal Procurement process. When people want to buy something, they want to do it quickly. Therefore, it can be said that people have a Procurement process objective of not wasting time. Amazon.com has found that online sales revenue increases 1 percent for every one-tenth of a second decrease in load time.[2] As a result, it makes download time an objective of its Sales process.

Examples of increasing synergy at CBI are shown in Figure 5-18. At CBI the Production process can support the objectives of the Sales process. If the Production process times are consistent, the delivery of a sale is rarely late. As a result, customers are satisfied and opportunities

---

[2] Jolie O'Dell, "Why Web Sites Are Slow and Why Speed Really Matters," Mashable, April 6, 2011. Available at: *http://mashable.com/2011/04/06/site-speed/*.

**FIGURE 5-18**

**Examples of Process
Synergy**

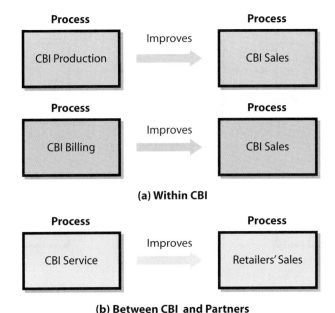

**Integrating Processes—Process Synergy**

for future sales are improved. The objective of the Sales process, repeat customers, is supported by the Production process.

A second example of process synergy is the support of the Sales process by the Billing process. When an accountant at CBI is contacted by a customer or the accountant contacts a customer to clarify a bill, the Billing process requires the accountant to share current pricing of products with the customer. More specifically, the accountant shares prices on products if the new price is better than the price on the bill, which, in turn, leads to future sales.

To improve process synergy with retailers, CBI can use its Service process to support the Sales processes of its customer retailers. For example, when a defective bike is returned to CBI from one of its retailers, the CBI Service process uses overnight shipping to give the retailer a new bike within 24 hours. As a result, the retailer's Sales process is improved, because each of CBI's retailers can promise customers 24-hour replacements.

SAP helps CBI achieve process synergy. SAP achieves process synergy by designing processes to work together. In the examples just given, the SAP Production process is designed to provide consistent production process times. The SAP Billing process can be configured to show current pricing data to billing agents. By using SAP processes, CBI can use a coherent set of processes that have been developed explicitly for mutual support. This is in contrast to CBI's previous processes, which were designed over time within different departments. These processes evolved using isolated databases, and each process was designed to achieve only its own objectives.

## SAP Integration Problems with Emerging Technologies

Earlier we said that the integration of customer-facing processes is called customer relationship management (CRM). When SAP is used to integrate customer processes, this module is called SAP CRM. However, SAP is not the only IS that supports customer process integration. Other emerging technologies that SAP must learn to integrate with include social CRM and cloud-based CRM.

SOCIAL CRM  As mentioned previously, one way customer processes are integrated is by sharing data. **Social CRM** is an information system that helps a company collect customer data from social media and share it among its customer-facing processes.

In today's social media environment, the vendor–customer relationship is complex and is not controlled by the vendor. Businesses offer many different customer touch points, and customers craft their own relationship with the business by their use of those touch points.

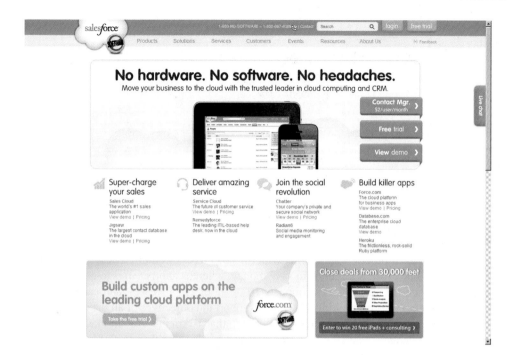

**FIGURE 5-19**

**Salesforce.com
Homepage**

Social CRM data is collected through interactions on Facebook, Twitter, wikis, blogs, discussion lists, frequently asked questions, sites for user reviews, and other social media. Social CRM systems collect and distribute this data to a variety of customer processes.

**CLOUD-BASED CRM: SALESFORCE.COM** **Salesforce.com** is the preeminent cloud-based CRM vendor. Rather than purchasing CRM software and installing it on site, companies utilize a pay-as-you-go plan to use the online software and run it off site at Salesforce.com. This payment arrangement is also called *software as a service*. With over 80,000 customer firms, Salesforce .com is growing rapidly, particularly with small to medium-sized firms. The Salesforce.com homepage is shown in Figure 5-19.

Salesforce.com helps a company integrate its customer processes in several ways. First, by keeping data in the cloud with Salesforce.com, a small company's data is stored in a format that is compatible with a wide variety of software. Because of the universal format, it is easier for the company to share this data among its various customer processes. Second, the software is scalable. A company can conduct a small-scale trial of the CRM software at one office to test the integration of its customer processes at one location before rolling it out to the whole company. Finally, start-up costs are zero; firms pay as they use the service without a big up-front contract. A company can therefore conduct its integration trial at one location without significant investment.

## Integration Challenges and Lessons

Although it is clear that SAP, social CRM, and cloud-based CRM can help integrate customer-facing processes, making integration a reality is challenging. First, with customer-facing processes, the measures of success are difficult to determine and can be debated. For example, you might ask what percentage of the increase in sales this year is due to integrated processes last year and what percentage of the increase is due to the economy, or having better products, or the new sales promotion?

Second, SAP and other CRM systems can be seen as a distraction by sales representatives. These representatives may see their job as building relationships with customers. They may view time spent with technology as time they could use to make commissions. Although a reasonable concern, it represents a common problem with information systems. Oftentimes the people who implement and use a system do not share in all the benefits they bring.

**PROCESS INTEGRATION CHALLENGES** As we close this discussion on integration of customer-facing processes, let's step back from sales integration and look at the bigger picture. Why is integrating any set of business processes hard?

**FIGURE 5-20**

**Process Integration
Lessons**

**To integrate processes:**

| |
|---|
| Make the goals and measures of the integrating processes explicit. |
| Data must flow from process to process. |
| Businesspeople must understand other parts of the business. |

One source of difficulty is that each process impacts many other processes. If sales only impacted service and not a host of other processes, integration would be much easier. However, the Sales process also impacts the processes that hire salespeople, train them, and promote them. The objectives of each process can conflict with the objectives of other processes. For example, the objectives of one process might be to save money, whereas another tries to grow sales. Now broaden this. When the Sales process impacts 10 or 15 other processes, and each process has multiple objectives, conflicts multiply. Trying to support the objectives of all the other processes simultaneously can be like finding one movie to go to that 10 friends will all like.

A second challenge is that all of the processes are in a state of change. Processes change, as we have mentioned in earlier chapters, due to technology changes, strategy changes, and product changes. Keeping all these processes working well together while they all change is difficult.

These challenges are not new. Ever since Henry Ford developed his assembly line the dream of process integration has been pursued, but with limited success. ERP systems give organizations a new way to tackle the challenges of process integration.

### Process Integration Lessons

Creating integrated processes is difficult, but some lessons have emerged. These are listed in Figure 5-20.

One lesson is that integration requires explicit objectives and measures of the integrating processes. If the objectives and measures of a process are not well known, integration is difficult. If you and your friends are trying to decide among restaurants or movies but no one shares their measures about what makes a good restaurant or movie, the challenge of picking a mutually satisfying solution becomes even harder. That is why for the last four chapters we have tried to be explicit about the objectives and measures of each process.

A second lesson is that integration requires data sharing. The key to flowing data is making the data compatible with a variety of software. If inventory data are stored in a database, and the salespeople want it on their smartphone, then the database must be compatible with the phone. If CBI wants to share sales forecast data with a wide variety of its retailers, it must make its data compatible with the software used in the industry. Although businesspeople do not need to know how to make data compatible, they should be able to ask compatibility questions.

A third lesson is that integration can occur when processes support other process objectives. This can only happen when businesspeople understand other parts of the business. Just as salespeople must know their customers' businesses and procurement processes in order to sell and integrate with them, they must also know how lead times are determined in their own firm's procurement process and how payments are processed in accounting in order to integrate with these other processes. When you are in business, make sure you know the objectives and measures for your company's processes.

## Q7. How Does E-Commerce Integrate Firms in an Industry?

In the past two chapters, we have discussed integration of processes between CBI and its partners. For example, in the last chapter CBI's Procurement process was integrated with its suppliers' Sales processes; here we considered CBI's Sales process and its customers' Procurement processes. However, process integration occurs on a larger scale and between all types of firms

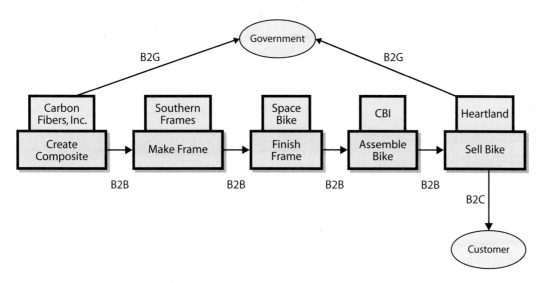

**FIGURE 5-21**

**E-Commerce
Integration**

and between firms and customers. In fact, the chain of organizations from the firm that creates the raw material to the firm that makes the final customer sale can be considered an integrated process, as shown in Figure 5-21. This integration of processes is achieved using e-commerce.

More specifically, **e-commerce** is a multifirm process of buying and selling goods and services using Internet technologies. Processes are also integrated when data are exchanged among firms on a private network, but here we focus on the public Internet and the open market it creates.

In Figure 5-21, composites, which are raw material for bike frames, are created by Carbon Fibers, Inc. The composites are sold to a frame manufacturer, Southern Frames, who makes the bicycle frames. The frames are sold to a frame wholesaler, Space Bike Composites in this scenario, where the frames are finished. CBI assembles the bikes and sells the finished product to retailers such as Heartland who, in turn, sells to a final customer.

The collection of these five firms and the five activities accomplished at each can be viewed as a process. Recall that a process is a series of activities accomplished by actors playing roles. In this example, a different enterprise plays each role in the E-commerce process.

In this process, and in all e-commerce, there is no unified or explicit strategy, because no one manager has the authority to specify a competitive strategy for the whole process. As a result, the e-commerce process has no universal objective. That said, most industries and participating firms pursue an implicit strategy and objective of reducing costs.

With each individual firm acting in its own best interest, an efficient supply chain emerges. **Emergence** is the way a complex system like an efficient supply chain emerges from the interaction of a large number of simple interactions. Computer simulations, the Web, social media, the stock market, and national elections also display emergent patterns from a large number of simple interactions.

This interorganizational e-commerce process is supported by **interorganizational IS**, which interact with each other via the public Internet. Interorganizational IS are IS used by more than one firm. Just as IS can improve intraorganizational process, IS can also improve interorganizational processes by improving their integration. Integration is achieved by sharing data. For example, each firm in Figure 5-21 might use an ERP system, and these systems may share purchase order, sales order, and inventory data. Another interorganizational system, say, in the health care industry, might share patient data in the form of electronic health care records; an interorganizational system in the defense industry might share classified military data.

By shifting our process focus beyond CBI and its partners to interorganizational e-commerce, we can better understand industry and market issues, such as merchant types, types of transactions, pricing, and disintermediation.

Figure 5-22 lists categories of companies that participate in e-commerce. The U.S. Census Bureau, which publishes statistics on e-commerce activity, defines **merchant companies** as those that own the goods they sell. They buy goods and resell them. It defines **nonmerchant companies** as those that arrange for the purchase and sale of goods without ever owning

**FIGURE 5-22**

**Merchant and
Nonmerchant List**

| Merchant Companies | Nonmerchant Companies |
|---|---|
| Business-to-consumer (B2C) | Auctions |
| Business-to-business (B2B) | Clearinghouses |
| Business-to-government (B2G) | Exchanges |

or taking title to those goods. With regard to services, merchant companies sell services that they provide; nonmerchant companies sell services provided by others. Of course, a company can be both a merchant and nonmerchant company.

### E-Commerce Merchant Companies

The three main types of merchant companies are those that sell directly to consumers, those that sell to companies, and those that sell to government. Each uses slightly different IS in the course of doing business. B2C e-commerce concerns sales between a supplier and a retail customer (the consumer). IS that support the Sales process of B2C companies are typically **Web storefronts** that customers use to enter and manage their orders. Amazon.com, REI.com, and LLBean.com are examples of companies that use Web storefronts.

B2B e-commerce refers to sales between companies. As Figure 5-21 shows, raw materials suppliers and other firms use interorganizational IS like ERP systems to integrate B2B supply chains.

**B2G**, or **business-to-government** merchants, sell to governmental organizations. In Figure 5-21, the composite raw material supplier and the bike retailer might sell their products to government agencies.

### Nonmerchant E-Commerce

The most common nonmerchant e-commerce companies are auctions and clearinghouses. **Auctions** match buyers and sellers by using an IS version of a standard auction. This application enables the auction company to offer goods for sale and to support a competitive-bidding process. The best-known auction company is eBay, but many other auction companies exist; many serve particular industries.

**Clearinghouses** provide goods and services at a stated price and arrange for the delivery of the goods, but they never take title. One division of Amazon.com, for example, operates as a nonmerchant clearinghouse, allowing individuals and used bookstores to sell used books on the Amazon.com Web site. As a clearinghouse, Amazon.com uses its Web site as an IS to match the seller and the buyer and then takes payment from the buyer and transfers the payment to the seller, minus a commission.

Another type of clearinghouse is an **electronic exchange** that matches buyers and sellers, similar to that of a stock exchange. Sellers offer goods at a given price through the electronic exchange, and buyers make offers to purchase over the same exchange. Price matches result in transactions from which the exchange takes a commission. Priceline.com is an example of an exchange used by consumers.

### How Does E-Commerce Improve Market Efficiency?

E-commerce improves market efficiency in a number of different ways. For one, e-commerce leads to **disintermediation**, which is the elimination of middle layers of distributors and suppliers. You can buy a bicycle from a typical " bricks-and-mortar" retailer like Heartland, or you can use CBI's Web site and purchase the bike directly from CBI. If you take the latter route, you eliminate the retailer. The product is shipped directly from CBI's finished goods inventory to you. You eliminate the retailer's inventory-carrying costs, and you eliminate shipping overhead and handling activity. Because the retailer and associated inventories have become unnecessary waste, disintermediation increases market efficiency.

E-commerce also improves the flow of price data. As a consumer, you can go to any number of Web sites that offer product price comparisons. You can search for the bike you want and sort the results by price and vendor reputation. You can find vendors that avoid your state sales tax or that omit or reduce shipping charges. The improved distribution of data about price and terms enables you to pay the lowest possible cost and serves ultimately to remove inefficient vendors. The market as a whole becomes more efficient.

From the seller's side, e-commerce produces data about price elasticity that has not been available before. **Price elasticity** measures the amount that demand rises or falls with changes in price. Using an auction, a company can learn not just what the top price for an item is, but also the second, third, and other prices from the losing bids. In this way, the company can determine the shape of the price elasticity curve.

Similarly, e-commerce companies can learn price elasticity directly from experiments on customers. For example, in one experiment, Amazon.com created three groups of similar books. It raised the price of one group 10 percent, lowered the price of the second group 10 percent, and left the price of the third group unchanged.

Customers provided feedback to these changes by deciding whether to buy books at the offered prices. Amazon.com measured the total revenue (quantity times price) of each group and took the action (raise, lower, or maintain prices) on all books that maximized revenue. Amazon.com repeated the process until it reached the point at which the best action was to maintain current prices.

Managing prices by direct interaction with the customer yields better data than managing prices by watching competitors' pricing. By experimenting, companies learn how customers have internalized competitors' pricing, advertising, and messaging. It might be that customers do not know about a competitor's lower prices, in which case there is no need for a price reduction. Or, it may be that the competitor is using a price that, if lowered, would increase demand sufficiently to increase total revenue.

## Process Integration and Your Business Future

One of the goals of this textbook is to help you become comfortable with processes and how they integrate. We first explained processes and then discussed how processes integrate a supply chain and the customer-facing processes within one firm. We also applied integration concepts to processes between firms. Our goal all along was to get to the following conclusion: *Process integration is essential to business.* As a result, it is essential to your future. In every job you will have, in every company large and small, you will play a role in many processes. If you are an accountant, your accounting classes will prepare you well to do those roles; if you are in sales, your marketing courses will get you ready for your roles as a salesperson. But in every job and in every role you play, you will be more effective if you keep the big picture, the process integration picture, in mind.

Process thinking will help you better understand your role in any process. Further, it will help you ask questions about process objectives and measures. It will also help make you aware of how the data from your process is used elsewhere and how your process supports the objectives of other processes. Finally, thinking about processes will help you see how IS can improve these processes.

Where there are business processes there is likely to be an ERP system. Whether you are an accounting, supply chain, marketing, or finance student, chances are that you will work with SAP or another ERP system on your very first job after college. As an accountant you will post payments and configure SAP to allow different payment schedules and to create automatic price discounts. As a salesperson, you may record every customer interaction in your CRM module, post and edit sales, and invent new reports that will help your company identify new trends and opportunities. These activities will impact other processes outside of your office. You and your employer will be pleased if by the time you start you have mastered some aspects of SAP so you can anticipate these impacts. So take this time to master the vocabulary in these chapters. Learn how to navigate to different screens and to move around within the screens. Think about processes and how ERP systems change and improve processes. If you can, do the tutorials in the Appendix, make mistakes, start over—learn beyond the book.

# Ethics Guide

## Are My Ethics for Sale?

Suppose you are a salesperson at CBI. CBI's sales forecasting system predicts that your quarterly sales will be substantially under quota. You call your best customers to increase sales, but no one is willing to buy more.

Your boss says that it has been a bad quarter for all of the salespeople. It's so bad, in fact, that the vice president of sales has authorized a 20 percent discount on new orders. The only stipulation is that customers must take delivery prior to the end of the quarter so that accounting can book the order. "Start dialing for dollars," she says, "and get what you can. Be creative."

Using CBI's CRM system, you identify your top customers and present the discount offer to them. The first customer balks at increasing her inventory, "I just don't think we can sell that much."

"Well," you respond, "how about if we agree to take back any inventory you don't sell next quarter?" (By doing this, you increase your current sales and commission, and you also help CBI make its quarterly sales projections. The additional product is likely to come back next quarter, but you think, "Hey that's then and this is now.")

"OK," she says, "but I want you to stipulate the return option on the purchase order."

You know that you cannot write that on the purchase order because accounting won't book all of the order if you do. So you tell her that you'll send her an e-mail with that stipulation. She increases her order, and accounting books the full amount.

With another customer, you try a second strategy. Instead of offering the discount, you offer the bikes and accessories at full price, but agree to pay a 20-percent credit in the next quarter. That way you can book the full price now. You pitch this offer as follows: "Our marketing department analyzed past sales using our fancy new CRM system, and we know that increasing advertising will cause additional sales. So, if you order more product now, next quarter we'll give you 20 percent of the order back to pay for advertising."

In truth, you doubt the customer will spend the money on advertising. Instead, they'll just take the credit and sit on a bigger inventory. That will kill your sales to them next quarter, but you'll solve that problem then.

Even with these additional orders, you're still under quota. In desperation, you decide to sell product to a fictitious company that is "owned" by your brother-in-law. You set up a new account, and when accounting calls your brother-in-law for a credit check, he cooperates with your scheme. You then sell $40,000 of product to the fictitious company and ship the bikes to your brother-in-law's garage. Accounting books the revenue in the quarter, and you have finally made quota. A week into the next quarter, your brother-in-law returns the merchandise.

Meanwhile, unknown to you, SAP is scheduling bike assemblies. The assembly schedule reflects the sales from your activities (and those of the other salespeople), which indicate a sharp increase in product demand. Accordingly, it generates a schedule that calls for substantial assembly increases and schedules workers for the assemblies. SAP also increases the procurement of parts and frames from suppliers to meet the increased demand.

## DISCUSSION QUESTIONS

1. Is it ethical for you to write the e-mail agreeing to take the product back? If the e-mail comes to light later, what do you think your boss will say?
2. Is it ethical for you to offer the "advertising" discount? What effect does that discount have on your company's balance sheet?
3. Is it ethical for you to ship to the fictitious company? Is it legal?
4. Describe the impact of your activities on next quarter's inventories.

# Active Review

Use this Active Review to verify that you understand the material in the chapter. You can read the entire chapter and then perform the tasks in this review, or you can read the text material for just one question and perform the tasks in this review for that question before moving on to the next one.

## Q1. What are the fundamentals of a Sales process?

Define *sale* and explain the activities and subactivities in the Sales process. Explain the overriding principle of sales. Locate the Sales process within the value chain.

## Q2. How did the Sales process at CBI work before SAP?

Explain the major activities in the Sales process at CBI before SAP and identify the actor who accomplishes each activity and what data are used. Explain how the Sales process is different at CBI for new customers. Identify the two reasons that Sue's sale was disapproved.

## Q3. What were the problems with the Sales process before SAP?

Explain the problems in the Sales process for sales, the warehouse, and accounting.

## Q4. How does CBI implement SAP?

State CBI's competitive strategy. Describe the efficiency objective and how it will be measured. Identify the two effectiveness objectives and the measures used to assess each one.

## Q5. How does the Sales process work at CBI after SAP?

How is the Pre-Sales Action activity different after SAP is implemented? Explain the major activities in the Sales process after SAP. Specify what data each actor supplies for each activity and what SAP does once each actor saves the data on his or her screen. Explain the general benefits of SAP's new Sales process for CBI. Describe how the new process improves the effectiveness and efficiency objectives.

## Q6. How can SAP improve the integration of customer-facing processes at CBI?

Describe CRM. Explain the Promotion and Service customer-facing processes. Describe how the Sales process can be integrated with other processes by sharing data and by process synergy. Explain social CRM and how it can be used to improve a company's sales. Describe the advantages of using Salesforce.com or another cloud-based CRM vendor. Why is integrating customer-facing processes a challenge? Explain the two main challenges to integrating business processes and the lessons learned about process integration.

## Q7. How does e-commerce integrate firms in an industry?

Define *e-commerce*. What makes the E-commerce process different from a process within a business? Explain emergence and give an example. Describe an interorganizational IS. How do merchant and nonmerchant companies differ? Explain the three types of nonmerchant companies. Describe how e-commerce can lead to disintermediation and to price elasticity data. Explain how process integration impacts your business future.

# Key Terms and Concepts

Auction  *144*
Business-to-business (B2B)  *129*
Business-to-consumer (B2C)  *129*
Business-to-government (B2G)  *144*
Clearinghouse  *144*
Customer relationship management
   (CRM)  *138*

Disintermediation  *144*
E-commerce  *143*
Electronic exchange  *144*
Emergence  *143*
Interorganizational IS  *143*
Merchant company  *143*
Nonmerchant company  *143*

Posting  *136*
Price elasticity  *145*
Sales  *128*
Salesforce.com  *141*
Social CRM  *140*
Web storefront  *144*

# Using Your Knowledge

1. This chapter introduced the Service process and the Promotion process:
   a. Diagram each process with a BPMN.
   b. For each process, specify efficiency and effectiveness objectives and measures appropriate for CBI.
   c. What new IS technologies could CBI use to improve these processes, as specified by your measures in item b?
   d. How can these two processes be integrated with each other?

2. Which of the four nonroutine cognitive skills (abstract reasoning, systems thinking, collaboration, or experimentation) did you use to accomplish exercise 1?

3. Even after SAP is implemented, input errors can still be made. What kinds of errors can Wally, Sue, and Ann still make? Describe a particularly harmful mistake that each can make and how the process could be changed to prevent that error.

4. Think of a company that you buy a product or service from. Specify the touch points you share with that company. Do you believe the company does a good job collecting data from these encounters?

5. Think of another company who you purchase from and that you are disappointed with. Identify the customer-facing process that may be at fault. Specify how that process could be improved.

6. Using the example of a fast-food restaurant or coffee shop, identify three processes that must integrate well for the outlet to run smoothly. Specify what data the processes must share or which processes can support the objectives of other processes. Give an example of how the processes not integrating well would be apparent to you, as a customer.

# Collaboration Exercise 5

Collaborate with a group of fellow students to answer the following questions. For this exercise do not meet face to face. Your task will be easier if you coordinate your work with SharePoint, Office 365, Google Docs with Google+ or equivalent collaboration tools. Your answers should reflect the thinking of the entire group, and not just that of one or two individuals.

Groupon offers a "Daily Deal" through its Web site *www.groupon.com*. Groupon originated in Chicago in 2008 and quickly spread to other cities in North America and then around the world. Groupon offers a Daily Deal in each of its geographic areas each day. If a specified minimum number of customers accept the deal, the deal becomes available to everyone who signed up. The coupon for each deal is made available to participating customers the day following its announcement. If the minimum number of customers is not met, the deal is cancelled for all.

For example, a popular health spa may offer through Groupon a $50 savings on a $125 weekend pass. If the minimum number of customers was set at 500 and, for purposes of this example, 800 accept the offer, then the 800 are notified that "The deal is on." Groupon charges each customer's credit card for $75. Groupon stores customers' credit card data so that customers can accept and participate in deals with minimal fuss. By charging the credit cards for each customer, Groupon receives cash up front. The next day, each of the 800 customers who purchased the Groupon can log into Groupon, navigate to their list of Groupons, and print their $125 voucher. They take the voucher to the spa and redeem it on arrival.

Participating firms, such as the spa, do not pay Groupon up front. Groupon takes a percentage of the $75 for each customer and pays the spa the rest. Visit Groupon at *www.groupon.com* to read more about the process.

As a team, complete the following:

1. Create a process diagram in BPMN to show this process *within* Groupon.
2. Create a process diagram in BPMN for the spa that shows activities from contacting Groupon for the first time through the end of the spa's promotion.
3. What are the objectives of each process? Label each as either an effective or efficient objective.
4. What measures should both firms use to assess accomplishment of the objectives identified in step 3?
5. Describe how Groupon's IS support this process.
6. Groupon's Procurement process integrates with the spa's Sales process. How is this integration accomplished?
7. Groupon's Sales process integrates with a customer's Procurement process. How is this integration accomplished?
8. What other IS (social media, smartphones, etc.) could Groupon use to improve its Promotion or Sales process?

## ACTIVE CASE 5: SAP SALES PROCESS TUTORIAL

A tutorial for the Sales process using SAP is included in the appendix to this chapter, Appendix 5. The tutorial leads the student through a Sales process that sells 5 bicycles to a customer called Philly Bikes. Once the tutorial is complete, students should answer the following questions.

Here are the questions at the end of the exercise.

### Questions

1. If you completed the Case Study/Tutorial in Chapter 4, how is the Sales process in SAP similar to the Procurement process in SAP? In what important ways are they different?

2. Create a screen capture of an SAP screen. Underneath the image, provide an answer to each of the following questions:
   a. In which of the activities does this screen occur?
   b. What is the name of the screen?
   c. What is the name of the screen that precedes it? What screen comes after it?
   d. What actor accomplishes this activity?
   e. Describe an error that this actor could make on this screen that SAP will prevent.

3. Make an informal diagram of the four main actors—the Customer (Philly Bikes), Sales (Sue), the Warehouse (Wally), and Accounting (Ann). Draw arrows that show the data that flows between each of the actors during this process. Number

the arrows and include on each arrow what data are included in the message.

4. Using the same four main actors, this time show with the arrows how the material (the bikes) moves.

5. One concern of a business is fraud. One fraud technique is to create customers who are not customers but who are co-conspirators. The conspirator inside the business credits the account of the coconspirator for payments that were never actually received. For this fraud scheme to work, who at CBI has to take part? How can SAP processes decrease the chance of this type of fraud?

6. Select any of the main activities or subactivities in the Sales process and:
   a. Specify what event triggers this activity to occur.
   b. Identify what activity follows this activity.
   c. For one data entry item, describe what would happen in the rest of the process if that entry was erroneous.
   d. For one data entry item, describe what limits (controls) you would put in place on the data to prevent the type of error described in item c.

7. Having completed one or both tutorials, make two suggestions about how:
   a. SAP could make their software easier to use.
   b. the tutorial(s) could be improved to help new students learn about processes and SAP.

# APPENDIX 5—SAP SALES TUTORIAL

This tutorial follows the Sales process shown in Figure 5A-1. The top of this diagram appears in Chapter 5 as Figure 5-3. This top figure shows the three main Sales activities—Sell, Ship, and Payment, and the subactivities (Create Sales Order, etc.). At the bottom of Figure 5A-1, we have added the eight steps included in this tutorial. To keep this tutorial simple, we begin with step 3, Create a Sales Order.

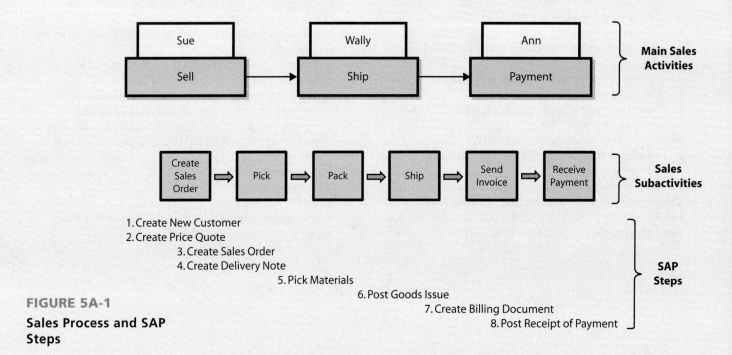

**FIGURE 5A-1**

**Sales Process and SAP Steps**

1. Create New Customer
2. Create Price Quote
3. Create Sales Order
4. Create Delivery Note
5. Pick Materials
6. Post Goods Issue
7. Create Billing Document
8. Post Receipt of Payment

## First Exercise

In this first exercise, we will sell five black Deluxe Touring bicycles to Philly Bikes. While our company in this tutorial is Global Bike, Inc., our actors—Sue, Wally, and Ann—and our Sales process are from Chuck's Bikes. Log in using data provided by your instructor (see Figure 4A-2).

### 1   Create New Customer

Skipped—does not apply to this first exercise, it is introduced later.

### 2   Create Price Quote

Skipped—does not apply to this first exercise, it is introduced later.

### 3   Create Sales Order

This first step, creating a sales order, is accomplished by a salesperson, at CBI, this is Sue. From the SAP Easy Access screen (Figure 5A-2), navigate to the Sales Order page by selecting:

*Logistics > Sales and Distribution > Sales > Order > Create*

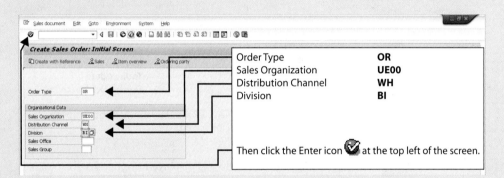

When you double-click Create, the next screen to appear is the Create Sales Order: Initial screen (Figure 5A-3). As in the tutorial in Chapter 4, the last two digits in Sales Organization in Figure 5A-3 are zeros, not the letter "O."

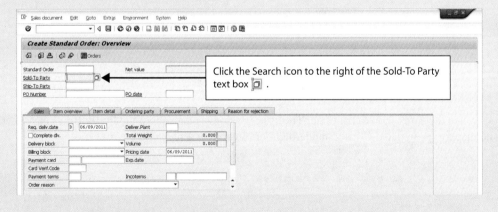

The next screen to appear is the Create Standard Order: Overview screen (Figure 5A-4). This screen may look familiar; it is Figure 5.9 from Chapter 5.

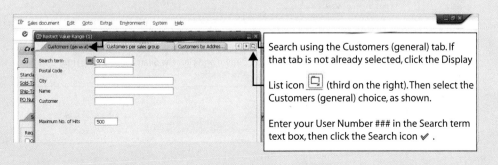

This will produce the pop-up search window shown in Figure 5A-5.

153

A list of potential customers is shown (Figure 5A-6).

**FIGURE 5A-6**

**Customer List Screen**

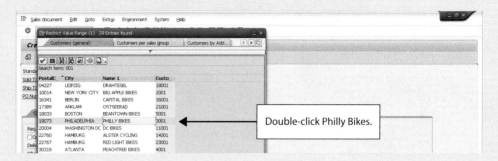

After you select Philly Bikes, you are returned to the Create Standard Order: Overview screen (Figure 5A-7). Notice that the Philly Bikes ID number appears in the Sold-To Party box. The PO number (65430 in this exercise) was specified by Philly Bikes and included in the sales order to provide the link between their purchase order and our sales order.

**FIGURE 5A-7**

**Create Standard Order: Overview Screen**

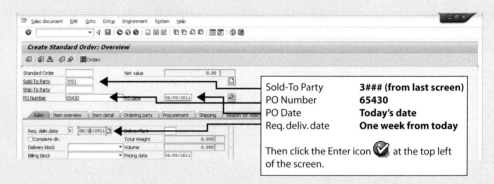

Click the Enter icon, and a warning pop-up window is displayed (Figure 5A-8).

**FIGURE 5A-8**

**Pop-up Warning Screen**

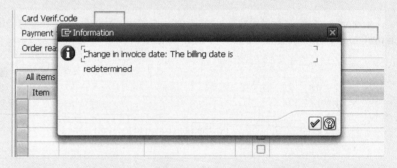

Click the Enter icon to continue. The system retrieves data about the Philly Bikes customer and displays an updated Create Standard Order: Overview screen (Figure 5A-9).

**FIGURE 5A-9**

**Create Standard Order: Overview Screen**

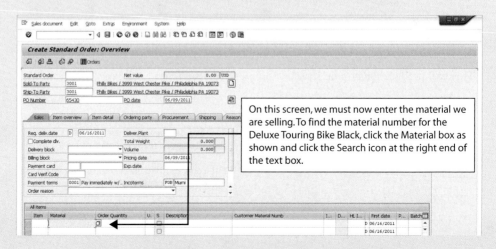

This will load the material search pop-up screen (Figure 5A-10).

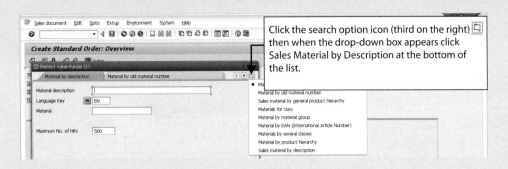

This will reload a new search pop-up screen (Figure 5A-11).

This will show you the sales material you can sell (Figure 5A-12).

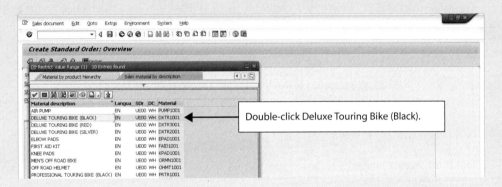

This returns you to the Create Standard Order: Overview screen. The material number for the Deluxe Touring Bike (Black) is now displayed in the Material column (Figure 5A-13).

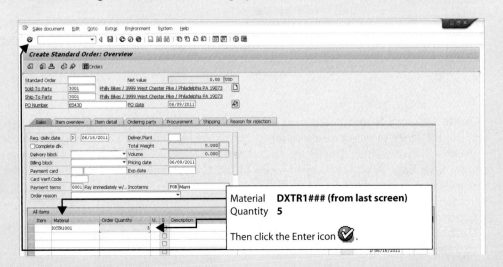

The system will check availability and retrieve Item Number, Total Weight, Net Value, and other data to complete your sales order, as shown in Figure 5A-14.

**FIGURE 5A-14**

**Create Standard Order: Overview Screen**

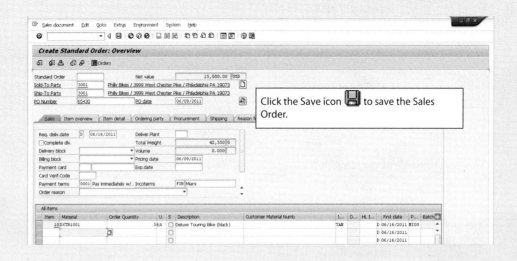

**FIGURE 5A-15**

**Standard Order Number Screen**

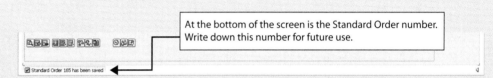

The sales order is now complete. To return to the SAP Easy Access Screen click on the exit icon as shown in Figure 5A-16.

**FIGURE 5A-16**

**Toolbar Screen**

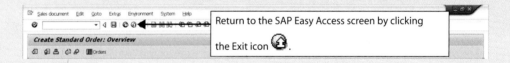

The Easy Access Screen can be returned to its original structure by clicking on the SAP Menu icon (Figure 5A-17).

**FIGURE 5A-17**

**Easy Access Screen**

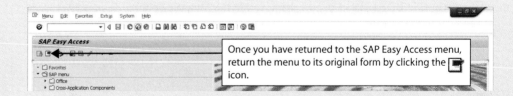

## 4 Create Delivery Note

To initiate the series of warehouse activities—Pick and Ship (called Post in SAP)—we must first create a Delivery Note. This is the second and last step accomplished by a salesperson. From the SAP Easy Access screen, navigate to the Create Outbound Delivery with Order Reference screen by selecting:

*Logistics > Sales and Distribution > Shipping and Transportation > Outbound Delivery > Create > Single Document > With Reference to Sales Order*

When the Create Outbound Delivery with Order Reference screen appears (Figure 5A-18), the Order number should automatically load, and it should correspond to the number you just created in the Sales Order step. Note that our Shipping point is our Miami plant, and the second digit is the letter "I," not the number 1.

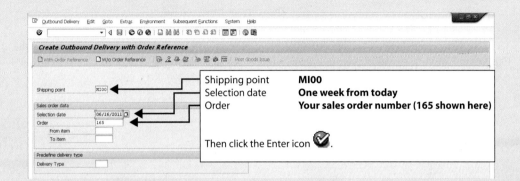

**FIGURE 5A-18**

**Create Outbound Delivery Screen**

The Create Outbound Delivery screen is displayed containing the data from the sales order (Figure 5A-19).

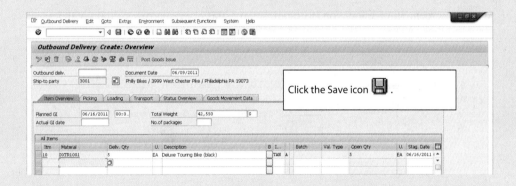

**FIGURE 5A-19**

**Create Outbound Delivery Screen**

By saving the document, the SAP system ensures that the material is available and can meet the specified delivery date. The SAP system assigns a unique number to this delivery document and displays it at the lower-left corner of the Status bar (Figure 5A-20).

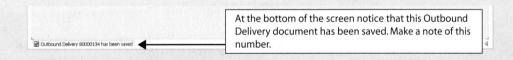

**FIGURE 5A-20**

**Outbound Delivery Number Screen**

Return to the SAP Easy Access screen by clicking the Exit icon.

## 5  Pick Materials

### *Logistics > Sales and Distribution > Shipping and Transportation > Outbound Delivery > Change > Single Document*

When a sales order is picked, the material is moved from its storage location and moved to its packing area. This picking step and the next step, posting, is accomplished by the warehouse manager, at CBI this is Wally. To do this, we must change the delivery document. The first screen in this step is the Change Outbound Delivery screen (Figure 5A-21).

FIGURE 5A-21

**Change Outbound
Delivery Screen**

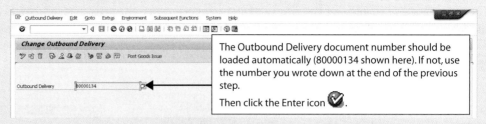

The Outbound Delivery Change: Overview screen will appear (it is very similar to the Outbound Delivery Create: Overview screen in the previous step). Notice in the item detail section that the Item Overview tab has been selected (Figure 5A-22).

FIGURE 5A-22

**Outbound Delivery
Change Screen**

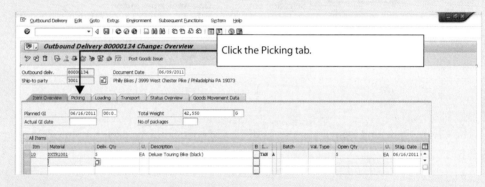

On this screen, Storage location (SLoc) may appear as a very narrow column with its visible heading shortened as "S…" (Figure 5A-23).

FIGURE 5A-23

**Outbound Delivery
Change Screen**

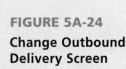

Again, a message in the Status bar appears that confirms that the outbound delivery document is once again saved. It is the same document number you created in step 4. Return to the SAP Easy Access screen by clicking the Exit icon.

## 6  Post Goods Issue

*Logistics > Sales and Distribution > Shipping and Transportation > Outbound Delivery > Change > Single Document*

When posting occurs, possession of the material transfers from Global Bike to Philly and inventory at Global Bike is reduced. Legal ownership of the material also changes hands. The first screen that appears in this step, Change Outbound Delivery (Figure 5A-24), is the same as the first and last screen in the previous step (Figure 5A-21).

FIGURE 5A-24

**Change Outbound
Delivery Screen**

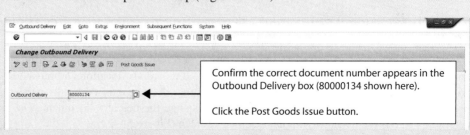

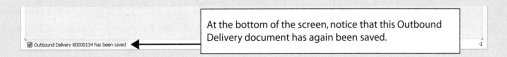

**FIGURE 5A-25**

**Outbound Delivery Number Screen**

At the bottom of the screen, notice that this Outbound Delivery document has again been saved.

Return to the SAP Easy Access screen by clicking the Exit icon.

## 7    Create Billing Document for Customer

*Logistics > Sales and Distribution > Billing > Billing Document > Process Billing Due List*

This step creates an invoice for the bikes that have been shipped. This invoice is sent to the customer. This step, and the final step, posting receipt of the payment, is done by an accountant, at CBI this is accomplished by Ann. The first screen is the Maintain Billing Due List screen (Figures 5A-26).

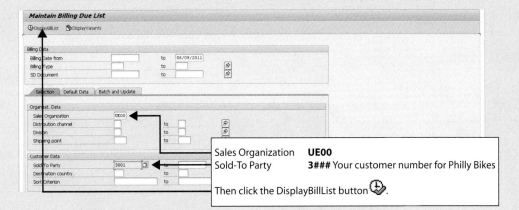

**FIGURE 5A-26**

**Maintain Billing Due List Screen**

| Sales Organization | **UE00** |
| Sold-To Party | **3###** Your customer number for Philly Bikes |

Then click the DisplayBillList button.

**FIGURE 5A-27**

**Maintain Billing Due List Screen**

Click the Collective billing document button.

Click the Collective Billing Document icon, and the background color of this row will disappear.

**FIGURE 5A-28**

**Maintain Billing Due List Screen**

This completes the Billing step, you do not need to click Enter or Save. Return to the SAP Easy Access screen by clicking the Exit icon twice.

## 8    Post Receipt of Customer Payment

*Accounting > Financial Accounting > Accountants Receivable > Document Entry > Incoming Payments*

In the previous step, we sent Philly Bikes a bill. It has now sent us a $15,000 payment. In this step, we record receipt of that payment. The first screen is the Post Incoming Payments: Header Data screen (Figure 5A-29).

**FIGURE 5A-29**

**Post Incoming Payments Screen**

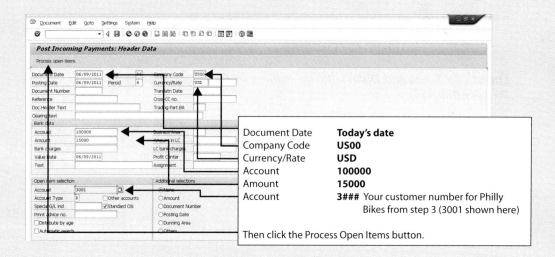

| | |
|---|---|
| Document Date | **Today's date** |
| Company Code | **US00** |
| Currency/Rate | **USD** |
| Account | **100000** |
| Amount | **15000** |
| Account | **3###** Your customer number for Philly Bikes from step 3 (3001 shown here) |

Then click the Process Open Items button.

**FIGURE 5A-30**

**Post Incoming Payments Process Open Items Screen**

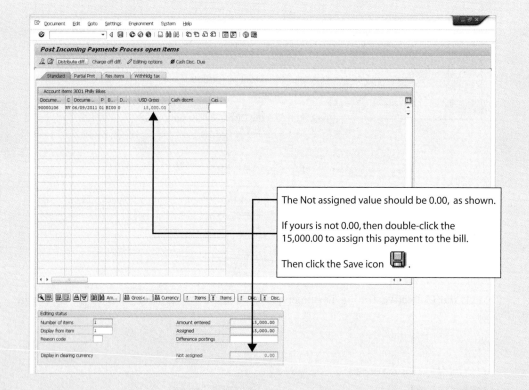

The Not assigned value should be 0.00, as shown.

If yours is not 0.00, then double-click the 15,000.00 to assign this payment to the bill.

Then click the Save icon 🖫.

**FIGURE 5A-31**

**Payment Document Screen**

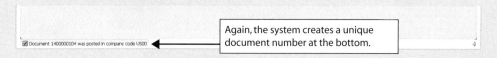

Again, the system creates a unique document number at the bottom.

Return to the SAP Easy Access screen by clicking the Exit icon. This will generate a pop-up window that is misleading (Figure 5A-32). There is no data to be lost at this point, so click Yes. You are finished with the first exercise.

## You Try It 1

You will sell 10 Professional Touring Black Bikes to Philly. All the data necessary is included before each step.

This is PO 65431, the PO date is today, and the requested delivery date is 1 week from today. Ship the order a week from today. Use Miami as the shipping point. The total price is $32,000.

## 3 Create Sales Order

*Logistics > Sales and Distribution > Sales > Order > Create*

Data needed:

| | |
|---|---|
| Order Type | **OR** |
| Sales Organization | **UE00** |
| Distribution Channel | **WH** |
| Division | **BI** |

When these four inputs have been made, your screen will look like Figure 5A-33.

FIGURE 5A-33

**Create Sales Order Screen**

Data needed:

| | |
|---|---|
| Sold-To Party | **3### (3001 shown here)** |
| PO Number | **65431** |
| PO date | **Today's date** |
| Req. delv.date | **One week from today** |

After entering these four data items, click the Enter icon and then click the check icon on the pop-up warning message. The Create Standard Order: Overview screen appears, as shown in Figure 5A-34.

**FIGURE 5A-34**

**Create Standard Order Screen**

**FIGURE 5A-34**

**Create Standard Order Screen**

Enter the material data:

| | |
|---|---|
| Material | **PRTR1###** |
| Order Quantity | **10** |

After entering these two data items, click the Enter icon and then the Save icon.

## 4   Create Delivery Note

*Logistics > Sales and Distribution > Shipping and Transportation > Outbound Delivery > Create > Single Document > With Reference to Sales Order*

Data needed:

| | |
|---|---|
| Shipping point | **MI00** |
| Selection date | **One week from today** |
| Order | **Your sales order number (automatic, from step 3)** |

Same screens as the first exercise.

## 5   Pick Materials

*Logistics > Sales and Distribution > Shipping and Transportation > Outbound Delivery > Change > Single Document*

Data needed:

| | |
|---|---|
| SLoc | **FG00** |
| Picked Qty | **10** |

After you have made these two inputs, your screen will look like Figure 5A-35.

**FIGURE 5A-35**

**Outbound Delivery Change Screen**

## 6   Post Goods Issue

*Logistics > Sales and Distribution > Shipping and Transportation > Outbound Delivery > Change > Single Document*

Same screens as the first exercise.

## 7   Create Billing Document for Customer

*Logistics > Sales and Distribution > Billing > Billing Document > Process Billing Due List*

Data Needed:

| | |
|---|---|
| Sales Organization | **UE00** |
| Sold-To Party | **3### Your customer number for Philly Bikes** |

After clicking the Display Bill List button and the Collective Billing Document button, the Maintain Billing Due List screen appears, as shown in Figure 5A-36.

**FIGURE 5A-36**

**Maintain Billing Due List Screen**

## 8   Post Receipt of Customer Payment

*Accounting > Financial Accounting > Accountants Receivable > Document Entry > Incoming Payments*

Data needed:

| | |
|---|---|
| Document Date | **Today's date** |
| Company Code | **US00** |
| Currency/Rate | **USD** |
| Account | **100000** |
| Amount | **32000** |
| Account | **3### (3001 shown here)** |

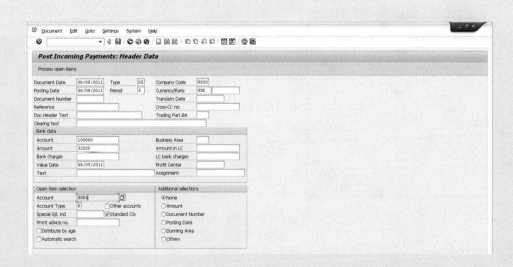

**FIGURE 5A-37**

**Post Incoming Payments Screen**

After clicking the Process Open Items button, the Post Incoming Payments Process Open Items screen will appear as shown in Figure 5A-38.

**FIGURE 5A-38**

**Post Incoming Payments Process Open Items Screen**

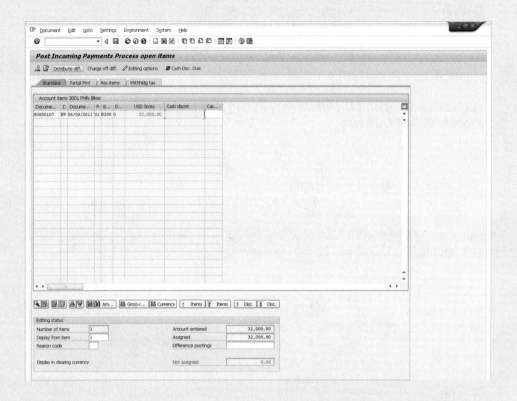

### You Try It 2

Sell three Deluxe Touring Black Bikes to a new customer—Cycle Works—and give it a price quote. The Cycle Works data can be found on the following New Customer screens (Figures 5A-39 through 5A-45).

### 1   Create New Customer

*Logistics > Sales and Distribution > Master Data > Business Partner > Customer > Create > Complete*

**FIGURE 5A-39**

**Customer Create: Initial Screen**

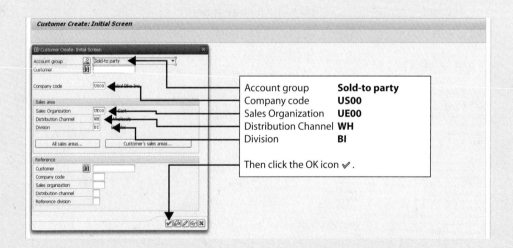

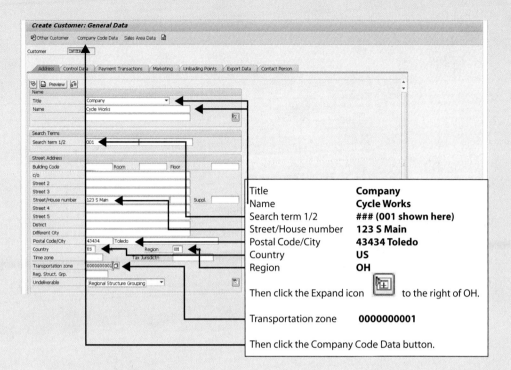

**FIGURE 5A-40**

**Create Customer: General Data Screen**

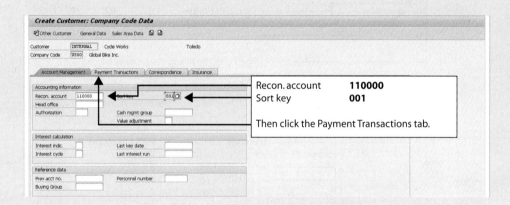

**FIGURE 5A-41**

**Create Customer: Company Code Data Screen**

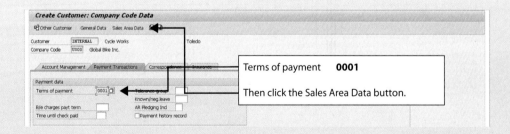

**FIGURE 5A-42**

**Create Customer: Company Code Data Screen**

**FIGURE 5A-43**

**Create Customer: Sales Area Data Screen**

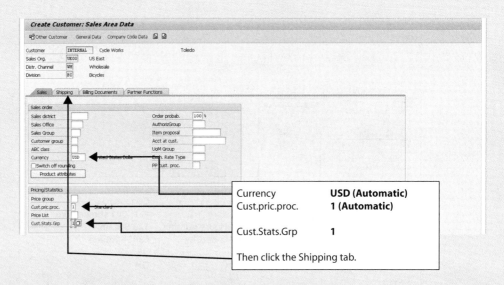

**FIGURE 5A-44**

**Create Customer: Sales Area Data Screen**

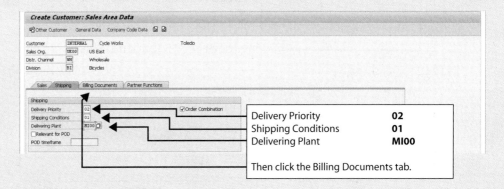

**FIGURE 5A-45**

**Create Customer: Sales Area Data Screen**

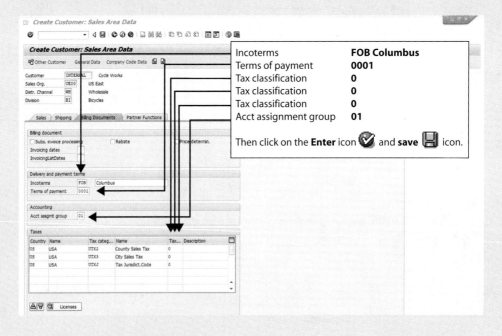

A new customer is created (Figure 5A-46).

**FIGURE 5A-46**

**Create Customer Number Screen**

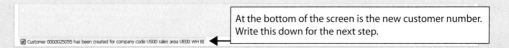

## 2   Create Price Quote

*Logistics > Sales and Distribution > Sales > Quotation > Create*

Cycle Works, our new customer, has asked for a price quote on Deluxe Black Bikes (Figures 5A-47 and 5A-48). Bikes you will sell to them in step 3.

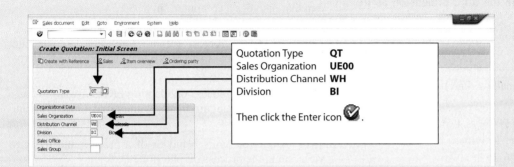

**FIGURE 5A-47**

**Create Quotation Screen**

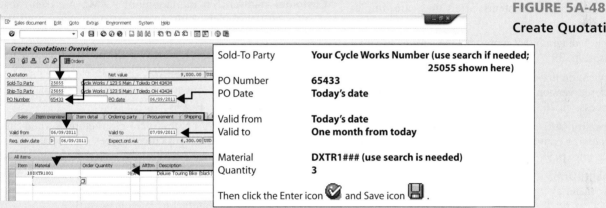

**FIGURE 5A-48**

**Create Quotation Screen**

Record the Quotation number at the bottom of the screen.

## 3   Create Sales Order

In this step, create a sales order to sell the three Deluxe Touring Black Bikes to Cycle Works. To do this, navigate to the Sales Order page as shown in Figure 5A-2, then after you have entered the four data fields as shown in Figure 5A-49, click on "Create with Reference"—see Figure 5A-49. Enter your Quot. number from the step 2: Create Price Quote. The PO is 65433, the PO date is today, and the Req. Deliv. Date is a week from today. Later, in step 8, record a payment from Cycle Works for $9,000. All the other data is the same as in the first exercise.

**FIGURE 5A-49**

**Create with Reference Sales Order Screen**

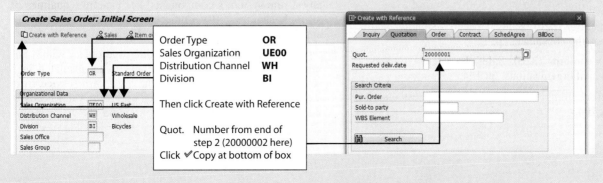

# Glossary

**3D printing.** Also called *additive manufacturing*; a process of depositing successive layers of material to manufacture objects. Just as current printers deposit ink in two dimensions, 3D printing deposits material in three dimensions, layering material in the third dimension as it dries. **p. 101**

**ABAP.** SAP's high-level application language that is used to enhance the functionality of an SAP implementation. It is frequently used to format the data in reports. **p. 74**

**Access.** A popular personal and small workgroup DBMS product from Microsoft. **p. 9**

**Activity.** A task within a business process. **p. 4**

**Actor.** A resource that carries out activities. An actor could either be a human or a computer. **p. 5**

**Analysts.** Sometimes called *systems analysts* or *business analysts*, these employees have specialized training or education that enables them to support, maintain, and adapt the information systems after they are implemented. **p. 64**

**As-is diagram.** A diagram that represents the current situation and processes. **p. 39**

**Auction.** Application that matches buyers and sellers by using an e-commerce version of a standard, competitive-bidding auction process. **p. 26**

**Augmented reality (AR).** Technology that superimposes data or graphics onto a computer-generated display of the physical environment. **p. 99**

**Bill of material (BOM).** A structure or description that specifies the raw materials, quantities, and subassemblies to create a product. **p. 68**

**Bottleneck.** When a limited resource greatly reduces the output of an integrated series of activities or processes. **p. 98**

**Bullwhip effect.** Phenomenon in which the variability in the size and timing of orders increases at each stage up the supply chain, from customer to supplier. **p. 97**

**Business process.** A sequence of activities for accomplishing a function. **p. 4**

**Business Process Management Notation (BPMN) Standard.** A standard set of terms and graphical notations for documenting business processes. **p. 4**

**Business-to-business (B2B).** Sales between companies. **p. 129**

**Business-to-consumer (B2C).** Sales between a supplier and a retail customer (the consumer). **p. 129**

**Business-to-government (B2G).** Sales between companies and governmental organizations. **p. 144**

**Buy-in.** A term for selling a product or system for less than its true price. **p. 104**

**Clearinghouse.** Entity that provides goods and services at a stated price and arranges for the delivery of the goods, but never takes title to the goods. **p. 144**

**Computer-based information system.** An information system that includes a computer. **p. 8**

**Computer hardware.** Electronic components and related gadgetry that input, process, output, store, and communicate data according to the instructions encoded in computer programs or software. **p. 7**

**Configuration.** The process of adapting ERP software to conform to customer requirements without changing program code. **p. 62**

**Control.** A control limits behavior of a process and reduces variation in the process output **p. 37**

**Criteria.** Factors that humans use when conceiving information from data. **p. 15**

**Customer relationship management (CRM).** A system that integrates customer-facing processes and managing all the interactions with customers. **p. 138**

**Data.** Recorded facts or figures. One of the five fundamental components of an information system. **p. 7**

**Disintermediation.** Elimination of one or more middle layers in the supply chain. **p. 144**

**Dynamic processes.** A process whose structure is fluid and dynamic. Contrast with structured processes. Collaboration is a dynamic process; SAP order entry is a structured process. **p. 17**

**E-commerce.** A multifirm process of buying and selling goods and services using Internet technologies. **p. 143**

**Effective.** A process objective that helps achieve organizational strategy. **p. 32**

**Efficient.** A resource-oriented process objective; a process is efficient if it creates more output with the same inputs or the same output with fewer inputs. **p. 32**

**Electronic exchange.** Site that facilitates the matching of buyers and sellers; the business process is similar to that of a stock exchange. Sellers offer goods at a given price through the electronic exchange, and buyers make offers to purchase over the same exchange. Price matches result in transactions from which the exchange takes a commission. **p. 144**

**Emergence.** Attributes of a system that are not attributes of any of the system's components. For example, qualities of a supply chain, such as efficiency or throughput, that do not appear as qualities of any part. **p. 143**

**Encapsulation (encapsulated).** Hiding one object within another; for example, with SOA logic is encapsulated in a service. Encapsulation isolates the logic of a service from the services that use it. No service user knows nor needs to know how the service is performed. **p. 45**

**Enterprise application integration (EAI).** The integration of existing systems by providing layers of software that connect applications and their data together. **p. 56**

**Enterprise resource planning (ERP).** A suite of software, a database, and a set of inherent processes for consolidating business operations into a single, consistent, information system. **p. 57**

**Epicor.** A company primarily known for its retail-oriented ERP software, although it is broadening its penetration in other industry segments. **p. 71**

**Executive support systems (ESS).** Information systems that support strategic processes. **p. 32**

**Finished goods inventory.** Completed products awaiting delivery to customers. **p. 86**

**Five-component framework.** The five fundamental components of an information system—computer hardware, software, data, procedures, and people—that are present in every information system, from the simplest to the most complex. **p. 7**

**Human resources processes.** Organizational process that assesses the motivations and skills of employees; creates job positions; investigates employee complaints; and staffs, trains, and evaluates personnel. **p. 35**

**Industry-specific platform.** An ERP system configuration that is appropriate for a particular industry, such as retail, manufacturing, or health care. **p. 73**

**Infor.** A company that pursued an acquisition strategy to consolidate many product offerings under one sales and marketing organization. Infor sells an ERP product for just about anyone in just about any industry. **p. 71**

**Information.** (1) Knowledge derived from data, where *data* is defined as recorded facts or figures; (2) data presented in a meaningful context; (3) data processed by summing, ordering, averaging, grouping, comparing, or other similar operations; (4) a difference that makes a difference. **p. 12**

**Information silos.** Islands of automation; information systems that work in isolation from one another. **p. 41**

**Information system (IS).** A group of components that interact to produce information. **p. 7**

**Inherent processes.** Process designs included in an ERP product that may be implemented by the organization. **p. 64**

**Internal control.** Systematically limiting the actions and behaviors of employees, processes, and systems within the organization to safeguard assets and to achieve objectives. **p. 90**

**Interorganizational information system (IS).** Information systems that support processes and activities that span two or more independent organizations. **p. 143**

**Inventory turnover.** The number of times inventory is sold in a given period, commonly a year. **p. 90**

**Invoice.** An itemized bill. **p. 87**

**Just in time (JIT).** A delivery method that synchronizes manufacturing and supply so that materials arrive just as the manufacturing process requires them. **p. 61**

**Linkage.** Process interactions across value chains. Linkages are important sources of efficiencies and are readily supported by information systems. **p. 37**

**Management information system (MIS).** An information system that helps businesses achieve their goals and objectives. **p. 32**

**Managerial processes.** Processes that concern resource use; includes planning, assessing, and analyzing the resources used by the company in pursuit of its strategy. **p. 32**

**Manufacturing resource planning (MRPII).** A manufacturing information system that schedules equipment and facilities and provides financial tracking of activities. **p. 61**

**Material requirements planning (MRP).** Software used to efficiently manage inventory, production, and labor. **p. 61**

**Measures (metrics).** Quantities that are assigned to attributes; in the process context, measures help assess achievement of process objectives. **p. 36**

**Merchant company.** In e-commerce, a company that takes title to the goods it sells. The company buys goods and resells them. **p. 143**

**Metrics.** Also called measures, these are quantities assigned to attributes. **p. 36**

**Microsoft Dynamics.** A suite of ERP products licensed by Microsoft. The suite is composed of four ERP products, all obtained via acquisition: AX, Nav, GP, and SL. AX and Nav have the most capability, GP is smaller and easier to use. Although Dynamics has over 80,000 installations, the future of SL is particularly cloudy; Microsoft outsources the maintenance of the code to provide continuing support to existing customers. **p. 71**

**Module.** A suite of similar applications in an ERP system; examples include manufacturing and finance. **p. 73**

**NetWeaver.** The SAP application platform that connects SAP to hardware, third-party software, and output devices. NetWeaver provides an SOA interface that eases the integration of SAP with non-SAP applications. **p. 74**

**Nonmerchant company.** An E-commerce company that arranges for the purchase and sale of goods without ever owning or taking title to those goods. **p. 143**

**Objective.** A goal that people in an organization have chosen to pursue. In the process context, managers develop and measure objectives for each process. Objectives fall into two categories: effectiveness and efficiency. **p. 32**

**OMIS model.** A process to help improve business processes. The model requires that each process have explicitly stated objectives, the measures be clearly identified and improved, and information systems be considered to help achieve the objectives. **p. 35**

**Operational processes.** Common, routine, everyday business processes such as Procurement and Sales. **p. 32**

**Ought-to-be diagram.** A diagram of suggested improvements to a current process. **p. 39**

**Outbound logistics processes.** Processes that collect, store, and distribute products to buyers. **p. 33**

**People.** As part of the five-component framework, one of the five fundamental components of an information system; includes those who operate and service the computers, those who maintain the data, those who support the networks, and those who use the system. **p. 7**

**Posting.** When the legal ownership of a material that has been sold is transferred from the seller to the buyer. **p. 136**

**Price elasticity.** A measure of the sensitivity in demand to changes in price. It is the ratio of the percentage change in quantity divided by the percentage change in price. **p. 145**

**Procedures.** Instructions for humans. One of the five fundamental components of an information system. **p. 7**

**Process blueprints.** In an ERP application, a comprehensive set of inherent processes for all organizational activities, each of which is documented with diagrams that use a set of standardized symbols. **p. 64**

**Procurement.** Obtaining goods and services. **p. 84**

**Procurement process.** The operational process for acquiring goods and services. **p. 33**

**Purchase order (PO).** A written document requesting delivery of a specified quantity of a product or service in return for payment. **p. 85**

**Purchase requisition (PR).** An internal company document that issues a request for a purchase. When accepted, data from the purchase requisition is used in the purchase order. **p. 92**

**R/3.** One of the most best known versions of SAP. It was the first truly integrated system that was able to support most of organizations' major operational processes. **p. 74**

**Radio-frequency identification (RFID).** Computer chips that help identify and track items. As small as, and soon to be as cheap as, a postage stamp, RFID chips broadcast data to receivers that can display and record the broadcast data. **p. 99**

**Raw materials inventory.** A repository of parts and sub-assemblies procured from suppliers that are used to produce products to be stored in the finished goods inventory. **p. 86**

**Repository.** A collection of records, usually implemented as a database. **p. 6**

**Resources.** The items necessary to accomplish an activity such as people, computers, data and document collections. **p. 30**

**Returns management process.** A process that manages the returns of faulty products for businesses. **p. 96**

**Role.** A set of activities in a business process; resources are assigned to roles. **p. 5**

**Roll up.** To compile, total, and summarize data. For example, daily sales are "rolled up" into monthly sales. In accounting systems, transactions are "rolled up" into common accounting reports such as balance sheets and income statements. **p. 89**

**Sales.** An operational outbound process comprised of three main activities—Sell, Ship, and Payment. **p. 128**

**Sales processes.** A process that records the sales order, ships the product and bills the customer. **p. 34**

**Salesforce.com.** The preeminent cloud-based CRM vendor. **p. 141**

**SAP AG.** The world's most successful ERP vendor. SAP AG is the third largest software company in the world. The core business of SAP AG is selling licenses for its SAP software solutions and related services. In addition, it offers consulting, training, and other services for its software solutions. **p. 72**

**SAP Business Suite.** The new name for SAP's integrated software platform. The SAP Business Suite runs on NetWeaver. **p. 74**

**Sarbanes-Oxley Act (SOX).** A federal law requiring companies to exercise greater control over their financial processes. **p. 62**

**Service.** In SOA, a repeatable task that a business needs to perform. **p. 42**

**Six Sigma.** A popular strategy for process improvement that seeks to improve process outputs by removing causes of defects and minimizing variability in the process. **p. 39**

**Service-oriented architecture (SOA).** A design in which every activity is modeled as an encapsulated service, and exchanges among those services are governed by standards. **p. 42**

**SOA standards.** Processing standards used to implement service-oriented architecture. They include XML, WSDL, SOAP, and numerous other standards. **p. 45**

**Social CRM.** An information system that helps a company collect customer data from social media and share it among their customer facing processes. **p. 140**

**Software.** Instructions that direct the operation of a computer. **p. 7**

**Strategic processes.** Business processes that seek to resolve issues that have a long-range impact on the organization. These processes have a broad scope and impact most of the firm. **p. 32**

**Structured processes.** Formally defined, standardized processes that support day-to-day operations such as accepting a return, placing an order, computing a sales commission, and so forth. **p. 17**

**Supplier evaluation process.** A strategic process that determines the criteria for supplier selection and adds and removes suppliers from the list of approved suppliers. **p. 96**

**Supplier relationship management (SRM) process.** A process that automates, simplifies, and accelerates a variety of supply chain processes. SRM is a management process that helps companies reduce procurement costs, build collaborative supplier relationships, better manage supplier options, and improve time to market. **p. 96**

**Supply chain management (SCM).** The design, planning, execution, and integration of all supply chain processes. SCM uses a collection of tools, techniques, and management activities to help businesses develop integrated supply chains that support organizational strategy. **p. 96**

**Swimlane.** In a BPMN diagram a swimlane indicates all the activities in a process accomplished by a particular role. **p. 5**

**System.** A group of components that interact to achieve some purpose. **p. 7**

**Technology development processes.** A support activity in the value chain; includes designing, testing, and developing technology in support of the primary activities of an organization. **p. 35**

**Three-way match.** The activity within the procurement process that ensures that the data on the invoice matches the data on the purchase order and the goods receipt. **p. 87**

**Train the trainer.** Training sessions in which vendors train the organization's employees to become in-house trainers in order to improve training quality and reduce training expenses. **p. 63**

**Transaction processing system (TPS).** An information system that supports operational decision making. **p. 32**

**Web storefront.** In e-commerce, a Web-based application that enables customers to enter and manage their orders. **p. 144**

# Index